The People's Money

THE URBAN AGENDA

Series Editor, Michael A. Pagano

A list of books in the series appears at the end of this book.

The People's Money

Pensions, Debt, and Government Services

Edited by Michael A. Pagano
University of Illinois at Chicago

PUBLISHED FOR THE
COLLEGE OF URBAN PLANNING
AND PUBLIC AFFAIRS (CUPPA),
UNIVERSITY OF ILLINOIS AT CHICAGO,
BY THE UNIVERSITY OF ILLINOIS PRESS
Urbana, Chicago, and Springfield

The College of Urban Planning and Public Affairs of the University of Illinois at Chicago and the University of Illinois Press gratefully acknowledge the publication of this book was assisted by a grant from the John D. and Catherine T. MacArthur Foundation.

Library of Congress Control Number: 2019947746

Contents

Preface and Acknowledgments

Cities and other local governments across the nation have yet to see their revenue streams return to the pre–Great Recession era. Data collected annually on the fiscal condition of US cities estimated that cities' general-fund revenues are just 98 percent of what they were in 2006 in constant dollars.[1] Yet taxpayers and fee payers, the people who elect their representatives for the purpose of providing for the people's health, safety, and welfare, demand an adequate level of government services. Moreover, they demand that borrowed funds used to build the city's infrastructure be paid back to the lender and that the pensions be fully funded to support the workforce when it retires. These demands from the people for good public services have increasingly clashed with the escalating costs of providing infrastructure and pensions, resulting in challenging fiscal times even as the nation's general economy has improved.

The paradox of fiscal challenges for cities and other local governments in a time of improving economic conditions was the focus of the 2018 annual UIC Urban Forum, held on the campus of the University of Illinois at Chicago. The theme of the conference was "The People's Money: Pensions, Debt, and Government Services." The challenge confronting US cities is no more evident than in Illinois, where city fiscal challenges are compounded by the state's fiscal crisis. Papers and panels were convened around the manifold challenges of mounting pension and health insurance liabilities, deferred infrastructure maintenance and investment, fiscal architectures not firmly connected to economic growth engines, uncertainty surrounding financial and legal entanglements between the private sector and city government, the changing municipal bond market, and cities' creative approaches to meeting their residents' needs.

The 2018 UIC Urban Forum was cochaired by Cook County Board president Toni Preckwinkle and UIC Chancellor Michael Amiridis. The event was held on September 13, 2018, and attracted four hundred students, community activists, private citizens, government and nonprofit leaders, and many others. The opening keynote address was presented by Preckwinkle, who reminded the audience of the critical challenges local governments face today, especially as pension costs soar and the costs of services continue to escalate. The closing keynote address was presented by former New York lieutenant governor Richard Ravitch, who reflected on his five decades of public service in support of viable and reasonable financial systems for state and local governments.

Between the two keynote addresses were three lively panels designed to address critical financial challenges facing local governments today and in the future. The first panel, titled "Who Gets What and Why? Cities and the People's Money," was moderated by the *Wall Street Journal*'s Heather Gillers. She engaged the budget directors of the largest American city, New York, and the third largest, Chicago, Melanie Hartzog and Samantha Fields, respectively, by encouraging a conversation about the similarities and differences between the two cities' fiscal policies. The second panel focused on the possibilities of municipal bankruptcy. Richard Greene, of Barrett and Greene, Inc., moderated a panel called "When Governments Go Broke: Lessons from Puerto Rico and Detroit." The panelists were Ana Matosantos, Puerto Rican Oversight and Financial Management Committee board member and former California state budget director, and Boysie Jackson, Detroit's chief procurement officer. The last panel was a sober discussion of the lasting effects of dealing with fiscal challenges by "kicking the can down the road." It was titled "The Sins of Our 'Fathers': Inheriting Pension Burdens." Chris Morrill, the executive director and CEO of the Government Finance Officers Association, and Laurence Msall, president of the Civic Federation, were engaged in a lively discussion, moderated by Katherine Barrett of Barrett and Greene, Inc., about how to prevent future pension crises.

The staff who ensured the conference's smooth operation and who dedicated months of work to assure its success included Jennifer Woodard, Norma Ramos, Brian Flood, and Casey Sebetto at UIC and Karla Bailey of Jasculca Terman Strategic Communications. For seven years, the UIC Urban Forum benefited from the critical events planning skills of Jenny Sweeney. Casey Sebetto, a graduate student in the Department of Urban Planning and Policy, also assumed responsibility for editorial assistance and manuscript supervision.

The 2018 UIC Urban Forum's external board of advisors included the following:

- Clarence Anthony, executive director, National League of Cities
- MarySue Barrett, president, Metropolitan Planning Council
- Henry Cisneros, former Secretary, HUD; former mayor, San Antonio; founder and chairman, CityView
- Rahm Emanuel, mayor, Chicago
- Lee Fisher, dean, Cleveland-Marshall College of Law, Cleveland State University; advisor, CEOs for Cities
- Karen Freeman-Wilson, mayor, Gary, Indiana
- Bruce Katz, The New Localism
- Jeff Malehorn, executive advisor/board member, World Business Chicago
- Toni Preckwinkle, president, Cook County Board
- Julia Stasch, president, John D. and Catherine T. MacArthur Foundation
- Joseph C. Szabo, executive director, Chicago Metropolitan Agency for Planning
- Susana Vasquez, associate vice president, Civic Engagement, University of Chicago

The annual UIC Urban Forum offers thought-provoking, engaged, and insightful conferences on critical urban issues in a venue to which all of the world's citizens are invited.

Note

1. Christiana McFarland and Michael A. Pagano, *City Fiscal Conditions in 2017* (Washington, DC: National League of Cities, 2017).

Michael A. Pagano
Director of the UIC Urban Forum
Dean, College of Urban Planning and Public Affairs,
University of Illinois at Chicago
July 2019

PART ONE
OVERVIEW

Introduction

CASEY SEBETTO

Shortly after the September 2018 Urban Forum, the federal government's fiscal year (FY) ended and revealed a notable increase in the US deficit. At the federal level, decreasing revenues caused a 17 percent increase in the budget deficit between fiscal years 2017 and 2018, totaling $779 billion.[1] This huge deficit at the federal level places increasing pressures on state, county, and municipal governments to provide infrastructure and public service funding. Across the United States, governments are grappling with decreasing revenues coupled with increasing costs for public services, infrastructure maintenance and development, and pension funding.

The unfunded pension obligations of state and local governments are growing in the United States. Moody's Investors Service reported that fiscal year 2017 saw an increase in net pension liabilities for all fifty states. Total unfunded liabilities reached $1.6 trillion—147.4 percent of state revenue. This was up from $1.3 trillion—122 percent of state revenue—in fiscal year 2016.[2]

A conversation on the people's money, with focuses on pensions, debt, and government services, was well set in Chicago, where the city, county, and state are all facing severe financial issues. The state of Illinois holds both the nation's largest unfunded pension liability as a percentage of state revenue—600.9 percent of approximately $250 billion[3]—and the lowest state credit rating. As of 2017, Cook County had around $69 billion in unfunded pension liability,[4] while currently Chicago has approximately $28 billion.[5] The 2018 Urban Forum gathered local and national scholars, experts, government workers, and policy makers to analyze and discuss the difficult financial climate, how we got there, and what the future may hold.

The Urban Forum program director and dean of UIC's College of Urban Planning and Public Affairs, Michael Pagano, greeted the room and set the stage for the day. He spoke of a collective passion to improve our cities, advance our children's education, and improve the movement of people and goods, and he noted that to achieve these goals as a society, we need to come to some agreement on how these desires, needs, rights, and aspirations are paid for. General taxes and fees contributed to by all through a variety of forms provide a resource base for public services to be delivered, while the public officials elected can set limits on how much of these services are received. In addition to these taxes and fees, another trend has emerged in paying for government services—borrowing with bonds and debt. In the morning's keynote address, Toni Preckwinkle, president of the Cook County Board of Commissioners, revealed several emergent themes that would resurface throughout the afternoon, including transparency, efficiency, and reform.

WHO GETS WHAT AND WHY? CITIES AND THE PEOPLE'S MONEY

In the 2019 fiscal year, Chicago will have the smallest budget deficit since 2007. Still, the city's deficit is projected to be $97.9 million.[6] Alternatively, New York City's 2019 fiscal budget, agreed upon in June, is not only balanced but will add $125 million to the city's general reserve fund, raising that fund to more than $1 billion.[7] To discuss what fiscal management lessons can be shared between these two cities, the budget directors of New York City and Chicago, Melanie Hartzog (New York City Mayor's Office of Budget Management) and Samantha Fields (City of Chicago), sat down to offer a view from inside.

BUDGETS ARE ABOUT TOUGH CHOICES. WHEN DRAWING UP A BUDGET EACH YEAR, WHAT ARE THE PRESSURES AND CONSIDERATIONS TO FUND A VARIETY OF SERVICES FROM CONSTITUENTS, COUNCIL MEMBERS, AND OTHER STAKEHOLD-ERS? New York City and Chicago have very different budgets, in both size and scope. For fiscal year 2019, New York City's budget was approximately $90 billion; Chicago's proposed budget for 2019 for all local funds is $8.86 billion.[8] One factor of their vast difference is that Chicago has separate budgets for many of its government agencies, such as the Chicago Housing Authority, Chicago Transit Authority, Chicago Public Schools, and the Chicago Park District. Similar agencies in New York City, apart from the Metropolitan Transportation Authority, are combined within one budget, as the city is a unified government.

Melanie Hartzog explained that the New York City budget is guided by a set of priorities: maintaining a key level of reserves, examining revenue estimates to ensure their anticipation isn't overestimated, and debt service. These priorities are guided by Mayor Bill de Blasio's goals of being a progressive government that is both fiscally prudent and aggressive. New York City's fifty-one council members have been supportive of these efforts, aiding in their implementation. The main drivers of the budget are labor, debt service, and education. Including labor as one of the main drivers was strategic. Hartzog explained that "when the mayor came into office, all of the collective bargaining contracts had been expired for some time. . . . It was a priority to settle those. From a financial management perspective, it gives continuity, knowing what those costs will be. Within those settlements include significant health care savings to offset the costs of labor settlements and retroactive payments."

Labor costs are also a main driver of Chicago's budget. Chicago has roughly thirty-five thousand employees, around 90 percent of whom are unionized. These labor-related obligations and increases are built into the budget each year, continuously constraining funding. Also like New York City, an additional driver of the budget is debt-service payments. A third driver of Chicago's budget is pension obligations. While two of the three drivers mentioned by Fields include financial obligations, and although Mayor Rahm Emmanuel has worked to narrow Chicago's budget gap, the shortcomings persist. Chicago could note New York's prudence, and also learn from Cook County, which includes Chicago. During her keynote address, Toni Preckwinkle stated, "I believe that the most important obligation of government is to craft and pass a budget." When she entered office in 2010, there was a budget gap of $487 million. Since then her administration has closed $2.1 billion in budget gaps and cut expenditures by more than $850 million. "Ensuring that the budget is balanced each year involves a great deal of pulling, tugging, and collaboration with not just commissioners who ultimately must pass the budget, but also with the independently elected officials who run county offices."

WHERE MONEY GOES IS ONE FACET OF A BUDGET, BUT WHERE THE MONEY IS COMING FROM IS ANOTHER. New York City and Chicago have very different revenue sources for their annual operating budgets. New York relies heavily on property taxes, sales tax, and income tax. In Chicago much of the property tax goes toward liabilities, as opposed to the general operating fund, leaving the city with a much greater dependence on other taxes and fees. Specifically,

Chicago's property taxes are split three ways: debt-service payments, pension obligations, and a levy for the Chicago Public Library system.

Fields explained that the city aims to design revenue streams that are fairly diverse so that there is no reliance on just one source or industry. Diverse revenue sources ensure that services are maintained and impacts minimal when unforeseeable disruptions to those sources arise, such as changes in state funding. A recent tax introduced in Chicago is the ground transportation tax. By putting a regulation structure in place for the fairly new ride-sharing industry, the city was able to integrate a corresponding taxing structure. The city is being cautious in projecting those revenues, as it is a newer industry, there is limited data, and they don't know when it will plateau. Still, the ride-sharing industry is becoming one of the city's larger taxpayers; the 2018 budget overview estimates that the ground transportation tax will exceed its initial projections by $41 million.[9]

In New York City, property taxes constitute a considerable portion, and the highest percentage, of incoming revenues, at 29 percent.[10] Personal income taxes make up the next highest amount of taxes coming in, but in terms of total incoming revenue, behind property taxes is state and federal funding—with the state contributing more than the federal government. Hartzog explained that this is largely driven by state education aid and that this large revenue stream was severely impacted this past year when the state budget presented $700 million in cuts and cost shifts, $500 million of which came to New York City. However, an unanticipated growth in personal income tax was able to offset the state budget cuts.

During the past year, personal income tax dollars in New York City were around $1.3 billion above the adopted budget forecast and $2.3 billion above the previous fiscal year. Hartzog stated that this unanticipated significant growth was largely a onetime occurrence and due to three factors—higher than anticipated Wall Street bonuses, the Trump tax bill, and the repatriation of funds (oversees funds coming back into the city and state)—and that it was the last year hedge-fund managers could repatriate funds from an Obama-era tax change. While both New York City and Chicago experienced recent unanticipated tax growth, both were cautious in their assessment of what that means for the future and stressed the importance of conservative revenue estimating so as not to overproject their income.

HOW DO YOU MANAGE THE RESPONSIBILITIES OF THE LONG-TERM LIABILITIES THAT CITIES FACE? New York City recently announced its collective bargaining settlements, which included significant health care savings. In the last round, the city achieved approximately $1.3 billion in annual health care savings and anticipate $1.9 billion in savings in the next round. Not only does that bend the curve for existing health care costs, but it also achieves savings for long-term liabilities. Additionally, Hartzog's office has an agreement with the Municipal Labor Committee, composed of all city unions, to look at long-term structural health care cost savings. Similar to the city's general reserve fund achievement, a partnership with the city council has aided in creating a Retiree Health Trust Fund that is currently funded at $3.5 billion and continuing to grow each year.

Chicago is currently in the process of negotiating all of its collective bargaining agreements, and part of the mandate given by Mayor Emmanuel is to ensure that they have some health care savings that will translate into savings for the city in the long run. One form these savings will take is in increased health care contributions on behalf of the employee. Additionally, the city does not provide all retirees with health care. Instead, the city offers a "bridge to opportunity" for retirees to take advantage of certain pricing to carry them from their retirement into the Medicaid/Medicare age groups. The mayor also implemented a corporate-inspired program that incentivizes employees to have periodic health check-ins and attend workshops or programs. The city is anticipating that by ensuring its workforce has regular visits with their doctors, emergency medical costs will be decreased, thereby saving money over time.

Long-term liabilities include future operating and capital costs and pension payments and liabilities. Additionally, for many governments, including Chicago and New York City, long-term liabilities include debt-service payments. Fields explained that in Chicago, a lot of the debt is general obligation (GO) debt that is backed by property tax and has a reduced credit rating because the debt limits have been reached. To provide more stability and certainty in the city's debt-service planning, it was able to change their variable debt rate to a fixed rate. To do this, the city's chief financial officer went to the mayor and the state to receive authority to approve the creation of a Sales Tax Securitization Corporation. This securitized a portion of the sales tax revenue so that some of the GO debt could be refinanced at a much lower rate, helping with debt-service payments. New York City also initiated the Citywide Savings Program, a collaborative effort that reexamines internal processes and policies while promoting efficiency, and over the course of two fiscal years, the city achieved around $2 billion in savings.[11]

Toni Preckwinkle also spoke of working to put Cook County on more sound financial footing by being more "judicious and careful about how we incur and pay down debt." Since 2011 her administration has paid down the county's debt by $450 million—12 percent. They have also limited any rise in debt service to 2 percent. Those efforts have allowed Cook County to borrow at much lower costs than other large local governments in the state.

Funding and debt associated with pensions is an additional long-term liability governments are facing, specifically when there is not enough funding in the budget to cover their liabilities. New York City and Chicago are both facing unfunded pension liabilities. New York has a mandate to fully fund its $50 billion unfunded liability by 2034. In Illinois a large part of the budget is dedicated to pensions; the state's pension obligations and funding represent over 25 percent of the state budget. Being judicious and implementing best management practices for these liabilities, similar to the actions implemented regarding debt service and collective bargaining, will be crucial moving forward.

SINS OF OUR "FATHERS": INHERITING PENSION BURDENS

Illinois currently holds both the largest state pension deficit and the lowest state credit rating. The state has $130 billion in unfunded pension liability,[12] Cook County had around $69 billion as of 2017,[13] and currently Chicago has approximately $28 billion.[14] Taxpayers today and in the future are on the hook for this high pension burden. Who will bear the responsibility of paying this future liability, and what prompt solutions can be applied today? Chris Morrill, executive director and chief executive officer of the Government Finance Officers Association (GFOA), and Laurence Msall, president of the Civic Federation, joined the event to help discuss these questions.

ALTHOUGH THE SITUATION IN ILLINOIS IS SIGNIFICANT, THE STATE IS NOT ALONE IN FACING PROBLEMS OF UNFUNDED PENSION LIABILITIES. TO FIND A SOLUTION, YOU FIRST NEED TO UNDERSTAND YOUR PROBLEMS. HOW DID SO MANY US GOVERNMENTS FIND THEMSELVES IN THIS SITUATION?   Many jurisdictions, states, and localities have been faced with pension crises. Chris Morrill explained the recent timeline of national events, beginning in 2001, when the aggregate funded ratio of government pensions was 103 percent. Because of this surplus, many governments used additional funds to improve various benefits. This continued until shortly before the Great Recession hit, when the aggregate funded rate was around 87 percent. Following the Great Recession, governments were generally hit in two considerable ways: a decline in revenues and corresponding declines in equity.

When revenues began to decline due to the Great Recession, governments struggled to keep services fully funded and functional. To ensure that services continued, they often stopped making annual required contributions to the pensions, perhaps with an optimistic outlook that the recession would be a short-term event and the budget would be able to catch up and balance later. Subsequently, pensions—70–80 percent of which are often in the equity market—saw a dramatic decrease in their values due to equity tanking. From there, funding ratios continued to fall. Consequently, more than 70 percent of states and around 60 percent of localities made tough decisions and reformed their pensions. Some of these governments were able to apply the reforms to existing employees versus applying the reform only for new hires, but most state laws didn't allow for it, so, alternatively, reforms were applied moving forward.

While pension funding rates haven't returned to 2001's over 100 percent funded level, more recent years have seen improvements. Overall, government pensions have stayed in the 70–72 percent funded range over the past three years, from 2015 to 2018. These improvements are the results of tough decisions. The impacts of those tough decisions aren't always immediately visible, but they become apparent over time. Chris Morrill stated that he believes over the next ten to twenty years, improvements will continue and that the overall pension funding rate for governments will continue progressing toward the ideal 100 percent. Government pensions aren't issues everywhere, though. The real challenges lie ahead for the governments, such as Chicago and the state of Illinois, that need to not only make their current contributions but also play catch-up.

THE PENSION PROBLEM IN ILLINOIS AND CHICAGO: WHAT ARE THE LESSONS FROM THE ROAD TO DEFICIT?   Laurence Msall outlined that the current financial conditions at the state and local levels were initiated through a series of bad decisions by politicians who, mostly, are no longer in office. In the mid-1980s, the then governor and Illinois General Assembly passed a statute that mandated an automatic 3 percent compounded cost-of-living adjustment (COLA) annually for all Illinois state government retirees. The courts have interpreted that statute as a contract, and it has been unchangeable, even though it wasn't identified to the legislature or to the public how the state can meet that increasing payment. A large portion of the state's unfunded pension liability is driven by this and the failure to make contributions in association with the cost of the program. This is an example of a fundamental issue of such reforms—when a benefit is changed without a long-term plan for implementation and maintenance.

In Chicago, looking back to 2001, the city employee retirement system was 93 percent funded, the Chicago police were 70 percent funded, and Chicago teachers were 100 percent funded. At the state level, Illinois had funded 80 percent of its annual bill that year. The first report that the Pew Charitable Trust issued on pensions came out the month that the Great Recession officially began and focused on the years of 1997–2006; the report was authored by Richard Greene and Katherine Barrett, who monitored two of the Urban Forum's panels. Barrett noted that prerecession, when more money was still coming into states, Illinois was still not funding its annual bills. In 2006 the state made 33 percent of its annual required contributions. This was a steep decline from two years earlier, in 2004, when Illinois's required payments were 111 percent funded.[15]

Chris Morrill outlined what he considered to be the three drivers of ongoing unfunded pension ratios: the level of benefits, annual contributions, and investment returns. Looking back to 2006, Illinois wasn't making its annual required contributions, even in better years. Morrill suggested that those are the times when governments should consider overpaying so that they are prepared for worse years, and some states are making a conscious effort to do so. Underfunding annual contributions usually leads to the inability for governments to take advantage of longer-term investments, lessening their investment returns. And finally, those annual contribution amounts are dependent on the level of benefits being offered. In Illinois there were, until 2011, very generous retirement benefits for government employees.

RECENT REFORMS: ARE THEY IMPROVING THE SITUATION?   There are multiple pension systems in Illinois, so while the state system is currently 35 percent funded, the Illinois Municipal Retirement Fund is 93 percent funded. The Illinois General Assembly created the IMRF to direct local governments on what to do with their pensions. However, the state is not under the same restrictions, and the municipal system does not include Chicago, Cook County, or the 650 state police and fire pensions. Under this system, if a city doesn't make its actuarial required contribution dictated by the IMRF board, then the IMRF can intercept with state resources that would have gone to the municipality. Msall stated that the Civic Federation advocates that as a part of comprehensive reform, there is no reason to maintain so many separate pension funds. Consolidating local government pensions, including police and fire, into the Illinois Municipal Retirement Fund would benefit from concentrated staffing and expertise.

The Illinois General Assembly has initiated some reforms to the state system by creating a second tier for new hires, which is something that has been done in other states with some success. The second tier is less gener-ous than its predecessor and puts a limit on the size of the benefit that a person can receive. The new second tier follows Social Security limitations, so new government employees in Illinois are capped at a pensionable sal-ary based on Social Security; currently, that amount is around $107,000. Even more recently, a third tier of benefits has been proposed. Eventually, we will see the impact of these reformed benefits. Additionally, the general assembly passed legislation in May 2018 to create an experiment to save on those who are still promised the 3 percent compounded benefit structure. In 2018 retirees will have the option that if they're retiring in the next couple of years, instead of taking the 3 percent COLA, the state will give them 70 percent of the value of that benefit with a reduced 1.5 percent COLA that is not compounded. The pension contribution has been reduced by about $423 million in FY 2019's budget based on the theory that this experiment will create savings, but if it doesn't, the underfunded pension amount will continue to increase.[16]

As a solution for Chicago's problem, Mayor Rahm Emanuel has floated the idea of borrowing $10 billion to prop up the city's pension funds in the form of issuing a $10 billion pension obligation bond. This may not be an example of adopting best practices to solve a problem. Pension obligation bonds operate by selling these bonds to the debt market, paying on the inter-est rate, and investing the remaining dedicated funds in equities or deriva-tives. Should those investments prove profitable, the difference is used to make payments toward the pension deficit. But both the Civic Federation and the Government Finance Officers Association have concerns. Msall noted that, while they have not fully analyzed this proposal, they would like to see a comprehensive long-term plan. The GFOA generally does not recommend these bonds due to their high-risk nature. Additionally, they can crowd out debt capacity, impacting other debt needs, such as infrastructure.

During her keynote address, Cook County Board president Toni Preck-winkle shared that her team has developed and implemented a plan to prevent insolvency in the years ahead by providing increased contributions to the pension fund. The county has dedicated supplemental funding to shore up the pension fund by approximately $350 million annually over the statutory required contribution. They have been able to create these funds by increas-ing the sales tax by a penny. Prior to the decision to raise the sales tax, the county's pension fund shortfall was increasing by a million dollars a day. Now, "the county is on track to pay the full supplemental pension payment and will have paid early $1 billion over the past three years to shore up our pension fund."

ILLINOIS, COOK COUNTY, AND CHICAGO ARE IN SERIOUS SITUATIONS WITH THEIR PENSIONS. WHY SHOULD PEOPLE CARE ABOUT THIS PERSONALLY, AND WHAT COULD THE FUTURE HOLD? Traditionally, state and local governments have supplemented their budgets with federal funding. As stated earlier, the US federal government's deficit in FY 2018 totaled $779 billion, and it is expected that this will further limit available supplemental funding. Illinois is currently in its own financial crisis, presumably exacerbated by the lack of federal funding, and signifying that they have limited resources available for assisting local governments with problems. With limited financial resources available, tough decisions need to be made regarding budget allocation. Dedicating funds to meet required pension obligations—or to pay down a pension deficit—decreases the amount of the budget available for other sectors. Financial resources are necessary for providing services, and as those resources diminish, public services will also decline.

Fiscal year 2019 was the first year that Illinois had a full budget since FY 2016. However, Laurence Msall noted that the budget left unanswered massive issues related to its unpaid bills. For example, the state was able to provide more resources to fund education, but at the cost of shorting the pension funds again. So, Msall continued, Illinois is continuing with its irresponsible behavior of not funding its pensions according to what the actuaries identify as the required contribution. The problem continues to grow, and the solutions aren't matching the size of the problem.

Toni Preckwinkle discussed how Cook County has dealt with both a budget and a pension funding deficit during her time in office, essentially by adopting best practices. While they may not pay off immediately, in the long term, results will surface. This long-term view is essential, because realistically problems won't be solved in the next few years. But if long-term perspectives are adopted, if our governments begin to plan for thirty years in the future while making improvements immediately, progress can be made. Morrill summed this up by stating, "When is the best time to improve your pension? Ten years ago. When is the second best time? Today."

WHEN GOVERNMENTS GO BROKE:
LESSONS FROM PUERTO RICO AND DETROIT

In 2013 the City of Detroit filed for the largest municipal bankruptcy in US history at approximately $18 billion;[17] in 2017 the commonwealth of Puerto Rico was the largest debt default in US history and may surpass Detroit in its coming bankruptcy-like proceedings for its current debt of more than $70 billion.[18] What happened, who pays, and which lessons from these events can be learned? Is bankruptcy an option for Illinois municipalities? Joining this conversation was Ana Matasantos, board member of the Puerto Rican Oversight and Financial Management Committee (PROMESA), and Boysie Jackson, chief procurement officer for the City of Detroit.

IMAGINING THE METAPHOR OF BEING IN A TUNNEL AND SEEING LIGHT AT THE END OR COMING OUT THE OTHER SIDE, IT COULD BE SAID THAT DETROIT IS NEAR THE END, WHILE PUERTO RICO IS SOMEWHERE IN THE MIDDLE. WHAT WERE THE EVENTS THAT LED TO THE DARKNESS, AND HOW DID THINGS GET SO BAD?   What happened in both Puerto Rico and Detroit can be seen happening in many places: fundamental economic issues, significant population decline, and unsustainable spending that is propped up with debt. Ana Matasantos explained that in Puerto Rico, unsustainable financial commitments were made and followed by a delay in addressing those issues with a high usage of debt. Debt funded the existing deficits and depleting pension funds, eventually leading to $70 billion in public debt and a pension obligation of $50 billion. This situation had been escalating for some time and worsened when the island was hit with two massive hurricanes within one month in 2017. Similarly, Detroit saw an escalating debt problem that built for many years, eventually leading to its $18 billion problem. Boysie Jackson stated that the city did not have a good and integrated financial system. Instead, the mind-set had been "go do it, and later we'll come back and find the money."

At its peak, in 1950, Detroit's population was around 2 million. Over about ten years, between 2000 and 2010, population fell from around 951,000 to about 714,000,[19] exacerbated by GM's, Ford's, and Chrysler's bankruptcies. Often, it was talent leaving the state because of a lack of good jobs and a disconnect between the city and the universities. In addition to people leaving the city, people were abandoning homes and walking away from cars—blight was a significant problem. It was not uncommon for a person to abandon his or her house in one part of the city and go to another area of the city due to home assessment and appraisal values—these people owed more on their homes than they were worth, so they would abandon those homes for a new house with a low appraisal value. And with declining population came declining city revenues and declining public services; people were losing confidence in bus service, the police department, and other services.

Over the past ten years in Puerto Rico, nearly 500,000 people have left for the mainland, declining the island's population by roughly 15 percent, from around 3.5 million to around 3 million.[20] The decline preceded 2017's Hurricane Maria and continued afterward, but the exact portion of the decline attributable to the hurricanes is still unknown because it has yet to become clear how many people will return. Similar to Detroit, the issue of which portions of the population are leaving is significant. Puerto Rico has been losing its younger population, meaning that it is increasingly becoming an older population, with a poverty rate of almost 50 percent.

FOLLOWING DRAMATIC POPULATION LOSS, HOW DO YOU GET THE PEOPLE BACK? HOW CAN ECONOMIC DEVELOPMENT BE EMPLOYED TO REACH THE YOUNGER POPULATION?   Jackson stated that 2018 was the first year that Detroit had an increase in residents returning to the city and that a key contributor was getting financials secured for the public services they depend on. Some of those services were as simple as functioning street lights and filled potholes; others were more complex, like reviving bus services and the quality of education in public schools. A second key contributor was partnerships and community engagement. The mayor's office reached out to citizens and block clubs, who provided ideas on what they thought would be good for the city. They also reached out to universities and institutions to inquire about what might attract talent back to Detroit. A third contributor was decreasing crime. The Federal Bureau of Investigation had once labeled Detroit the most dangerous city in the United States. Boysie explained that they had to work on that image while improving public health and safety to turn things around.

Financially, a key contributor for Detroit was emphasizing the budget process and the budget director's role. Economic development and better budgeting were motivated because Jackson knew that "for every million I save, that's one police officer, one more ambulance, one more bus to improve services. As services improve, people will become more confident in the city and want to move back." In the past five years, Detroit was able to implement performance management initiatives to assist in driving and enforcing standard operating procedures. Now there are metrics associated with city administration that the community can access. "The police chief can stand up now and say, 'This is how long it takes for a 911 call', 'This is how frequently the bus runs,'" and that information can be depended on by citizens. Additionally, these metrics help the administration to measure their progression as they continue to evolve.

For more than eighty years, Puerto Rico offered favorable tax treatment for US companies. The federal government initiated these incentives as a driver of economic growth and tool for industrializing the island, but that practice began to be phased out in 1996. This phaseout occurred without another strategy in place to generate growth, and that change is a factor in the island's underlying economic challenges.[21] The Financial Oversight and Management Board for Puerto Rico along with the Puerto Rican government are currently working through economic development strategy, how they plan to become more competitive, and ways in which they can offer more opportunity. While there are differences of opinion, Matasantos said that one of the areas everyone agrees is a priority is transforming the island's energy infrastructure to become more reliable and affordable. "Puerto Rico has very costly energy, and it's also very unstable. It's not unusual to have significant power outages that have impacts on equipment. In some ways, people carry a second mortgage with the payment of electricity. So making that more reliable and affordable is an important priority." Another priority is restoring fiscal balance and stability.

Differences of opinion have emerged around topics such as reforming labor laws to restore growth and opportunity. Some in Puerto Rico believe that focusing on sectors such as energy transformation will promote growth. But Matasantos stated that there has yet to be the economic plan that PROMESA and the government think will turn things around that everyone is on board with. But she does believe that it is emerging. Referencing the 2017 hurricanes, she elaborated that "it is hard to think of it as a positive when there's been so much individual loss and devastation. But it does mean that there's an influx of more than $60 billion into infrastructure and other opportunities. So in some ways, this can provide an influx of capital to be able to support some of the transformation that without these funds, it was hard to see where it would come from." Specifically, energy, transportation, and housing are some of the areas that would benefit from increased spending.

CHICAGO IS NOT WITHOUT ITS PROBLEMS, BUT NOT AS DIRE AS EITHER OF THESE GOVERNMENTS HAVE FACED. WHAT PIECES OF ADVICE DO YOU HAVE FOR CHICAGO AND OTHER MUNICIPALITIES THAT WILL HELP THEM AVOID BECOMING THE DETROIT OR PUERTO RICO OF THE FUTURE?   Similar to Detroit and Puerto Rico, Chicago is witnessing both population decline and the consequences of unsustainable spending that is propped up with debt. The year 2017 marked the third year in a row that the Chicago metropolitan area lost residents; of the five most populated cities in the United States, it was the only one to see a decline.[22] Not only has Detroit begun to see its population grow, but as of February 2018 the city marked its third year with a balanced budget, and its general fund had an operating surplus of $53.8 million.[23]

There was consensus between Matasantos and Jackson on the advice they would give for avoiding a situation similar to theirs. Governments, policy makers, and leaders need to understand the problem that they are trying to solve and ensure that there is a strong long-term plan for getting there. Simply put by Matasantos, "Where are you, where are you trying to go, and what are the real options that can actually be responsive to the problem?"

Regarding financial options such as pension bonds, Matasantos noted that "one has to think about the cost of capital and the impact of delay." Those making financial decisions regarding pensions need to understand that they "pay now or pay more later." Jackson also spoke of understanding the comprehensive financial situation and planning for the future. In Detroit they transitioned from a one-year budget to a four-year financial plan while becoming more centralized. Previously, departments would spend, and later the budget director would find the money to cover it. Moving forward, the city focused on building relationships with city council, the county, and the mayor to establish priorities and budgets, promoting understanding and transparency. Also important was cultivating relationships with citizens. Engaging the people is an important piece of advice. Information, whether it is about the pension deficit, Medicaid, or a park, needs to be communicated clearly and in a common frame.

CONCLUSION

States and municipalities are facing enormous pressure as they are challenged with slowly increasing revenues paired with increasing expenditures and obligations. This is evident in the decline of infrastructure nationwide and the increasing cost of education and health care. As resources become ever more restricted, difficult decisions are made, whether those decisions are increasing the government's income, shorting financial obligation payments, or cutting funding to public services and programs.

In his closing keynote address, Richard Ravitch, former lieutenant governor of New York, addressed the seriousness of the problems jurisdictions across the country are facing. He called on political action and citizen involvement as the key to progression and reform. "Do politicians care? Yes. Are they willing to take the controversial steps to solve it? No. In our system, if you can kick the can down the road, you will." The time to stop kicking the can is now, before debt and deficits grow larger and before another municipality finds itself in a similar position to Detroit or Puerto Rico. Cities in thirty states have the constitutional authority to file bankruptcy, and eight have done so since 2010.[24] Ana Matasantos offered advice for avoiding these types of situations: "You have to understand what problem you're trying to solve, what is the best assessment of the facts, and try to present the information . . . in a common frame so that folks can decide their relative priorities and make policy choices."

There is a need for more accessible information on public finance to inform the public. This information can be distilled through efforts from educated journalists. A well-informed public can further hold politicians accountable for action that is efficient and transparent—and there are indications of this happening. When asked about anything positive happening in Illinois related to pensions, Laurence Msall added, "It is positive to have this conference. . . . It would not have been imagined twenty years ago in Illinois that people would want to talk about pensions. Public awareness and academic awareness [are] much higher." Like awaiting the long-term benefits of current reforms, there is optimism that the benefits of amplified public and academic awareness will emerge through elected officials unafraid to take on these issues. In both Chicago and Illinois, there is possibility for these shifts to begin soon.

During her keynote address, Toni Preckwinkle spoke of her initial run for the Cook County Board of Commissioners in 2010 and its focus on transforming the government to more truly serve its residents. She had realized that they had to rethink the way Cook County did business in order to transform it, because for too long "Cook County had been content to put a new coat of paint on the house when what it needed was a top-to-bottom rehab." Once voted into office, she tasked her transition team with creating a report that outlined a plan to structurally reform Cook County government. The transition team outlined thirty-seven initiatives that had the intent to make Cook County more efficient, more transparent, and more responsive.

Illinois, Chicago, and municipalities throughout the United States can work toward a future, hopefully nearer than it is far, with elected representatives, supported by their well-informed constituents, who are unafraid to take on challenges and make tough decisions regarding our collective financial future.

Notes

1. Kate Davidson, "U.S. Government Deficit Grew 17% in Fiscal 2018," *Wall Street Journal*, October 15, 2018, www.wsj.com.

2. Rob Kozlowski, "Moody's: Unfunded Liabilities for 50 States Jump to $1.6 Trillion in Fiscal Year 2017," *Pensions and Investments*, August 27, 2018, www.pionline.com.

3. Kozlowski, "Moody's."

4. Greg Hinz, "Cook County Governments Owe $139 Billion—Up to 30% in Six Years," *Crain's Chicago Business*, November 6, 2017, www.chicagobusiness.com.

5. Greg Hinz, "City Hall Floats Idea of Huge Pension Borrowing Plan," *Crain's Chicago Business*, August 3, 2018, www.chicagobusiness.com.

6. Elizabeth Campbell, "Chicago Faces Lowest Budget Gap since 2007 in Coming Fiscal Year," *Bloomberg*, July 31, 2018, www.bloomberg.com.

7. Jeff Coltin, "Five Things to Know about the NYC Budget Deal," *City and State New York*, June 11, 2018, www.cityandstateny.com.

8. City of Chicago, Mayor Rahm Emanuel, 2019 Budget Overview, "Proposed 2019 Budget: Key Reforms, Savings and Investment," www.cityofchicago.org, 23.

9. City of Chicago, Mayor Rahm Emanuel, 2018 Budget Overview, "Proposed 2018 Budget: Key Reforms, Savings and Investment," www.cityofchicago.org, 11.

10. New York City Independent Budget Office, "Understanding New York City's Budget: A Guide," July 2017, www.ibo.nyc.ny.us, 7.

11. Mayor's Office of Management and Budget, the City of New York Executive Budget Fiscal Year 2019, "Citywide Savings Program," April 2018, www1.nyc.gov, 2.

12. Institute for Illinois' Fiscal Sustainability at the Civic Federation, "Illinois Passes Budget on Time; Fiscal Challenges Remain," June 8, 2018, www.civicfed.org.

13. Hinz, "Cook County Governments Owe $139 Billion."

14. Hinz, "City Hall Floats Idea."

15. Pew Center on the States, "Promises with a Price: Public Sector Retirement Benefits," principal authors Katherine Barrett and Richard Greene, December 2007, www.sanjoseca.gov, 63.

16. Karen Pierog, "Savings from Illinois' Pension Buyout Plan Could Fall Short," Reuters, May 31, 2018, www.reuters.com.

17. Pete Saunders, "Detroit after Bankruptcy," *Forbes*, April 24, 2016, www.forbes.com.

18. Laura Sullivan, "How Puerto Rico's Debt Created a Perfect Storm before the Storm," NPR, May 2, 2018, www.npr.org.

19. World Population Review, "Detroit, Michigan, Population 2018," June 3, 2018, http://worldpopulationreview.com.

20. Arelis R. Hernandez, "Exodus from Puerto Rico Grows as Island Struggles to Rebound from Hurricane," *Washington Post*, March 6, 2018, www.washingtonpost.com.

21. Marc D. Joffe and Jesse Martinez, "Origins of the Puerto Rico Fiscal Crisis," Mercatus Center, George Mason University, April 2016, www.mercatus.org.

22. Kristen Thometz, "Chicago Population Drops for 3rd Straight Year," WTTW News, May 24, 2018, https://news.wttw.com.

23. Annalise Frank, "Detroit Posts Third Year of Balanced Budgets; State Oversight Could End Soon," *Crain's Detroit Business*, February 2, 2018, https://news.wttw.com.

24. Brad Plumer, "Detroit Isn't Alone. The U.S. Cities That Have Gone Bankrupt, in One Map," *Washington Post*, July 18, 2013, www.washingtonpost.com.

PART TWO

WHITE PAPERS

Local Government Long-Term Liabilities

Pensions, Other Postemployment Benefits, and Infrastructure

MARTIN J. LUBY, GARY STRONG, AND DAVID SAUSTAD

In a previous era, discussion of local government long-term liabilities would likely induce sleepiness for most except maybe some accountants, public finance academics, fiscal watchdogs, and a very small slice of the citizenry.[1] This is no longer the case. The chronic underfunding of pensions, other postemployment benefits (OPEBs), and infrastructure maintenance and investment over the past several decades has created serious fiscal challenges for local governments—challenges that have been a topic of considerable interest in recent years. Many local governments continue to be challenged by ballooning pension and other postretirement benefits that cause these governments to reduce spending in everyday services and programs as well as to defer funding of infrastructure maintenance or to scrap investments in new capital projects altogether.[2]

This chapter aims to provide a general primer on this topic. First, we report on the size of the underfunding problem for US local governments in terms of three areas: pensions, other postemployment benefits, and deferred infrastructure maintenance and investment. Second, we explore various hypotheses that seek to explain why local governments underfunded these areas. Third, we detail the fiscal and policy consequences from such underfunding of long-term liabilities. The chapter concludes with a discussion of options available to make local public officials more accountable so that such underfunding of long-term liabilities is less likely to occur in the future.

SIZE OF THE PROBLEM

Pensions

The underfunding of pensions has received the most attention among local government long-term liabilities. For most local governments, pensions are structured as a defined-benefit plan whereby local government workers defer part of their compensation to be deposited into pension funds along with contributions made by the sponsoring government. These contributions, along with interest earnings from the fund, are used to make pension payments to these government employees, and sometimes their spouses, in retirement for as long as they live. The local government has flexibility in terms of the timing and amount of its contributions. The misuse of this flexibility has been one of the driving factors in the underfunding of local government pensions.

Local governments must account for their long-term pension obligations on an accrual basis. Thus, they must report the actuarial accrued liability, the actuarial value of assets, the unfunded liability, the funded ratio, and the annual required contribution (ARC) payment. All of these statistics have received considerable attention in the past decade or so, given the size of the underfunding problem for this type of long-term liability. However, the calculation of these statistics is not without controversy. More specifically, there has been considerable debate on the actual mechanics of estimating pension underfunding at the state and local government levels. This debate is generally beyond the scope of this paper but revolves around three areas: the proper discount rate, differentiating pension payments related to past and future service, and the calculation of asset values based on multiyear averages.[3]

Table 1 summarizes studies that have estimated long-term liabilities at the local government level in the United States. Joshua Rauh of Stanford has often been cited in his estimations of local government pension liabilities. Rauh estimates the pension funding deficits for the largest forty cities and twenty-five counties based on 2015 data.[4] In terms of dollar underfunding, the forty largest cities reported total unfunded pension liabilities of $163.61 billion, while the twenty-five largest counties reported $51.9 billion in total unfunded pension liabilities, for a combined total of $215.51 billion. Rauh argues, however, that local governments use overly optimistic assumed investment returns when calculating their ARC payments and further exacerbate the problem by using a discount rate for future obligations that mirrors the potentially inflated assumed investment returns. In 2015 the liability-

Table 1. Estimates of pension and OPEB unfunded dollar amounts at the US local government level

	Pension amount	OPEB amount	Data year	Sample
Rauh	$558 billion	No estimate	2015	40 largest cities, 25 largest counties
Munnell et al.	$2.94 trillion	$328 billion	2014	46% of counties, 43% of cities, and 26% of school districts
Pew	$99 billion	$118 billion	2009	61 key cities
GAO	No estimate	$129 billion	2008	39 large local governments

weighted average expected return was 7.6 percent. Rauh rediscounts future liabilities with a more conservative 2.77 percent, based on a risk-free Treasury bond–based return. Rauh calls the Treasury-based rediscounted estimate the Market Value Liability (MVL). This methodology leads to far higher funding deficit estimates and paints a much grimmer picture. Using the MVL, the underfunding for the forty largest cities jumps to $407.38 billion, while the underfunding for the twenty-five largest counties jumps to $151.08 billion, for a combined total of $558.46 billion.

The funding ratio of total accrued assets versus total accrued liabilities tells a similar story, with wide variability between stated and MVL funding ratios. The City of Chicago has the lowest funding ratio, with a stated funding ratio of 36 percent and an abysmal 19.9 percent MVL funding ratio, while Fresno has the highest funding ratio, with a 112 percent stated funding ratio and an MVL funding ratio of 64 percent. These obligations translate into heavy burdens as a share of local government revenue. In 2015 Chicago had the highest percentage of its own revenues going to cover pension obligations at a whopping 23.1 percent, while eleven of the other forty biggest cities had more than 10 percent of their own revenues consumed by pension obligations.

Just like with dollar underfunding and funding ratios, the fiscal obstacle becomes even more daunting if MVL is used instead of expected investment returns. If MVL is used, eleven of the forty biggest cities would need to spend over 20 percent of their own revenues in order to avoid a rise in future pension obligations, with Chicago needing to spend a staggering 44.5 percent of its own revenue. With the exceptions of Detroit, Miami, Philadelphia, New Orleans, Nashville, Indianapolis, Sacramento, and Long Beach, all thirty-two of the other biggest cities contributed far less than was needed to prevent a future rise in unfunded pension liabilities, which indicates that the problem will continue to grow over time. The twenty-five largest counties displayed correspondingly low funding ratios, with Wayne County, Michigan, showing the lowest funding ratio at 31.6 percent, and Macomb County, Michigan, showing the highest funding ratio at 76.7 percent. Fresno County, California, had the highest percentage of their own revenue consumed by pension obligations at 37.6 percent, but that number jumps to a disabling 61.3 percent if MVL is used. Similarly, if MVL is used, Cook County, Illinois, and Orange, San Diego, and Kern Counties in California would need to contribute more than 40 percent of their own revenues to avoid increasing liabilities.

Another oft-cited researcher on postretirement underfunding is Alicia Munnell. Munnell and Aubry analyzed data from 2014 for pension plans administered by 178 counties, 173 cities, and 415 school districts in an attempt to determine how much of the burden from state cost-sharing plans was the responsibility of local governments.[5] Their analysis determined that a full 60 percent of the pension liabilities in state-administered pension plans falls squarely on local governments, which translated to a combined $2.94 trillion in total pension obligations. Munnell and Aubry did not address any of the MVL/discounting issues that Rauh argues, but their data showed that eleven of the fifty biggest cities had pension contributions that accounted for over 20 percent of their own revenues. Although Munnell and Aubry's sample was quite robust, their data covers only 46 percent of counties, 43 percent of cities, and 26 percent of school districts. The Pew Charitable Trusts analyzed 2010 data for a sample of sixty-one key cities across the country, including the largest city in each state and all other cities with a population greater than 500,000, and showed similar results.[6] In fiscal year 2009, the cities in their sample displayed $99 billion in unfunded liabilities. They also ran a follow-up analysis of forty cities in their sample for 2010 and found that their unfunded pension liabilities had grown by 15 percent from 2009. Although these studies captured a wide sample of local governments, they were far from exhaustive, so the estimates of total pension obligations are conservative in terms of covering the entire landscape of local governments.

Other Postemployment Benefits

Other postemployment benefits represent additional deferred compensation that most local governments also provide their employees. The largest OPEB is retiree health insurance that these governments subsidize for their workers in retirement. Historically, most governments have not prefunded their OPEB liabilities like they have for pensions. Rather, these governments paid for these costs on a pay-as-you-go basis as an annual expense. Due to the sharp rise in health care costs and health insurance premiums, the Government Accounting Standards Board (GASB) promulgated new guidelines in 2007 (GASB 45) that required governments to account for their OPEB liabilities on an accrual basis rather than cash basis. GASB 45 incentivized some researchers to estimate state and local OPEB liabilities on individual government and national aggregate bases, as has been performed for pensions.

Munnell and Aubry's sample of 2014 data for 46 percent of counties, 43 percent of cities, and 26 percent of school districts estimates a combined total of $369.3 billion in local OPEB liabilities, with only $41.3 billion in current assets, leaving $328.1 billion in liabilities unfunded. The Pew Charitable Trusts also performed an analysis of their sample of sixty-one key cities on their OPEB liabilities.[7] The key cities had an estimated $118.2 billion in OPEB liabilities that translated to an anemic 6 percent funded ratio. The Government Accountability Office (GAO) ran a more limited study of thirty-nine large local governments based on 2008 data and found that their unfunded OPEB liabilities exceeded $129 billion.[8] There was significant variability between these local governments, ranging from only $15 million for a county in Arizona to a staggering $59 billion for New York City. The GAO found similar funding ratios as the aforementioned Munnell study, reporting that of the thirty-nine local governments only thirteen had set aside any assets to prefund their OPEB liabilities, with the remaining twenty-six local governments holding zero assets, which led to an estimated funding ratio of only 5 percent.

OPEB plans typically use much lower discount rates than pension plans due to their unfunded nature, with counties and school districts using an average discount rate of 4.9 percent and cities use a slightly higher average discount rate of 5.6 percent. This lower discount rate may lead to less controversy surrounding their methodology, but some analysts may argue that the rate is still too high. OPEB benefits are somewhat more flexible than pension obligations in that municipalities have more freedom to adjust benefits by increasing deductibles and co-pays or increasing the percentage of the premium paid by the employee. This flexibility could provide some relief to local government budgets, but that relief could be politically difficult to enact, as reducing health benefits often leads to widespread public outcry. As with the pension estimates, the OPEB estimates cover only an incomplete cross-section of local government obligations, so these estimates must be considered conservative in terms of covering the entire landscape of local governments.

Infrastructure

Infrastructure, the third category of underfunding, is not technically a long-term liability but rather refers to the condition of a government's physical capital assets. However, disinvestment in the nation's infrastructure essentially represents a liability, as such investment will have to be made sometime in the future, at which point it will require more resources than if such investment was made today.

Before providing formal estimates of such infrastructure deficits, we must understand what this concept of infrastructure really entails. The American Society of Civil Engineers (ASCE) classifies infrastructure into sixteen categories: aviation, bridges, dams, drinking water, energy, hazardous waste, inland waterways, levees, parks and recreation, ports, rail, roads, schools, solid waste, transit, and wastewater.[9] Hume compresses these categories, creating a five-prong taxonomy of infrastructure: horizontal (streets, bridges, sewers, water systems, etc.), technology (broadband, cellular service, electricity grid), creative (parks, libraries, nature spaces, etc.), mush sector (investments in schools, hospitals, higher-education facilities), and federal and state (investments in other infrastructure run by the federal and state governments that impact local government infrastructure such as harbors and interstate highways).[10]

The popular press has well documented the lack of investment made by all US levels of government in infrastructure over the past few decades. In fact, President Trump recognized the acuteness of such policy challenge by including infrastructure funding as a prominent plank in his presidential campaign. Probably the most comprehensive estimate of the state of the United States' infrastructure is made by the American Society of Civil Engineers every four years. Considering all three levels of government, the ASCE gave the United States a grade of D+ (which represents a grade of "poor") in its most recent estimate in 2017.[11] These engineers estimate that it would require $4.6 trillion in infrastructure investment to bring the nation's infrastructure to a state of "good" repair by 2025. As of 2017, only 55 percent had been committed to this infrastructure need, which represents a $2 trillion funding gap. While this report does not break out funding responsibility by level of government, other analysts have claimed that state and local governments own 90 percent of nondefense government physical assets and estimate that 75 percent of the funding for these assets have historically been the responsibility of state and local governments.[12] According to the US Census Bureau's 2015 Annual Surveys of State and Local Government Finances, state and local governments made $334 billion in direct expenditure capital outlays in 2015. Local governments made $210 billion in capital outlays, while state governments made $124 billion in capital outlays.[13] This represents a split of 63 percent to 37 percent between local and state governments in capital spending.

Based on a $2 trillion funding gap in which state and local governments own 90 percent of the physical assets and bear 75 percent of the costs of the assets they own, subnational governments in the United States would be responsible for $1.35 trillion of the $2 trillion infrastructure deficit (that is, $2 trillion × 90% × 75%). Assuming a 63–37 split between local and state governments, local governments in the United States would bear $850 billion of the infrastructure deficit. Of course, there is likely much diversity in the infrastructure deficit among local governments. The 2017 American Society Civil Engineers evinces this diversity by assigning states different ratings as well as ratings across different types of assets that may be more or less the responsibility of local governments.

WHY UNDERFUND?

With the underfunding size of local government long-term liabilities detailed, we now explore the possible causes of such underfunding. Not surprisingly, the underfunding problem does not seem to have just one or two causes but is due to a multitude of factors. The extent of influence of these factors is dependent on the local government. For some local governments, many of these factors are "in play" in terms of contributing to the underfunding problem, whereas maybe only one or two of these factors drive the problem in other governments.[14] We describe these factors in terms of four broad categories: political, institutional, fiscal, and financial.

Political Factors

The political causes of underfunding long-term liabilities are commonly cited in the popular press.[15] The shortsighted nature of decision making is often attributed as an inherent problem of elected officials who often make decisions mainly to maximize the likelihood of their success at the next election.[16] Erick Elder and Gary Wagner use data from ninety-one state and local pension plans from 2001 to 2010 to show that greater electoral competition, legislative term limits, and higher rates of legislative turnover lead to pension underfunding. Further, they find that term limits reduce average pension funding ratios by about 10 percentage points. Theoretically, public choice theory related to the concept of "fiscal illusion" provides support to the notion that government officials often make financial decisions in the short-term fiscal interests of the taxpayers that also provide electoral benefits to current politicians.[17] For example, at the state and local levels, there are many tangible examples of the way in which governments use debt to mask deficits and defer hard taxing and spending choices.[18] The underfunding of pensions and the lack of prefunding OPEB liabilities clearly fit into this category. To the extent elected officials defer spending in these areas, they can spend more money in other policy areas that curry favor with the citizenry. One of these policy areas is often infrastructure in which the benefits of prominent capital projects are instantly visible to the public through a traditional ribbon-cutting ceremony.[19] Alternatively, skirting their prefunding responsibility of pensions and OPEBs provides additional revenues that local governments can use to justify cutting taxes or providing rebates (for example, increasing the homestead exemption for property owners) to its taxpayers.

Of course, it "takes two to tango" in terms of the political nature of the underfunding decisions described above. It has been widely documented that many Americans have an aversion to both higher taxes and a reduction in the level of government services they are used to receiving.[20] For example, Pew Research Center surveys since 2009 have found that majorities in both political parties favor maintaining or increasing government spending in all budget areas except unemployment benefits,[21] while Gallup has reported during the same period that more than half Americans think their federal income taxes are too high in most years.[22] In the 1970s and 1980s, the "starve the beast" experiment was attempted in which the federal government reduced taxes as a mechanism to force government spending cuts. This experiment has been widely viewed as a failure. William Niskanen shows that the reduction in federal revenues between 1981 and 2005 saw an increase in federal spending, the exact opposite effect of what "starve the beast" intended.[23] What seems obvious now is that citizens "want their cake and eat it too"—they want lower tax burdens but do not want a concomitant reduction in government services to accompany such lower tax revenues. Thus, local elected officials, in shortsightedly underfunding pensions and OPEBs to free up money to either spend elsewhere or return to their taxpayers, are acting quite rationally, in a political sense, by responding to the incentives provided to them by the ones who placed them in office.

Institutional Factors

The institutional causes of underfunding long-term liabilities mainly relate to restrictions on the fiscal autonomy of local governments. The increase in tax and expenditure limitations (TELs) at the state and local levels has in many cases reduced local governments' ability to meet their fiscal needs.[24] Currently, most states have placed binding property tax limitations on cities, while eight states have established expenditure limitations.[25] Sharon Kioko, using data on county governments between 1970 and 2004, found that TELs negatively impacted counties' unrestricted cash reserves. With fewer cash reserves, local governments will find it difficult to navigate through economic recessions. Moreover, property tax limitations can reduce the amount of revenue local governments realize from their most important revenue source. State restrictions on the types and structure of other local government taxes have the same effect. At the same time, in the context of statutory or constitutional spending limitations, demands for increased local government spending have not abated both because of increased citizenry demands and as a result of increased devolution of government responsibilities from the federal and state levels to the local level.[26] In this context of smaller than possible fiscal resources and increased spending needs alongside expenditure caps, local governments are incentivized to defer prefunding pensions and OPEBs to address such mismatch on the two sides of the government ledger.

Increased restrictions on the amount and type of debt local governments can issue for infrastructure purposes has a similar effect. Many local governments are restricted by voter approval on the amount of debt they can sell to fund capital projects. In many parts of the country, securing voter approval for such bond financing has been difficult to achieve even as interest rates have been historically low for almost two decades.[27] Absent such approval, governments rely on funds on hand or pay-as-you-go financing to fund such projects. Given the scarcity of resources on hand at all levels of governments over the past few decades, restrictions on debt financing have had a de facto result of significantly slowing investment in infrastructure. Of course, local governments have tried to get around these debt restrictions by creating other financial instruments, like revenue bonds, that may not be subject to voter referendum. These attempts were successful years ago, but as the citizenry has become more aware of such financial gamesmanship, it seems such efforts by local governments have diminished.[28] For instance, in 2016, a group of California residents created Proposition 53, a referendum on requiring voter approval of revenue bonds exceeding $2 billion. California voters narrowly defeated the proposition. However, the creation of the proposition shows that voters are becoming more aware of state and local government usage of revenue bonds.

The creation of fiscal institutions like TELs and debt limitations was intended, at least partly, to help local governments keep their long-term fiscal house in order. However, such limitations are blunt instruments that have many perverse effects, including the underfunding of long-term liabilities.[29] Moreover, they are a sort of "drive by" policy response in that they are restrictions put in place by a higher level of government to achieve a particular result without ongoing monitoring. On the contrary, a different type of institutional response in lieu of (or in addition to) TELs and debt restrictions would be active fiscal oversight of local governments by the state government. Many analysts argue that greater oversight by the state would result in fiscal decision making that would have been in the better long-term fiscal interests of the local government.[30] Unfortunately, many states have no institutional oversight of local governments, while many others are obligated to make relatively minimal effort. For instance, a Pew Charitable Trusts study found that only eight states had systems in place that detected when local governments became "fiscally distressed."[31] Thus, it seems likely that such lax institutional oversight contributed to the shortsighted decisions of local governments to underfund their pensions, OPEBs, and infrastructure investment.

Fiscal Factors

In addition to political and institutional causes, fiscal issues have contributed in a number of ways to the underfunding of local government long-term liabilities. First, the declining base of the sales tax has resulted in slower growth of sales tax revenues compared to the growth of the economy as a whole. The base has declined as a result of two changing consumption patterns. First, the US economy has increasingly become a more service-based and less goods-based economy, with many services not taxed at the state and local levels.[32] Second, US consumers over the past three decades have increasingly bought their goods online, with such purchases often untaxed or taxed at lower rates.[33] Both of these buying patterns have reduced the base of the sales tax, which has reduced the available resources for local governments to fund long-term liabilities. The declining sales tax base has also reduced capital spending, since many local governments sell bonds backed by their sales tax revenues. To the extent that the sales tax based has been narrowed, there are fewer sales tax revenues available to support such bonds, which results in smaller bond sales to fund capital spending.

On the spending side of the fiscal equation, local governments, like the federal government, state governments, private-sector firms, and individuals have been budgetarily challenged by escalating health care costs over the past couple of decades.[34] At the local level, these budgetary expenses have increased as a result of increased health care premiums for current employees and greater health care costs associated with more expensive medical care provided by local governments, as well as an increase in the population served by local government health care providers as individuals choose not to purchase insurance due to rising premiums.[35] Like any other spending pressure, increased expenditures on health care costs in the current budget leave less resources available for other spending, including on pensions, OPEBs, and infrastructure.

Financial Factors

There are a number of possible financial causes to the underfunding of local government long-term liabilities. While the concepts of "financial" and "fiscal" are related, we use the term "fiscal" to identify government revenue and spending causes, whereas the term "financial" mainly relates to financial decision making, often connected to capital market decisions or changes in the financial markets associated with such underfunding. The obvious first financial cause of underfunding relates to the deep recession experienced by local governments in 2007–8. The value of pension investments declined considerably as a result of the financial crisis, as equity and other asset values dropped dramatically.[36] In some parts of the country, the decline in property values as a result of the subprime mortgage crisis put downward pressure on property tax revenues, which also resulted in a reduction in government resources to fund pensions, OPEBs, and infrastructure investments.[37] However, many of these pension funds have witnessed significant growth in recent years, while property values have recovered in most parts of the country since the Great Recession. Given such recovery, we need to be careful relying on some of the pension funding estimates described previously that were estimated only at the onset of such asset-price rebound.

Some local governments employed financial instruments that were greatly affected by the financial crisis. For example, the use of interest-rate swaps and auction-rate securities resulted in much higher debt-service costs than expected for many of these governments during this time. The *Wall Street*

Journal reported a $1.25 billion estimate from the Service Employees Union International of the cost of interest-rate swaps for a sampling of US cities that were dealing with significant budget challenges in 2010.[38] To the extent greater than expected resources were allocated to pay debt-service and termination payments on these instruments, less money was available for pensions, OPEBs, and infrastructure spending. This was not lost on various stakeholders of local government finances. For example, the Chicago Teachers Union demanded that the Chicago Public Schools renegotiate with the investment banks that marketed these financial instruments, given the stress they put on school finances.[39]

The decision by local governments to use another financial instrument, pension obligation bonds, has had a mixed impact on pension finances. POBs are municipal bonds in which the sale proceeds are used to fund a portion of the unfunded pension liability. Under a POB, the government is hoping the return on the pension-bond proceeds is greater than the cost of the debt. To the extent such return is greater, the unfunded liability is reduced by the difference. However, if the return is less, the unfunded liability actually becomes greater than if the government did not sell the POB. Munnell, Aubry, and Cafarelli found that POBs had a negative average real return between 1992 and 2009 but a small gain when the period was extended to 2014.[40] However, the success of POBs is heavily reliant on timing, so POBs sold in the late 1990s often continue to have a negative return, while POBs sold in the early 2000s garner a positive return. Moreover, Munnell, Aubry, and Cafarelli found that POBs tend to be used by governments under the most financial pressure, which are precisely the sorts of entities that should be reducing their financial risk, not increasing it through the use of a financial risky instrument like a POB. In any event, for some governments, POBs have helped their pension underfunding, while for others they have hurt their position.

Illustrating the zero-sum nature of the underfunding of liabilities situation for local governments is the decision by some governments to use new revenues for pensions. Given that the gravity of the pension funding situation is compounded by the political difficulty in raising taxes and fees, some governments have turned to user fees that are more acceptable to the public to help fund pensions.[41] For example, the City of Chicago implemented a four-year phase-in between 2017 and 2021 of a new water and sewer utility tax to make newly mandated pension payments.[42] In the past, water and sewer fees were used primarily to fund capital improvements to the city's water and wastewater system. City residents received a separate water and sewer bill but were generally supportive of it because they understood what such a bill was funding. As such, the city has been able to embark on a consistently sizable capital program related to its water and sewer infrastructure. The tax-benefit linkage has been eroded by adding pension funding to the use of water and sewer taxes, so it is unclear how citizens will view future increases in this tax necessary for capital spending. More urgently, the implementation of the new water and sewer tax to fund pensions reduces the future opportunity for the city to use these specific revenues for the traditional capital improvements it has made in the past.

Another financial cause could also be classified as a political one. For some local governments, elected officials made the financial decision to provide enhanced pension benefits or offer early retirement programs.[43] These financial decisions were made to provide short-term operating budgetary relief, as they either removed salaries altogether from the payrolls (via the early retirement program) or reduced the size of demand for annual increases in current employee salaries (by promising larger pension benefits in the future). In both cases, these financial decisions enhanced the size of pension underfunding either by creating more generous pension benefit formulas or by pushing people onto the pension rolls earlier. No doubt these promises were political in nature, but there was a degree of poor financial decision making in play as well. For example, in 2002 the state of Illinois implemented an early retirement initiative that was estimated to cost $622 million in additional unfunded pension liability but ended up costing $2.5 billion, which represents a misestimation of $1.8 billion. The error in estimation was mainly due to underestimating how many and what types of employees would avail themselves of the early retirement initiative.[44] That size of estimation error is indicative of a substantial degree of financial policy mismanagement.

Two financial factors have had a mitigating impact on the underfunding of long-term liabilities. The first financial factor relates to the provision in the federal American Recovery and Reinvestment Act that created the Build America Bond program. The BAB program was a direct-subsidy bond program that provided local governments a 35 percent subsidy of their interest payments on the sale of taxable BABs. This represented a generous financial subsidy that led state and local governments to issue more than $181 billion in BABs in 2009 and 2010 (the BAB program expired on December 31, 2010). With the help of the BAB program, municipal bond issuance for 2009 and 2010 was $532 and $547 billion, respectively. Municipal bond issuance in 2011, the year after the BAB program's sunset, was $394 billion. Since 2011 municipal bond issuance has not exceeded $470 billion, with several years in the high $300 million range.[45] Thus, it appears that this federal policy increased spending on infrastructure beyond what it would have been without implementation of the BAB program.

The second mitigating financial factor has been the historically low level of interest rates over the past fifteen years. As interest rates have declined and stayed low in this time period, local governments have been afforded the ability to sell lower cost debt, either to refinance existing debt to create budgetary savings or to fund new capital investment. It is impossible to determine how much additional debt was sold for new capital projects that otherwise would not have been sold absent the favorable interest rates. However, we can draw some tentative conclusions from the trend in bonds sold to refinance old debt. Specifically, more than 40 percent of municipal bonds on average per year by par value since 2000 have been sold to refinance existing debt. This composition has only accelerated in recent years, with 2016 seeing 58 percent of par value municipal bonds sold for refunding purposes.[46] These interest cost savings provide additional resources for local governments to increase their prefunding of pensions or OPEB liabilities, pay for other programmatic spending, or issue more debt to fund infrastructure. Thus, it is likely that the advantageous interest-rate environment has improved the underfunding of long-term liabilities over what it otherwise would be for many local governments.[47]

CONSEQUENCES OF UNDERFUNDING

With the size of the problem detailed and its potential causes identified, we now turn to an exploration of the various consequences of local government underfunding of long-term liabilities. We group these consequences into three categories: budgetary, economic, and intergovernmental relations.

Budgetary Consequences

The first budgetary implication from underfunding is straightforward. Underfunding pension and OPEB liabilities in past and current budgets means that future budgets will entail greater resources to satisfy these commitments. Such greater budgetary allocations to OPEBs and pensions means spending in other areas such as public safety, education, and health care is crowded out. Related to this chapter, it also may mean funding for investment in infrastructure is reduced as well. Of course, the deeper and the more prolonged a local government underfunds it long-term liabilities, the more difficult and painful it is to address at some point in the future. The state of Illinois offers an illustrative example of this. Illinois has underfunded its pension liabilities for decades, which has resulted in an annual structural budget gap that has persisted for more than a decade. This budgetary deficiency has been a significant factor in the state holding the lowest credit rating of all fifty US states, which speaks to the severity of the problem and the budgetary pain that will likely need to occur to rectify it.[48] For example, according to the Fiscal Futures Project at the University of Illinois, it could take almost two decades for the state of Illinois to eliminate this structural budget gap, even if it restrains spending to the lowest growth rate observed by state governments over the past twenty years.[49]

Another budgetary consequence of underfunding pensions and OPEBs, as previously described, is that revenues normally earmarked for other purposes (including infrastructure) are now used to make up payments to the pension funds and OPEB liabilities. The City of Chicago's use of a water and sewer tax that would normally be earmarked to maintain the city's capital infrastructure related to its water and wastewater systems is an example of this consequence. Thus, in this case, the increase in funding to pension and OPEB liabilities with capital dollars reduces capital spending on a dollar-for-dollar basis.

The third budgetary consequence relates to a local government's financial condition as expressed by its credit ratings. In recent years, the credit-rating agencies (and investors) have paid much more attention to a local government's funding of its long-term liabilities.[50] Of course, these stakeholders have focused on the size of the government's unfunded pension liabilities and its OPEB requirements, as the size of these liabilities has the potential to severely hamper a government's ability to satisfy its creditors. However, the rating agencies have also begun to pay greater attention to the condition of a local government's infrastructure, as disinvestment in physical assets can have serious long-term economic consequences. For instance, in 2018 S&P Global Ratings commended Washington, DC, on its plan to determine funding for deferred maintenance on infrastructure. In the report, S&P warned state and local governments that if they did not create funding plans, they would risk hurting their credit ratings.[51] From a budgetary perspective, decreases in a local government's credit rating result in the government having to pay additional interest costs to investors in their debt obligations to compensate these investors for the additional risk of such financial instruments. For example, a general-obligation bond sale sold by the Chicago Public Schools in July 2017 priced at 490 basis points higher than a top-rated municipal bond on the same day.[52] Depending on the repayment source of the financial instrument, such additional borrowing costs will apply upward spending pressure on the local government's operating or capital budget and crowd out other spending in current operations or reduce the size of future infrastructure investment.

Economic Consequences

In addition to the more direct budgetary impact, the underfunding of long-term liabilities has significant economic consequences that arrive over both the short and the long term. First, as mentioned above, delays in funding a local government's long-term commitments will necessitate more dramatic revenue activities in the future. Depending on how acute the underfunding, this may involve significant tax and fee increases. Based on traditional economic theory, taxation creates deadweight loss, which is a loss in economic efficiency in the overall economy. Mathematically, the size of deadweight loss is a function of the square of the tax rate (in addition to the elasticity of supply and demand).[53] As such, deadweight loss increases quadratically with an increase in the tax rate. A local government that needs to increase taxes significantly can expect such policy action to result in significant deadweight loss and thus a reduction in economic efficiency.

Sizable unfunded liabilities also impact the economic decisions of firms and individuals.[54] For example, vendors to local governments may not provide their services or may price them higher than normal to local governments in which there is a risk of nonpayment due to the budgetary pressure of unfunded pensions and OPEB liabilities. More dramatically, individuals or business may not locate or may exit jurisdictions where they believe that their tax liabilities will sharply increase in the future to deal with these unfunded liabilities. A study by the Center for Retirement Research at Boston College found that a state's unfunded pension liability informs and motivates decisions to move. They note that negative media attention on a state's pension problems can affect the attractiveness of the state.[55] Further, these same firms may also not locate in these local governments if their physical infrastructure is deteriorating compared to other municipalities, both out of fear of future higher taxes to remedy the infrastructure problems and because they will not be able to avail themselves of adequate physical infrastructure. These locational decisions, while essentially indirect economic effects, will translate into direct future budgetary impacts when they result in a narrower tax base from which budget resources can be extracted.

In addition to distorting locational choices, it has long been understood that a government's crumbling physical infrastructure also imposes immediate economic costs beyond financial ones. Because infrastructure is so expansive, ranging from physical assets like roads and bridges to telecommunication systems to health care facilities to educational buildings, disinvestment has severe economic consequences. These impacts are varied and include reduced educational experiences and opportunities, less effective health care services, additional travel time, and missed business investment opportunities.[56] These impacts result in slower growth or declines (or both) in economic growth (gross domestic product), wages, productivity, employment levels, and income levels. The various stakeholders in local government experience these consequences in the short term, but they become only more pronounced over the long term as infrastructure neglect continues.

One could also view underfunding of long-term liabilities as a type of fiscal illusion that has implications for the size and scope of government. Fiscal illusion is an economic theory traditionally focusing on the revenue side of public budgets. Specifically, fiscal illusion describes how a government's use of nontransparent revenues makes taxpayers think government costs less than it actually does, which eventually leads to an increase in the size of government as these taxpayers come to enjoy the government services that these revenues fund.[57] A similar phenomenon is in place when a government underfunds pensions and OPEB liabilities or does not make the requisite investment in its infrastructure and instead provides other services with the revenues that should have been used to satisfy these previous unfunded commitments. If the taxpayers are ignorant of how this underfunding has effectively underwritten these additional services that they have now come to expect, appetite for government programs may grow and these taxpayers may demand the government expand its offerings.

Intergovernmental Relations Consequences

The extreme underfunding of local government long-term liabilities may also result in a shift in fiscal federalism. Local governments that need financial bailouts from their state government or changes in state law to help ameliorate their fiscal situation may find themselves in a weakened state going forward in terms of intergovernmental relations.[58] For example, the underfunding of pension and health care liabilities as well as sizable long-term bonded indebtedness contributed significantly to the decline in fiscal health of the City of Detroit.[59] This fiscal stress necessitated that the city seek help from the state of Michigan in 2012. Ultimately, Michigan governor Rick Snyder appoint Kevyn Orr as emergency manager of the city to oversee all financial operations. Subsequently, Orr recommended Detroit enter bankruptcy, which had to be approved by Governor Snyder. The case of Detroit offers an extreme example of how a local government can lose policy and fiscal autonomy as a result of underfunding its long-term liabilities.

Even if state intervention is not as extreme as in the case of Detroit, increased reliance on state assistance to help with underfunded pensions and health care or to provide additional funding for infrastructure introduces greater financial risk onto a local government's balance sheet. In terms of financial condition analysis generally, a local government's reliance on revenues from other levels of government reduces the local government's "stability of revenues." According to Granof and colleagues, "Failure to take advantage of appropriate intergovernmental grants can be rightfully interpreted as proof of poor management. But what a granting government gives, it can also take away. Therefore, a high or increasing ratio of intergovernmental revenues to total revenues is a sign of risk and hence is generally considered a negative fiscal characteristic."[60] While Granof and colleagues are cautioning about overreliance on intergovernmental revenues as a percentage of a local government's entire revenue base, the logic and risk can easily be applied to relying heavily on intergovernmental revenues to fund pensions, OPEBs, and infrastructure costs.

HOW CAN WE HOLD CITY OFFICIALS ACCOUNTABLE?

The previous sections of this paper detailed the size of the problem as well as its causes and consequences. We now evaluate some possible statutory and policy changes that have been advanced to better hold elected city officials accountable in ensuring that local governments adequately fund their long-term liabilities in the future. We have identified a menu of possible changes broken into three categories: institutional, political, and financial. We are not suggesting that all of these changes are advisable or feasible, but they do consist of an array of choices policy makers and the public may want to consider in better holding their elected officials more accountable in the future.

Institutional Changes

One possible institutional change that may reduce the likelihood of local governments underfunding their long-term liabilities is to increase the stringency of balanced-budget requirements, tax and expenditure limitations, or both. Such increase in stringency would include a statutory or even constitutional requirement that unfunded liabilities are reduced or funded at certain levels year over year in the context of the local government's annual budget process. Under such regime, local governments would be statutorily forced to deal with their long-term liability funding issues rather than providing these governments flexibility to address this fiscal area. Many local governments already have such statutory requirements, so changes would really be related to enhancing existing requirements. The 2017 state legislation that increased the City of Chicago's funding ramp of its municipal pension fund is an example of this approach.[61] Of course, all of the fiscal problems associated with TELs and balanced-budget requirements previously discussed would be present under such a regime. In addition, such increase in budget stringency would necessitate a reduction in the flexibility for governments to allocate their resources to other spending priorities.

Some have argued that a "no-bailout" policy from state governments onto local governments may incentivize these local governments to ensure their long-term liabilities are adequately funded.[62] Knowing that they will not be bailed out by their state government may induce local governments to pursue long-term prudent fiscal policies, including policies related to the funding of pension, OPEBs, and infrastructure. Related to this no-bailout strategy is the strengthening and expansion of municipal bankruptcy laws of which local governments can avail themselves. The basic logic of this policy option is that it has taken decades for select local governments to significantly underfund their long-term liabilities to the extent that it will be impossible for these governments to meet their financial commitments. The bankruptcy option with no state bailout would incentivize these governments to put their fiscal houses in order going forward to avoid the stain of bankruptcy. However, there are concerns that the fiscal, financial, and economic damage to a municipality by declaring bankruptcy is so substantial that the availability of such a strategy should be an absolute last option, if an option at all.

Related, another paper in this urban forum authored by James Spiotto offers some very creative institutional paths for dealing with unfunded long-term liabilities, specifically state and local government pensions. Spiotto focuses on strategies when "traditional pension reform efforts have been explored including raising taxes and reducing expenditures to the extent possible and more needed plan adjustments and modifications appear to be impossible legally or not possible on a consensual basis."[63] He offers four alternatives that policy makers may want to consider in this context: prepackaged Chapter 9 plan of debt adjustment; creation of a special federal bankruptcy court for insolvent public pension funds; creation of a Government Oversight, Refinance, and Debt Adjustment Commission "to assist when public pension reform is otherwise legally or practically impossible"; and model guidelines for a state constitutional amendment or legislative public pension funding policy for a greater government good. Spiotto's policy suggestions are most appropriate for local governments that are currently distressed in terms of their funding of long-term liabilities. As such, his suggestions are mainly remedies reflective of a retrospective approach rather than representing a prospective approach in terms of holding elected officials accountable in the future for funding long-term liabilities. However, to the extent Spiotto's policy suggestions lead to reduced pension liabilities owed by the local government, they can be viewed as an immediate strategy to "open up" funding for other government spending priorities like infrastructure, both for new projects and for deferred maintenance.

Another possible institutional change involves various state oversight efforts of local finances.[64] In his 2008 article detailing best practices related to preventing local financial crises, Charles Coe details three sequential categories of state oversight. First, states should actively monitor local government finances to predict fiscal stress. Second, in the event that local governments encounter financial problems, states should intervene quickly to provide aid to local governments, including the possibility of additional fiscal resources. Finally, in dire circumstances, states should take strong corrective actions such as requiring local governments to increase taxes or reduce costs. The approach that Coe lays out runs somewhat counter to the no-bailout approached advocated by Merrifield and Paulson. As such, it allows state governments to encroach on the fiscal autonomy of local governments in exchange for aid and policy direction. However, depending how such interventions are structured, it may lead to more quickly addressing fiscal issues, such as underfunding long-term liabilities, before the problem becomes so large that only draconian measures (if any) are suitable.

Finally, another institutional change is modification of the state oversight option. Recognizing that state oversight often entails relaxing local government's fiscal autonomy, it may not be attractive to many local governments, except the ones that are currently experiencing severe fiscal stress. To gain such local government support among a broader universe of local governments, perhaps a "trade" is possible between levels of government. For example, a local government may agree to greater state oversight if it is provided enhanced fiscal tools that will allow the local government to generally have more control over its finances. Such tools may take the form of greater flexibility on what it can tax, reduction in tax caps set at the state level, reduction in the provisional approach to revenue sharing, or the reduction in the possibility that such revenue sharing is able to be redirected by the state. Of course, some states may be averse to providing such additional flexibility out of concern that such flexibility is what enabled some local governments to underfund their long-term liabilities in the past.

Political Changes

One political change (which is also an institutional change) often advocated by government reformers relates to the short-term thinking of elected officials. It has always been the counterfactual issue of what an elected official would have done if from the start he or she did not have to run for reelection or that there would be only one reelection to worry about. That is, would we observe a difference in fiscal policy decisions related to long-term liability funding if an elected official was term limited? Would they be willing to make tough decisions that may not provide significant reelection benefits, such as properly funding a local government's long-term liabilities, including pensions and OPEBs as well as infrastructure maintenance, before such fiscal issues became serious problems? Would such term limits force elected officials to address fiscal issues quicker, given that their time in office would definitively be shorter? The recent effort by former Illinois governor Pat Quinn to get a binding referendum to limit mayoral terms in Chicago is evidence of this thinking.[65] However, the research on term limits in general has been murky in terms of resulting in better financial outcomes. In fact, some research on pension funding has shown that term limits are associated with greater rather than lower pension underfunding.[66]

Related to the concern of short-term decision making by politicians is the role of financial managers in the underfunding of long-term liabilities. While budgetary decisions are ultimately the responsibility of elected officials in the construction of public budgets, it should be a concern that more financial managers have not stood up to elected officials in neglecting their funding responsibilities. One would think that the reputational risk for financial managers that are complicit in such underfunding would incentivize them to more strongly encourage elected officials to make the required investments in funding postretirement benefits and infrastructure development. The Government Finance Officers Association, the primary professional association for financial managers in the government sector, provides active training and robust policy guidance on virtually all facets of financial management, including pensions and infrastructure. However, it is not clear that membership and being an active participant in GFOA have resulted in financial managers serving as an effective check on elected officials' natural inclination to act in their short-term financial interests. There are likely options for the GFOA to better serve its membership by more actively and strongly encouraging prudent financial management and shedding light on the causes and effects when this has not been present in specific municipalities.

Another political and institutional change relates to the form of government being associated with better fiscal choices related to long-term liabilities. That is, some argue that a city-manager form of government that professionalizes the management of city finances may lead to more prudent fiscal decision making in terms of long-term liability funding. That is, the strong-mayor form of government (or mayor-council) is inherently more political, which makes it susceptible to the short-term decision making often attributed to politicians in the context of making tough fiscal decisions. Unfortunately, the academic literature on the relationship between municipal structure and spending levels, which would support this line of thinking, is mixed at best, so it is difficult to claim that municipal structure is associated with fiscal decision making in one direction or another.[67]

Financial Changes

The final category of possible changes to better hold elected officials accountable involves mainly financial actions. The first option involves a recent development in the municipal bond market involving the state of Connecticut. In June 2018, Connecticut structured its latest bond sale to include a "bond lock" provision on the bonds. This covenant includes a pledge (which includes specific financial metrics) that the state will address its fiscal issues, including the funding of its long-term liabilities. The investor community responded favorably to the inclusion of this provision, as Connecticut saw strong demand for its June 2018 bond sale.[68] Local governments could offer a similar pledge that would force elected officials to deal with their fiscal issues or risk breaking a bond covenant that may result in a technical bond default. However, by providing such a covenant, the state does reduce its flexibility in managing its finances, and such flexibility may be needed in times of deteriorating fiscal conditions.

Another financial policy change relates to accounting standards. GASB 67, which was enacted in 2017, provides guidance on how state and local governments select a discount rate in valuing pension liabilities. Prior to GASB 67, many observers believed that state and local governments were overly generous in the selection of the discount rate that resulted in an artificially lower value of unfunded liabilities. GASB 67 advocated a blended approach that includes using a tax-exempt municipal bond rate to value the unfunded portion of a governments pensions. Some economists believe this blended approach is still deficient and would like for governments to value the entire funded and unfunded portions of their pensions using a low-risk bond rate. This would likely result in pension-plan liabilities increasing and funded ratios declining, which would put further pressure on local governments to increase their funding for these unfunded liabilities. However, such additional funding for pensions would result in less funding for other long-term liabilities such as prefunding OPEBs and spending on infrastructure. In addition, while local governments would revise their calculations of their pension liability under such a change, they are not required to fund their pensions based on this valuation, so it is unclear what net effect such a change would have.

The final category of financial policy change relates to the credit-rating agencies and, more generally, to better disclosure. As a result of the financial crisis of 2007–8, the credit rating agencies made some changes in how they provide bond ratings for state and local governments as well as better disclosing their rating approaches. For some local governments, including many local governments in Illinois, this meant that the rating agencies paid increasing attention to unfunded pensions, which resulted in downgrades for many of these governments.[69] Further emphasis on long-term liabilities by the rating agencies may provide disciplinary action and lead to greater funding action by these deficient local governments.

Related, in terms of disclosure, GASB 68, enacted in 2014, required state and local governments to include unfunded pension obligations as a liability on balance sheets, similar to long-term debt. It also enhanced the disclosures in terms of the notes to the financial statements and required supplementary information related to pensions. Expanding disclosures of other "underfunded liabilities" such as infrastructure investment would be a logical step and one toward which the credit-rating agencies seem to be moving in their rating determinations.[70] It may also incentivize local governments to address their lack of investment in their infrastructure portfolio, but, again, it would not require them to do so. In terms of OPEB liabilities, new GASB statements that went into effect in 2018 will likely lead to greater transparency for these local government liabilities. The impact on funding from these recent long-term liability transparency measures is still unclear, but they certainly represent attempts to better improve the fiscal practices of local governments.

CONCLUSION

The underfunding of long-term liabilities, including pensions and OPEBs as well as the deferral of infrastructure spending, continues to plague many local governments. While local government finances have generally improved in the decade since the onset of the Great Recession, many local governments continue to struggle with adequately funding these areas.[71] The causes of underfunding are myriad, and the consequences vary based on the previous fiscal policy choices made by local governments. While there is no shortage of changes that local governments can implement to mitigate such underfunding in the future, there are also no "silver bullets"; many of these changes may not be politically palatable, and some options used by other governments have been shown to offer mixed results in the past. Furthermore, some of these changes may come at a cost that local governments may not be willing to bear in terms of changing the balance of power between the state and local government. Nevertheless, many local governments need to consider changes in the way they make decisions related to the funding of their long-term liabilities, as such policy decisions in the past have resulted in serious fiscal pain that these governments continue to grapple with.

Notes

1. Since this paper was presented at an urban forum, it focuses primarily on local governments. The same causes, consequences, and options related to long-term liability underfunding can easily be applied to state governments, and, in fact, much of the previous research has either focused solely on the state level or combined state and local governments.

2. Joe Nation, "Pension Math: Public Pension Spending and Service Crowd Out in California, 2003–2030," Stanford Institute for Economic Policy Research, October 2017, https://siepr.stanford.edu.

3. Douglas J. Elliott, "State and Local Pension Funding Deficits: A Primer," Brookings Institution, December 3, 2010, www.brookings.edu.

4. Joshua D. Rauh, "Hidden Debt, Hidden Deficits: 2017 Edition," Hoover Institution, May 5, 2017, www.hoover.org.

5. Alicia Munnell and Jean-Pierre Aubry, "An Overview of the Pension/OPEB Landscape," Center for Retirement Research at Boston College Working Paper 2016-11, October 2016, https://crr.bc.edu.

6. Pew Charitable Trusts, "A Widening Gap in Cities: Shortfalls in Funding for Pensions and Retiree Health Care," January 2013, www.pewtrusts.org.

7. Pew Charitable Trusts, "Widening Gap."

8. Government Accountability Office, "State and Local Government Retirement Health Benefits," Report to the Chairman, Special Committee on Aging, US Senate, 2009, www.gao.gov/new.items/d1061.pdf.

9. American Society of Civil Engineers, "Failure to Act: The Impact of Infrastructure Investment on America's Economic Future," 2016, www.infrastructurereportcard .org/wp-content/uploads/2016/10/ASCE-Failure-to-Act-2016-FINAL.pdf.

10. Gord Hume, "What the Public Needs to Know about the Municipal Infrastructure Deficit," *Governing*, March 26, 2018, www.governing.com/.

11. American Society of Civil Engineers, "2017 Infrastructure Report Card," 2017, www.infrastructurereportcard.org/making-the-grade.

12. Elizabeth McNichol, "It's Time for States to Invest in Infrastructure," Center on Budget and Policy Priorities, 2017, www.cbpp.org/research/state-budget-and-tax/ its-time-for-states-to-invest-in-infrastructure#_ftn9; Congressional Budget Office, "Spending on Infrastructure and Investment," March 1, 2017, blog post of Chad Shirley, www.cbo.gov.

13. The 2015 Annual Surveys of State and Local Government Finances rely on a sample of local governments and thus are susceptible to sampling error. See www .census.gov/govs/local/.

14. Jerrell Coggburn and Richard Kearney, "Trouble Keeping Promises? An Analysis of Underfunding in State Retiree Benefits," *Public Administration Review* 70, no. 1 (2010): 97–108.

15. Christopher Burnham, "Why We Need to Keep Politics Out of Public Pensions," *Forbes*, June 5, 2018, www.forbes.com.

16. Erick Elder and Gary Wagner, "Political Effects on Pension Underfunding," *Economic and Politics* 27, no. 1 (2014): 1–27.

17. James Buchanan, *Public Finance in Democratic Process: Fiscal Institutions and Individual Choice* (Chapel Hill: University of North Carolina Press, 1967).

18. Robert Bifulco et al., "Debt and Deception: How States Avoid Making Hard Fiscal Decisions," *Public Administration Review* 72, no. 5 (2012): 659–67.

19. While governments have certainly underfunded their infrastructure needs as previously described, such underfunding would likely be even more significant if not for the political nature of capital spending. In this sense, government spending can be thought of as zero-sum. That is, for every dollar spent on capital projects that seek to enhance an elected official's electoral prospects, a dollar may be lost in funding pension and other long-term liabilities.

20. John Gramlich, "Few Americans Support Cuts to Most Government Programs, Including Medicaid," Pew Research Center, 2017, www.pewresearch.org/; Gallup, "Taxes," accessed August 29, 2018, https://news.gallup.com/poll/1714/Taxes.aspx.

21. Gramlich, "Few Americans."

22. Gallup, "Taxes."

23. William Niskanen, "Limiting Government: The Failure of 'Starve the Beast,'" *Cato Journal* 26, no. 3 (2006), citeseerx.ist.psu.edu/viewdoc/download?doi=10.1.1.5 78.3954&rep=rep1&type=pdf.

24. Sharon Kioko, "Impact of Tax and Expenditure Limitation on Local Government Savings," in *Local Government Budget Stabilization* (New York: Springer-Science and Business Media, 2015), 141–69.

25. Michael Pagano and Christopher W. Hoene, "City Budgets in an Era of Increased Uncertainty," Metropolitan Policy Program at Brookings, 2018.

26. Dave Swenson and Steven Deller, "Devolution or Convolution? The Changing Relationship between Federal, State and Local Governments," *Journal of Regional Analysis and Policy* 31, no. 1 (2001): 49–75; Bo Zhao and David Coyne, "Walking a Tightrope: Are U.S. State and Local Governments on a Fiscally Sustainable Path?," *Public Budgeting and Finance* 37, no. 3 (2017): 3–23.

27. Hannah Covington, "Minnesotans Reject School Bond Issues at Highest Rate in Years," *Minneapolis Star Tribune*, May 30, 2017, www.startribune.com.

28. Legislative Analyst's Office (State of California), "Proposition 53: Revenue Bonds. Statewide Voter Approval. Initiative Constitutional Amendment," 2016, https://lao.ca.gov/ballot/2016/Prop53–110816.pdf.

29. Craig Maher, Sungho Park, and James Harrold, "The Effects of Tax and Expenditure Limits on Municipal Pension and OPEB Funding during the Great Recession," *Public Finance and Management* 16, no. 2 (2016): 121–46.

30. Charles Coe, "Preventing Local Government Fiscal Crises: Emerging Best Practices," *Public Administration Review* 68, no. 4 (2008): 759–67.

31. Pew Charitable Trusts, "State Strategies to Detect Local Fiscal Distress," 2016, www.pewtrusts.org.

32. Legislative Analyst's Office (State of California), "Why Have Sales Taxes Grown Slower than the Economy?," 2013, https://lao.ca.gov.

33. Alana Semuels, "All the Ways Retail's Decline Could Hurt American Towns," *Atlantic*, May 23, 2017, www.theatlantic.com.

34. Joyce Manchester and Jonathan Schwabish, "The Long-Term Budget Outlook in the United States and the Role of Health Care Entitlements," *National Tax Journal* 63, no. 2 (2010): 285–305.

35. Increases in OPEB costs related to rising health insurance premiums have also been the result of the escalating cost of health care. However, this portion of the paper focuses on the causes of underfunding long-term liabilities like OPEBs, which, thus, results in our focus on current employee health insurance premiums.

36. Gavin Reinke, "When a Promise Isn't a Promise: Public Employers' Ability to Alter Pension Plans of Retired Employees," *Vanderbilt Law Review* 64, no. 5 (2011): 1673–1711.

37. Howard Chernick, Adam Langley, and Andrew Reschovsky, "The Impact of the Great Recession and the Housing Crisis on the Financing of America's Largest Cities," *Regional Science and Urban Economics* 41, no. 4 (2011): 372–81.

38. "Sampling of Interest Rate Swap Deals across the Country," *Wall Street Journal*, 2010, accessed on June 28, 2018, https://online.wsj.com/public/resources/documents/Interest_Rate_Swaps.pdf.

39. David Roeder, "Chicago Teachers Unions Say 'Swaps' Payments Sap Schools," *Chicago Sun Times*, July 3, 2011, https://chicago.suntimes.com.

40. Alicia Munnell, Jean-Pierre Aubry, and Mark Cafarelli, "An Update on Pension Obligation Bonds," Center for Retirement Research at Boston College, no. 40, July 2014, https://crr.bc.edu.

41. Thad Calabrese, "The Use of Locally Imposed Selective Taxes to Fund Public Pension Liabilities," in *For Your Own Good: Taxes, Paternalism, and Fiscal Discrimination in the Twenty-First Century*, ed. Adam J. Hoffer and Todd Nesbit (Arlington, VA: Mercatus Center, George Mason University, 2018), 263–88.

42. Civic Federation, "Chicago City Council Approves Water-Sewer Tax for Municipal Employees Pension Fund," September 22, 2016, www.civicfed.org.

43. Heather Kerrigan, "Early Retirement Incentives Making a Comeback," February 13, 2013, www.governing.com. There is considerable debate about the generosity of pension benefits to government workers especially compared to private-sector workers. This portion of the paper only focuses on financial policy decisions over the past few decades to enhance this generosity level rather than explore the debate on the general generosity of local government pension benefits. We feel such an approach is appropriate since this section details the possible causes of underfunding that have come into focus over the past decade.

44. Whet Moser, "Two Sobering Graphs about the Illinois Pension Crisis," *Chicago Magazine*, June 1, 2012, www.chicagomag.com.

45. Daniel Bergstresser and Martin J. Luby, "Changes in the Municipal Capital Markets since the Financial Crisis," working paper presented at the Brookings Institution sixth annual Municipal Finance Conference, 2017, www.brookings.edu/wp-content/uploads/2017/04/bergstresser.pdf.

46. Bergstresser and Luby, "Changes in the Municipal Capital Markets."

47. It is unclear the effect higher interest rates would have had on pension returns. Thus, while lower interest rates provided refinancing opportunities and the ability to issue less costly debt for capital, it may have reduced pension fund returns, thus reducing the overall long-term liability underfunding benefit to local governments.

48. Moody's Investors Service, "Unfunded US State Pension Liabilities Surge in Fiscal 2017 Due to Poor Investment Returns," August 27, 2018, www.moodys.com.

49. David Merriman, Chuanyi Guo, and Di Qiao, "No Magic Bullet: Constructing a Roadmap for Illinois Fiscal Sustainability," Fiscal Futures Project, University of Illinois Institute for Government and Public Affairs, March 1, 2018, https://igpa.uillinois.edu/report/FFP-FY2017-annual-update.

50. Moody's Investors Service, "Moody's Announces New Approach to Analyzing State, Local Government Pensions; 29 Local Governments Placed under Review," April 17, 2013, www.moodys.com.

51. Lynn Hume, "D.C. Gets Kudos for Its Approach to Infrastructure Maintenance," Bond Buyer, May 29, 2018, www.bondbuyer.com.

52. Yvette Shields, "Chicago Board of Education Pays a Steep Penalty to Price Bonds," Bond Buyer, July 10, 2017, www.bondbuyer.com.

53. Frank Ramsey, "A Contribution to the Theory of Taxation," *Economic Journal* 37 (March 1927): 47–61.

54. Jean-Pierre Aubry and Caroline V. Crawford, "Does Public Pension Funding Affect Where People Move?," Center for Retirement Research at Boston College, 2016, https://crr.bc.edu.

55. Aubry and Crawford, "Does Public Pension Funding Affect Where People Move?"

56. American Society of Civil Engineers, "Failure to Act."

57. Justin Ross and Sian Mughan, "The Effect of Fiscal Illusion on Public Sector Financial Management," *Public Finance Review* 46, no. 4 (2016): 635–64.

58. Pew Charitable Trusts, "The State Role in Local Government Financial Distress," July 23, 2013, www.pewtrusts.org.

59. Staci Zavattaro, "Organizational Implosion: A Case Study of Detroit, Michigan," *Administration and Society* 46, no. 9 (2014): 1071–91.

60. Michael H. Granof et al., *Government and Not-for-Profit Accounting: Concepts and Practices*, 7th ed. (Hoboken, NJ: Wiley, 2016).

61. Yvette Shields, "Chicago's Largest Pension Fund Not Out of Woods Yet," Bond Buyer, June 6, 2018, www.bondbuyer.com.

62. John Merrifield and Barry Poulson, "Illinois Is Better Off Bankrupt," Real Clear Policy, June 7, 2018, www.realclearpolicy.com.

63. James Spiotto, "When Needed Public Pension Reforms Fail or Appear to Be Legally Impossible, What Then? Are Unbalanced Budgets, Deficits and Collapse the Only Answer?," University of Illinois at Chicago 2018 Urban Forum paper, uicurbanforum.org/issues/files/2018/Public-Pension-Reforms-Spiotto.pdf.

64. Eric Scorsone, "Municipal Fiscal Emergency Laws: Background and Guide to State-Based Approaches," Mercatus Center working paper, 2014, www.mercatus.org; Charles Coe, "Preventing Local Government Fiscal Crises: Emerging Best Practices," *Public Administration Review* 68, no. 4 (2008): 759–67.

65. Kristen McQueary, "Don't Give Up on Term Limits for Mayor," *Chicago Tribune*, August 6, 2018, www.chicagotribune.com.

66. Elder and Wagner, "Political Effects."

67. Jered Carr and Shanthi Karrupusamy, "Reassessing the Link between City Structure and Fiscal Policy," *American Review of Public Administration* 40, no. 2 (2010): 209–28.

68. Paul Burton, "Connecticut Cites Bond Covenant in Oversubscribed Sale," Bond Buyer, June 11, 2018, www.bondbuyer.com.

69. Yvette Shields, "Pension Woes Take Toll on Illinois Local Government Ratings," Bond Buyer, July 12, 2018, www.bondbuyer.com.

70. L. Hume, "D.C. Gets Kudos."

71. National Governors Association, "State and Local Fiscal Facts, 2018," www.gfoa.org/sites/default/files/StateandLocalFiscalFacts2016.pdf.

Contemporary Fiscal Challenges and Positions of US Cities

YONGHONG WU, SHU WANG,

AND MICHAEL A. PAGANO

The Great Recession, by any measure, had a damaging impact on the nation and its cities. The national economy contracted, as did the economies of states, cities, and metropolitan regions; the fiscal position of the nation declined, as it did for states and municipalities. Real gross domestic product fell by nearly 6 percent between 2007 ($14.99 trillion, fourth quarter of 2007) and 2009 ($14.35 trillion, second quarter of 2009), which was the trough of the recession.[1] The losses were recovered by the third quarter of 2011 (rebounding to $15.02 trillion). Federal government revenues, primarily composed of income tax receipts, also declined but by even more, falling 21 percent between 2007 and 2009 ($2.66 trillion to $2.1 trillion, constant dollars), then rebounding to its prerecessionary level in 2013 ($2.77 trillion). States also witnessed a decline of more than 11 percent ($609 billion from $680 billion) in their general fund revenues between 2008 and 2010, rebounding to the prerecessionary levels in 2012.[2] Municipalities, after a decline of some 12 percent in general fund revenues between 2006 and 2012, have yet to experience the return of their fiscal position to prerecessionary levels.[3] The fiscal position of the federal government and the states appears to have been more resilient and robust than cities' fiscal position. What explains the less than resilient fiscal position of cities? This chapter explores the many constraints on city fiscal behavior, including most notably cities' legal position as creatures of their respective states and the wide variation in city fiscal positions as a consequence of the nesting of cities within a federal political system.

THE CONTEMPORARY FISCAL POSITION OF US CITIES

The national economic picture, which is painted in broad strokes as if all sectors have been growing and improving since the end of the Great Recession, is not always reflected in municipal coffers. One example can be found in the dynamic growth of consumer sales since the end of the Great Recession. Although retail sales surged after 2009 (the official end of the recession), the growth rate of retail sales tax collections was lower, however, due in large part to the fact that Internet sales taxes were in most cases not collected. This meant that state and local governments collected less retail sales tax revenue as a consequence of online sales than they would have had if those sales had been made in a brick-and-mortar store.

That issue, referred in many cases as prejudicial to Main Street merchants, was addressed by the Supreme Court at the end of its 2018 session.[4] No longer does "physical presence" in a material way need to be demonstrated, now that an electronic presence of most sellers is ubiquitous. Moreover, the Court ruled that a tax on Internet sales would not jeopardize interstate commerce. The seller is now required to collect and remit appropriate sales taxes. The impact on sales tax collections nationwide could be substantial. In the opinion of the Court, the majority cited the magnitude of the loss by noting: "In 1992, it was estimated that the States were losing between $694 million and $3 billion per year in sales tax revenues as a result of the physical presence rule. New estimates range from $8 to $33 billion. . . . The South Dakota Legislature has declared an emergency, S. B. 106, §9, which again demonstrates urgency of overturning the physical presence rule. The argument, moreover, that the physical presence rule is clear and easy to apply is unsound."[5] Most states' coffers will benefit from the new ruling, since forty-five states impose a retail sales tax, but only slightly more than half of the nation's municipalities will benefit. Those cities with a local option sales tax connect the purchase or consumption of goods (and, depending on the city, some services), which certainly is part of the "gross metropolitan product" of the city, to the city's fiscal architecture. As consumption increases, sales tax collections increase, and vice versa. The Court's ruling, then, may affect the fiscal position of a majority of cities, but many cities will not feel the decision's impact. Boston, for example, generated retail sales of approximately $11,500 per capita in 2010, yet because it is not permitted to adopt a local option sales tax, it collected nothing. Denver also generated approximately the same amount of retail sales on a per capita basis, but contributed nearly 20 percent of Denver's total revenues in 2010 because it does have the authority to tax retail sales.

These illustrations demonstrate a wider truth about municipal finance in the United States, namely, changes to a city's underlying economy are not always reflected in the city's revenue collections. In other words, if retail sales increase and a city is not authorized to levy a sales tax, it hardly matters. What does matter is a city's alignment of its taxing authority with the major drivers of its underlying economy.

A city's taxing (and fee) authority can include general taxes, such as a tax on retail sales, income or wages, and the ubiquitous property tax. Yet there are many others as well, including utility taxes, telecommunications taxes, water and sewer fees, building inspection fees, and property tax transactions. These are referred to as own-source revenues, which are the fees and charges over which a municipality has control. As table 1 indicates, the composition of cities' own-source revenues indicates that the category "Charges and misc. revenue" has generated more revenue than the ubiquitous property tax since the early 1980s. Charges and fees now amount to approximately two of every five dollars collected by municipalities, while property taxes have generated slightly less than one-third of own-source revenues. This shift in prominence from property tax domination to charges and fees is not likely to reverse itself. Indeed, user fees and charges will probably continue to grow in stature over time.[6]

A closer examination of the general fund (exclusive of all other funds, such as the capital improvement funds, enterprise funds, and special revenue funds)—which is the largest fund of municipal governments, accounting for approximately 55 percent of total municipal funds, and the fund over which city councils have the most discretion—reveals a troubling feature. According to the most recent data available on municipal general funds, cities' revenues to the general fund have yet to return to their prerecessionary levels in constant dollars. In other words, the fund that typically provides financial

Table 1. Own-source revenue

Revenue source	1977	1982	1987	1992	1997	2002	2007	2012
Property taxes	42.70%	32.73%	32.73%	29.40%	28.85%	29.09%	29.72%	32.41%
Sales and gross receipts taxes	15.84%	17.06%	17.06%	16.88%	17.10%	17.72%	16.92%	17.50%
Income taxes	8.47%	8.34%	8.34%	8.69%	8.61%	7.56%	8.77%	8.21%
Other taxes	4.16%	4.04%	4.04%	4.95%	4.68%	5.74%	6.18%	4.55%
Charges and misc. revenue	28.83%	37.84%	37.84%	40.09%	40.76%	40.13%	38.41%	37.33%

Source: Census Bureau, Government Finances.

Figure 1. Comparative general fund revenue recovery over three recessions

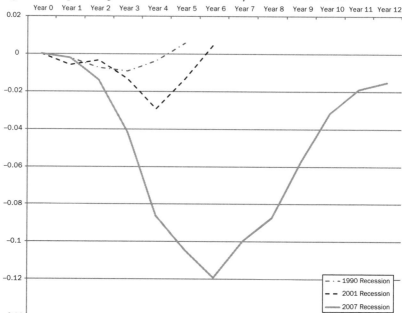

Source: Data collected from National League of Cities annual survey of "city fiscal conditions," including data for fiscal year 2018. An earlier version, including data through fiscal year 2017, was published in Christiana McFarland and Michael A. Pagano, *City Fiscal Conditions in 2017* (Washington, DC: National League of Cities, 2017).

support for cities' general operations, including police and fire services, has not rebounded to the pre-2007 levels (as of 2018), whereas the federal government's resources returned to prerecessionary levels in 2013.

Property taxes, which are collected on the assessed value of land and structures, have been improving over the past few years, but it is questionable whether the future growth in property values will approach the pre-hyper-growth era of the late 1990s. If that forecast holds, growth in real estate taxes will most likely be modest. Additional increases to the tax rate might grow municipal revenues in the future. In that same vein, however, increasing the tax rates on sales or income could also grow revenues for those cities with such an authority. Should it prove difficult politically (or legally) to raise tax rates, cities will continue to find services and activities to which a fee can be applied.

CITIES IN THE INTERGOVERNMENTAL CONTEXT

Cities operate within an institutional framework laid out by state governments. The framework enables cities to make fiscal decisions while imposing constraints on their behaviors at the same time, shaping the fiscal policy space of cities.[7]

Taxing Authority

First, for city fiscal capacity, taxing authority granted by the state greatly affects cities' ability to extract revenues from their economic base and the stability of revenue structure. Scholarship has often appraised revenue diversification as a tool to enhance revenue stability that enhances governments' resilience to the shocks in external economic environment.[8] However, the degree of diversification is dictated by the number of tax sources authorized by the state. To examine the variation of taxing authority in the United States, Christopher Hoene and Christiana McFarland rate municipalities based on whether they have the authority to levy property taxes, sales taxes, or income taxes; whether they can set the tax rate; and if the revenues are for general use (as opposed to earmarked for specific use).[9] The rating shows a wide variation across states in terms of fiscal authority. Pagano and colleagues examine main tax sources (property taxes, sales taxes, and income tax) among the one hundred largest cities[10] and find that the most common state fiscal structure is one in which a state allows its cities to levy two local option taxes. Most cities are granted the authority to impose a tax on real estate, a ubiquitous tax for municipal governments. More than 55 percent of all municipalities are granted the authority to levy a tax on retail sales, and approximately 11 percent can tax income or earnings.

How taxing authority is structured and administered at the local level adds complexity to the issue. Take income tax, for example; among the three major taxes, an income tax is used the least and, where authorized, varies in application and structure. In the state of Michigan, cities do not levy sales tax but have authority to levy income taxes. However, the income tax will have to be placed on the ballot and approved by local voters. Due to the administrative burden and possible political obstacles, only 18 out of 276 cities in Michigan have income tax as a tax source. In contrast, the local income tax is levied by nearly all municipalities in Ohio and Pennsylvania; in Ohio and Kentucky, the earnings tax is imposed on net business income and on wages earned at both the place of employment and the place of residence, meaning that it is also a commuter tax. How income as the tax base is defined also differs by state. Ohio and Kentucky cities can tax business profits at the same rate as individual income. Cities in Washington State can levy a business and occupancy tax on all businesses, including ones that sell services, as well as on incomes derived from working within the city boundary.

State Aid

Aid to cities provided by the states also affects the capacity cities have for service provision. How states distribute their funds to cities varies widely from state to state. States can provide discretionary funding or provide assistance through project- or need-based grants. Earmarking is another tool of state aid distribution, that is, designating some or all of a specific tax for a specific expenditure. States earmark different types of taxes for local governments' uses, including general and selective sales taxes, utility taxes, personal or corporation income taxes, and severance taxes.[11] Local governments other than school districts are the beneficiaries of earmarked state taxes in forty-six states; the taxes most commonly earmarked are motor fuel taxes (twenty-two states) and general sales taxes (seventeen states), and the most common expenditure is local roads and highways.

In theory, earmarking is a useful tool to enhance fiscal accountability because it allows voters to designate taxes to finance specific public services.[12] It also secures a revenue stream for functional responsibilities shouldered by local governments. In practice, how earmarked revenue affects local spending is more complicated. Earmarked funds can be fungible in that they can be used as a substitute for other sources of revenue,[13] and the impacts of the earmarked dollar on expenditures would be the same as general fund dollars. Earmarking can also provide cities with more flexibility. By providing a new line of funding for existing programs, it frees up moneys in the general fund that can now be used for other purposes. In this case, there will be increase in spending in the programs that are not funded by the earmarked taxes.[14] Alternatively, earmarking can draw more resources to the program that the earmarked dollars are designated for, leading to more spending for the earmarked program.[15] In this case, the spending for the earmarked program will increase, while the spending for nonearmarked programs decreases. Unfortunately, there is no comprehensive survey of how assistance to cities is structured in each state. Future research is needed to first understand common ways of state aid distribution and then assess their efficiency and equity.

To indicate the fiscal capacity of cities, we examine the change of revenue reliance by source of the 150 largest cities in the United States from 1977 to 2015.[16] It is important to first point out that there is variation of taxing authority in this sample. Although all cities have authority to levy property taxes, 14 cities do not have revenue generated from sales tax, and only 25 cities have authority to levy individual income tax and exercised such authority. As an important aspect of fiscal capacity, taxing authority lays down the foundation for cities' revenue structure.

Revenue reliance is measured by the percentage of a revenue source in city general revenue. We calculated the average revenue reliance by source across cities of each year. As shown in figure 2, property taxes remain the main revenue source for cities throughout this time. State aid is also an important part for cities' revenue structure and makes up around 15 percent of the general revenue. The change of state aid has remained stagnant after 2007 with a sign of decline. In contrast, the reliance on sales taxes has increased steadily overtime from 10 percent to 15 percent. In fact, the number of cities in the sample that exercise sales tax authority has also grown from 20 in 1977 to 25 in 2015. The trend suggests that cities are seeking more diversified revenue structure, but it would be possible only when states enable them to do so.

Figure 2. City revenue reliance by source from 1977 to 2015

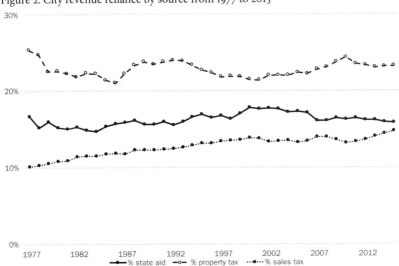

Source: US Census of Governments, http://datatoolkits.lincolninst.edu/subcenters/fiscally-standardized-cities/.

Second, various state fiscal policies constrain cities' fiscal discretion, including home rule and tax and expenditure limits (TELs), as additional key policies that lay out the architecture of the institutional framework within which cities operate.

Home Rule

Since the United States Constitution does not suggest what type of authority local governments should possess, nor are local governments mentioned at all, the Tenth Amendment reserves authority-giving powers to the states or to the people. Dillon's Rule and home rule are usually used as crude proxies for local government authority enabled by the state. In the case of *City of Clinton v. Cedar Rapids and Missouri River Railroad* (1868), Judge Dillon summarized his view of the relationship between the state government and local governments: "Municipal corporations owe their origin to, and derive their powers and rights wholly from, the legislature." Dillon's Rule allows a state legislature to control local government affairs, such as government structure, methods of financing service provisions, and the authority of enacting local-level policies. Related to the separation of powers, Dillon's Rule refers to a tool used by courts to construe grants of local government autonomy. Since the court becomes involved only when a case is brought before them, it exercises little control over local government autonomy, and when it does it operates in reactive fashion and interprets grants of authority from the state legislature.[17]

In contrast, home rule refers to a state constitutional provision or legislative action that provides a local government with self-governance ability.[18] The local authority is usually granted through local charters and state statutes, both of which are initiated by the state legislature. Unlike Dillon's Rule, which is a standard of statutory construction, that is, a court must not impose its own interpretation on a statute but should defer to the legislature to ascertain the legislative intent,[19] the power granted under home rule is usually limited to specific fields and subject to judicial interpretation. Theorists have made efforts to classify types of home rule in various ways, including by the way authority operates,[20] by the structure of the local authority,[21] or by the source of the authority.[22] Regardless of the classification, no type of home rule equates to total local freedom from state oversight.[23] There is also a wide variation across states in terms of the policy area over which local governments have discretion. Krane, Rigos, and Hill document how states define home rule differently and grant local governments different degrees of autonomy for different fields, such as functional responsibilities, administrative discretion, economic development, and revenue-raising power.[24] Even when local governments are granted with the home rule authority, in many states local policies are valid only when they are not contradictory to state statutes.

Tax and Expenditure Limits

Although property taxes are a major revenue source for most cities in the United States, states can impose limits on the level of property tax levied by local governments. The limits, also known as tax and expenditure limits, can be caps on millage rates, assessment growth, property tax levy growth, or combinations of these caps.[25] By 2015 twenty-nine states impose levy limits, thirty-two states impose rate limits, and fifteen states impose limits on assessed value growth.[26] Five states (Arizona, California, Colorado, Nebraska, and New Jersey) also impose limits on local revenue and spending growth. Figure 3 shows the types of TELs imposed by different states.

The limits vary by maximum allowable rate for growth; for example, Washington sets a ten-mill limit for local governments, whereas the rate limit in

Figure 3. TEL types by state (2015)

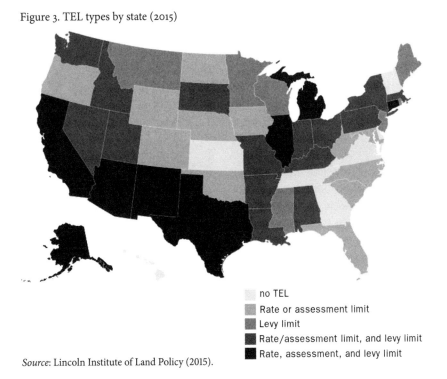

no TEL
Rate or assessment limit
Levy limit
Rate/assessment limit, and levy limit
Rate, assessment, and levy limit

Source: Lincoln Institute of Land Policy (2015).

Pennsylvania is set at twelve mill. This ceiling rate can also vary within one state by class of cities or by type of government. The administration of limits also differs from state to state. Massachusetts imposes a cap on municipal property tax levy at 2.5 percent. Texas administers its levy limit through a rollback rate; that is, levy increases are limited to the lesser of the rate to generate the same revenue as the prior year, which is called the effective rate, or the rollback rate. By constraining the accessibility of local governments to their economic base, TELs disconnect a city's growth in tax revenue from its economic growth.

It is noteworthy that the restrictiveness of TELs depends on the interaction between the design of TELs and local economic condition and taxing efforts. Consider a state that sets the limit on local assessment growth at 10 percent. This limit would constrain the property tax growth for cities where assessed values of properties grow at a rate greater than 10 percent but have no practical impact on cities where assessed values do not grow as fast. Mark Skidmore and Mehmet S. Tosun show counties in Michigan react to the state-imposed assessment cap differently, and the counties with faster growth of housing market suffer more from tax base erosion. Wang also constructed a measure that indicates the gap between legal ceilings of TELs and local tax levies.[27] The study shows different results regarding the effects of TELs when TELs are measured by the gap and by the TEL types, respectively. The difference suggests a more complex mechanism through which TELs affect local taxation when unique local characteristics are taken into account.

THE IMPACT OF SALT DEDUCTION ON STATE AND LOCAL GOVERNMENT FINANCES

In America's fiscal federalism, the state-local fiscal relationship is much more substantive and complex than that between the federal government and state-local governments. States are not created by the federal government, and the power to govern is constitutionally divided between the two levels of government. Since Congress and the executive branch have decentralized (and "devolved") more program responsibilities to states and localities starting in 1980s, state and local governments have been playing a primary role in domestic policy arenas.[28]

Although direct federal aid has been declining in significance to state and local government finances, federal government has continued subsidizing state and local governments in other indirect ways. For example, the interest income received by investors in state and local government bonds is not taxed by either federal individual or corporate income taxes. The federal tax exemption of state and local bond interest started when the federal income tax became constitutional in 1913. The exemption allows state and local governments to issue bonds at lower than market interest rates and therefore subsidizes state and local borrowing, particularly capital investments. Although the uses of tax-exempt debt by state and local governments have been restricted over the years, particularly in the Tax Reform Act of 1986, this form of federal subsidy has remained and even survived the most recent reform of federal tax system under the Trump administration.

Also dating from the first federal income tax act (the Revenue Act of 1913), another indirect federal subsidy through federal income tax system is to allow deductions for certain taxes paid to state and local governments. In itemizing deductions for federal income tax, taxpayers are allowed to include deductions for state and local property tax and general sales or income tax. By reducing the federal income tax base, a portion of state and local taxes (SALT) is offset by a lower federal income tax liability. For example, if one federal income tax filer paid $20,000 in state and local property and income taxes and her marginal federal income tax rate is 28 percent, she can reduce her federal income tax by $5,600.

The Tax Cuts and Jobs Act of 2017 places a $10,000 cap on deduction for certain states and local taxes.[29] Section 11042 reads: "This section temporarily limits individual deductions for certain state and local taxes to $10,000 per year ($5,000 for a married taxpayer filing a separate return). The limit does not apply to taxes paid or accrued in carrying on a trade or business or for expenses for the production of income."[30] The law still allows filers of federal income tax returns who choose itemized deduction to subtract state and local property tax and income tax or general sales tax from their federal taxable income within the limit. While the provision will reduce federal tax expenditures, it will affect almost all state and local governments, as some taxpayers will have to claim smaller amounts of taxes they pay to state and local governments. As a result, their federal income taxes will rise and after-tax incomes will shrink.

The impact of the cap on SALT deductions is moderated somewhat by two other provisions in the law. First, taxpayers are given higher standard deductions—$12,000 for single filers, $24,000 for married individuals filling joint returns, and $18,000 for heads of household. The increased standard deductions will eliminate the potential negative effects on some taxpayers as they switch from itemized deductions to the option of standard deductions. In addition, the law enacts a slightly lower tax-rate structure. For instance, the highest marginal tax rate is reduced from 39.6 percent to 37 percent. This may also reduce the potential negative effects of the cap on SALT deductions, particularly for taxpayers with quite high incomes.

Given the substantial variation in the percentage of filers who claim the SALT deduction and the amounts of the deduction, the impact of this cap is likely to vary across states, especially because the standard deduction increases, resulting in fewer filers who itemize deductions. Much of the attention has concentrated on a handful of large and rich states, such as California and New York. Other states will also feel the influence as well. The passage of the tax bill has received a great deal of attention from scholars and practitioners regarding how much it will affect state and local government finances. Some well-known think-tank organizations such as the Pew Charitable Trusts have come up with some initial estimates about the potential impact of this provision. According to their recent analysis, the impact of the cap on SALT deductions could be far-reaching because federal income tax filers in nineteen states who took the SALT deduction claimed more on average than the cap allowed in 2015, the latest year with available data.[31]

The SALT cap provision will increase federal income tax liability for certain federal income tax filers because they are not allowed to claim a SALT deduction beyond the limit. It will affect state and local finances because the after-tax incomes of certain taxpayers will be lower than without the cap. Using a data set from the Internal Revenue Service (IRS), we can estimate how many taxpayers are affected and the extent to which they will be affected and explore how the cap on SALT deduction will affect state and local government revenues and expenditures, in order to improve our understanding of the tax bill's impact on subnational government finances.

The source of data is the IRS Statistics of Income, Historic Table 2, "Individual Income and Tax Data, by State and Size of Adjusted Gross Income," for tax year 2015.[32] The data is based on administrative records of individual income tax returns (Forms 1040). Included in the data are federal income tax returns filed during the twelve-month period January 1–December 31, 2016.[33]

The data are available for multiple levels of filers' adjusted gross income (AGI). We calculate the percentage of filers who choose itemized deductions, the percentage of filers with itemized deductions who also claim SALT deductions, and the percentages of filers with itemized deductions who claim deductions for real estate taxes, general sales taxes, or state and local income taxes.[34] As shown in table 2, the three percentages move up as the AGI level gets higher with one exception: the percentage of filers with itemized deductions who claim general sales tax declines with higher AGIs. This makes sense because state and local income taxes tend to grow more rapidly with income than general sales tax, and taxpayers are required to select the larger of the two taxes in their deductions, not both. Another observation is that when filers itemize their deductions, most of them include the SALT deduction even when their AGIs are relatively low.

For the tax year 2015, the total number of federal income tax returns is 149,726,990, and about 30 percent of them used itemized deductions. Among the 44,671,840 filers who itemized deductions, 37,538,310, 9,545,210, and 32,956,930 claimed deductions for real estate taxes, general sales taxes, and state and local income taxes, respectively. After exclusion of taxpayers who would switch to the option of standard deductions allowed in the new tax law, we determine that 32,194,087 filers would still choose itemized deductions and that 30,790,309 of them would claim SALT deductions. The total deducted real estate taxes, general sales taxes, and state and local income taxes were $539 billion in 2015. After excluding the taxpayers who would switch to standard deductions, the total SALT deductions would be $474 billion if the new tax law were effective.

We expect that the excess of SALT deductions that would not be allowed under the new cap to vary by level of AGI. We first divide the total amount of SALT deductions by the number of filers who would claim deductions of SALT to calculate the average SALT deduction for each level of AGI. As shown in table 3, the average SALT deduction per filer rises with the level of AGI. In particular, the average SALT deduction per file is below $10,000 if the AGI is under $100,000. We further determine that 36 percent of the fil-

Table 2. Filers with itemized deductions and SALT deductions

Level of AGI	% of filers who would itemize deductions	% of filers with itemized deductions who ...		
		would deduct SALT	deduct state-local income taxes	deduct general sales taxes	deduct real estate taxes
AGI<$10,000	3.0	79.7	25.9	53.9	69.1
$10,000≤AGI<$25,000	4.4	87.7	39.6	48.2	67.2
$25,000≤AGI<$50,000	9.9	92.4	61.7	30.7	71.2
$50,000≤AGI<$75,000	20.6	94.7	72.7	22.0	81.3
$75,000≤AGI<$100,000	18.1	95.9	78.3	17.7	86.3
$100,000≤AGI<$200,000	76.0	97.0	82.1	14.9	90.6
$200,000≤AGI<$500,000	93.6	98.1	83.0	15.1	91.8
$500,000≤AGI<$1,000,000	93.2	99.0	84.7	14.3	93.4
$1,000,000≤AGI	91.5	99.3	87.9	11.4	94.2

Source: Authors' computation.

Table 3. Excess of SALT deductions

Level of AGI	Number of filers who would deduct SALT	Average SALT deduction per filer (in $000s)	Excess of SALT deduction per filer (in $000s)
$1 ~ $10,000	509,931	4.21	0.00
$10,000 ~ $25,000	1,257,291	3.54	0.00
$25,000 ~ $50,000	3,206,386	4.01	0.00
$50,000 ~ $75,000	3,884,944	5.50	0.00
$75,000 ~ $100,000	2,241,834	7.24	0.00
$100,000 ~ $200,000	13,520,160	11.08	1.08
$200,000 ~ $500,000	4,973,970	22.82	12.82
$500,000 ~ $1,000,000	797,700	54.35	44.35
$1,000,000 or more	398,090	273.55	263.55

Source: Authors' computation.

ers who would itemize SALT deductions will not be affected by the new cap provision. On the other hand, the remaining 64 percent of the filers itemizing SALT would not be able to claim the same amount of SALT deduction without the cap imposed because their average SALT deductions are beyond $10,000. The magnitude of the excess of SALT deductions per filer gets larger for filers with higher AGIs.

For the whole country, the aggregate excess of SALT deductions is about $219 billion. If there were the $10,000 cap on SALT in 2015, the filers would not have been allowed to claim $219 billion, or about 46 percent of total SALT deductions in that year.[35] We can also estimate the total excess of SALT deductions for each state and compare the excess amount to the state's total collection of SALT. As shown in table 4, the excess of SALT deductions as a percentage of total SALT varies substantially across states. Compared with their own SALT, the sizes of excess of SALT deductions are highest for California, Connecticut, New York, New Jersey, and Maryland and lowest for Alaska, South Dakota, Tennessee, Washington, and Mississippi. In other words, states such as California, Connecticut, New York, New Jersey, and Maryland will be mostly affected by the SALT cap provision because more than 25 percent of their SALT could not have been deducted if the cap were effective in 2015. On the other hand, some states will not be much affected. The total excess of SALT deductions is below 5 percent of total SALT revenues for nine states, including Alaska, South Dakota, Tennessee, Washington, Mississippi, North Dakota, Texas, New Mexico, and Wyoming.

The capped SALT deductions do not affect state and local tax revenues directly. Its direct impact is to reduce taxpayers' after-tax incomes. Some high-income taxpayers will face larger federal income tax liability because

Table 4. Excess of SALT deductions by state

State	Total excess of SALT deductions	Total SALT	Total excess of SALT deductions as percentage of total SALT
Alabama	0.57	10.60	5.41%
Alaska	0.01	1.71	0.76%
Arizona	1.47	20.10	7.31%
Arkansas	0.79	9.01	8.76%
California	62.80	185.00	34.03%
Colorado	2.22	20.50	10.82%
Connecticut	7.47	22.50	33.24%
Delaware	0.36	2.01	18.15%
District of Columbia	1.22	5.44	22.51%
Florida	4.70	48.90	9.63%
Georgia	3.76	30.40	12.38%
Hawaii	0.58	6.74	8.64%
Idaho	0.48	4.54	10.51%
Illinois	8.26	55.80	14.79%
Indiana	1.49	20.20	7.41%
Iowa	0.99	11.80	8.34%
Kansas	0.77	10.50	7.33%
Kentucky	1.17	12.10	9.70%
Louisiana	0.75	14.10	5.30%
Maine	0.51	5.55	9.12%
Maryland	6.92	27.00	25.65%
Massachusetts	8.58	35.60	24.08%
Michigan	2.89	32.20	8.97%
Minnesota	4.57	24.40	18.72%
Mississippi	0.34	8.11	4.15%
Missouri	2.07	18.10	11.43%
Montana	0.35	2.74	12.67%
Nebraska	0.72	7.99	8.95%
Nevada	0.44	7.48	5.84%
New Hampshire	0.39	4.16	9.31%
New Jersey	15.80	49.90	31.66%
New Mexico	0.29	6.23	4.60%
New York	44.30	137.00	32.25%
North Carolina	3.42	30.20	11.31%
North Dakota	0.13	3.07	4.21%
Ohio	4.16	42.70	9.74%
Oklahoma	0.89	10.70	8.29%
Oregon	3.20	13.00	24.64%
Pennsylvania	5.32	46.00	11.55%
Rhode Island	0.66	4.65	14.11%
South Carolina	1.20	13.30	8.98%
South Dakota	0.06	2.52	2.23%
Tennessee	0.46	14.80	3.08%
Texas	3.79	88.60	4.28%
Utah	0.88	8.72	10.06%
Vermont	0.33	2.68	12.25%
Virginia	5.05	29.80	16.97%
Washington	0.99	25.80	3.82%
West Virginia	0.31	4.88	6.40%
Wisconsin	2.70	21.70	12.45%
Wyoming	0.12	2.43	4.80%
US total	219.00	1220.00	17.87%

Source: Authors' computation.
Note: The tax revenues are in billions of dollars.

Table 5. The impact of the SALT cap on income

State	Level of AGI			
	$100,000 ~ $200,000	$200,000 ~ $500,000	$500,000 ~ $1,000,000	$1,000,000 or more
Alabama	/ (0.00%)	0.37% (2.11%)	1.11% (0.34%)	1.36% (0.15%)
Alaska	/ (0.00%)	/ (0.00%)	0.26% (0.29%)	0.37% (0.10%)
Arizona	/ (0.00%)	0.51% (2.75%)	1.50% (0.40%)	1.89% (0.19%)
Arkansas	/ (0.00%)	1.07% (2.09%)	2.15% (0.32%)	2.04% (0.14%)
California	0.47% (10.95%)	2.09% (4.79%)	3.66% (0.77%)	4.75% (0.40%)
Colorado	/ (0.00%)	0.69% (4.10%)	1.60% (0.60%)	1.93% (0.28%)
Connecticut	0.73% (13.85%)	1.95% (5.46%)	3.16% (1.06%)	3.27% (0.64%)
Delaware	/ (0.00%)	1.14% (3.09%)	2.31% (0.40%)	2.50% (0.18%)
District of Columbia	0.39% (12.13%)	1.82% (6.39%)	3.18% (1.06%)	3.30% (0.57%)
Florida	/ (0.00%)	0.33% (2.24%)	0.97% (0.43%)	1.31% (0.26%)
Georgia	/ (0.00%)	1.08% (3.09%)	1.98% (0.48%)	2.14% (0.22%)
Hawaii	/ (0.00%)	1.34% (2.64%)	2.96% (0.33%)	3.52% (0.13%)
Idaho	/ (0.00%)	1.29% (2.09%)	2.34% (0.34%)	2.37% (0.15%)
Illinois	0.26% (10.03%)	1.21% (3.71%)	1.97% (0.62%)	2.01% (0.31%)
Indiana	/ (0.00%)	0.81% (2.12%)	1.69% (0.34%)	2.04% (0.15%)
Iowa	0.18% (1.01%)	1.33% (2.49%)	2.24% (0.37%)	2.16% (0.14%)
Kansas	/ (0.00%)	0.76% (2.74%)	1.49% (0.44%)	1.78% (0.18%)
Kentucky	0.17% (0.93%)	1.35% (2.05%)	2.33% (0.31%)	2.21% (0.13%)
Louisiana	/ (0.00%)	0.55% (2.33%)	1.37% (0.38%)	1.37% (0.17%)
Maine	0.44% (1.16%)	1.75% (2.33%)	2.95% (0.32%)	3.09% (0.12%)
Maryland	0.60% (14.59%)	1.89% (4.96%)	3.21% (0.60%)	3.37% (0.26%)
Massachusetts	0.40% (12.75%)	1.45% (5.54%)	2.35% (0.90%)	2.50% (0.46%)
Michigan	/ (0.00%)	0.98% (2.55%)	1.81% (0.39%)	1.79% (0.17%)
Minnesota	0.22% (1.63%)	1.68% (3.76%)	3.21% (0.58%)	3.75% (0.25%)
Mississippi	/ (0.00%)	0.63% (1.64%)	1.54% (0.26%)	1.63% (0.10%)
Missouri	/ (0.00%)	1.08% (2.45%)	2.08% (0.39%)	2.31% (0.18%)
Montana	/ (0.00%)	1.24% (2.22%)	2.29% (0.35%)	2.56% (0.15%)

State	$100,000 ~ $200,000		$200,000 ~ $500,000		$500,000 ~ $1,000,000		$1,000,000 or more	
				Level of AGI				
Nebraska	0.18%	(0.98%)	1.37%	(2.57%)	2.42%	(0.41%)	2.07%	(0.18%)
Nevada	/	(0.00%)	0.04%	(1.91%)	0.79%	(0.33%)	1.23%	(0.20%)
New Hampshire	/	(0.00%)	0.64%	(3.62%)	1.22%	(0.43%)	1.78%	(0.17%)
New Jersey	0.84%	(13.61%)	2.09%	(5.80%)	3.37%	(0.93%)	3.77%	(0.44%)
New Mexico	/	(0.00%)	0.71%	(1.98%)	1.51%	(0.25%)	1.69%	(0.10%)
New York	0.97%	(10.99%)	2.49%	(4.08%)	3.92%	(0.77%)	4.56%	(0.51%)
North Carolina	/	(0.00%)	1.14%	(2.85%)	2.12%	(0.43%)	2.11%	(0.18%)
North Dakota	/	(0.00%)	0.17%	(2.36%)	0.97%	(0.48%)	1.55%	(0.22%)
Ohio	0.23%	(1.13%)	1.36%	(2.33%)	2.30%	(0.38%)	2.34%	(0.16%)
Oklahoma	/	(0.00%)	0.78%	(2.45%)	1.63%	(0.42%)	1.57%	(0.18%)
Oregon	0.61%	(10.90%)	2.06%	(3.16%)	3.27%	(0.45%)	3.42%	(0.18%)
Pennsylvania	0.25%	(1.43%)	1.17%	(3.18%)	1.89%	(0.50%)	1.73%	(0.22%)
Rhode Island	0.32%	(10.85%)	1.54%	(3.08%)	2.56%	(0.42%)	2.90%	(0.19%)
South Carolina	/	(0.00%)	1.03%	(2.38%)	1.93%	(0.37%)	1.89%	(0.16%)
South Dakota	/	(0.00%)	0.05%	(1.71%)	0.46%	(0.33%)	0.84%	(0.15%)
Tennessee	/	(0.00%)	0.02%	(1.97%)	0.47%	(0.33%)	1.05%	(0.14%)
Texas	/	(0.00%)	0.41%	(2.88%)	0.83%	(0.46%)	0.71%	(0.22%)
Utah	/	(0.00%)	0.90%	(2.68%)	1.72%	(0.43%)	2.04%	(0.20%)
Vermont	0.54%	(1.26%)	1.87%	(2.60%)	3.21%	(0.35%)	3.17%	(0.14%)
Virginia	0.12%	(12.66%)	1.20%	(4.98%)	2.16%	(0.57%)	2.36%	(0.25%)
Washington	/	(0.00%)	0.25%	(3.65%)	0.70%	(0.49%)	0.75%	(0.20%)
West Virginia	/	(0.00%)	1.14%	(1.62%)	2.23%	(0.24%)	2.60%	(0.08%)
Wisconsin	0.43%	(1.16%)	1.52%	(2.49%)	2.57%	(0.40%)	2.67%	(0.18%)
Wyoming	/	(0.00%)	/	(0.00%)	0.53%	(0.32%)	1.28%	(0.23%)
US total	0.19%	(9.02%)	1.38%	(3.32%)	2.43%	(0.53%)	2.95%	(0.27%)

Source: Authors' computation.

Note: Each percentage refers to the estimated reduction of income as a percentage of AGI of the filers who will be affected by the new tax law, followed by the percentage (in parentheses) of the filers who will be affected in all filers of federal individual income tax returns.

their allowable SALT deductions are capped at $10,000. About 13 percent of all filers of federal income tax will be affected by this cap. According to the median voter model, the demand for state and local government services will not change because it is very likely that this provision does not change the demand of the decisive median voters. However, there is concern that high-income taxpayers are likely to relocate from high-tax states to low-tax states because they are most affected. To estimate the impact on relocation of high-income taxpayers, we can examine the extent to which the cap on SALT will affect personal incomes.

We follow a four-step approach to estimate the effect on the filers' income. First, the excess of SALT deductions over the cap is determined for each level of AGI. Second, we calculate a weighted average marginal tax rate for each level of AGI by multiplying the shares of different types of filers (single, married filing jointly, and head of household) and the corresponding marginal federal income tax rates in 2018. Third, we multiply the excess of SALT deductions and the weighted average marginal tax rate. This would be the reduced personal income if the cap were effective. Last, we divide the reduced personal income by the total AGI of those who would be affected by the cap. This approximates the percentage reduction of personal incomes of those filers due to the cap provision. Table 5 presents the estimated percentage reduction of income as a result of the cap and the number of the filers who would be affected as a percentage of all filers of federal individual income tax returns.

It turns out that the cap provision will not have a large impact on personal incomes. For the whole country, the estimated reductions of income are 2.95, 2.43, 1.38, and 0.19 percent of the adjusted gross income of the affected filers with AGI at $1 million or more, $0.5 million to $1 million, $0.2 million to $0.5 million, and $0.1 million to $0.2 million, respectively. Filers in all states except Alaska and Wyoming will feel the impact if their AGIs are above $0.2 million a year. However, the magnitude of the impact is quite modest, between 0.02 and 4.75 percent of AGI. Those with an AGI at or over $1 million will see over 3.75 percent reduction of their incomes in four states: California, New York, New Jersey, and Minnesota. The estimated impact at the same top level of AGI is below 1 percent in Alaska, Texas, Washington, and South Dakota.

CONCLUSION

The aftermath of the Great Recession witnessed the rebounding of government revenues at federal, state, and municipal levels in the United States.

Unlike the federal and state governments, municipal governments have not yet fully recovered from substantial revenue losses to their general funds even ten years after the official ending of the recession. The sluggish recovery of municipal finances presents a major challenge to municipal governments. There are several underlying factors that have led to the current municipal fiscal situation.

The fact that the recovery of municipal general fund revenues does not keep pace with the rebounding economy indicates a problematic alignment of a city's economic base to its fiscal architecture. While a strong local economic base is the foundation of a city's fiscal capacity, a city's fiscal architecture is greatly shaped by state control. Through various constraints on local autonomy, states can constrain cities' fiscal capacity by setting limits on how much revenue a city can extract from its economic base. For instance, a strong retail sales sector cannot generate much tax revenue if the city does not have the authority to tax retail sales or if its authority is strictly limited. Slightly less than half of all municipalities are not granted the authority to levy a tax on retail sales, and about nine in ten cannot tax income or earnings. Almost half of the cities in the United States cannot directly benefit from the recent Supreme Court ruling regarding tax on online sales, although it is applauded as a major benefit for state and local governments. Although the majority of cities rely on property taxes, TELs impose limits on the growth rate of property taxes, and thus the recovery of the real estate market does not translate into the growth of tax revenue. Coupled with stagnant growth of state aid to cities, cities are left with fewer resources at the same time they are asked to do more.

Although the federal government plays a lesser role in shaping municipal fiscal decisions, changes at the federal level can have an impact on city revenues, directly by reduced federal aid and indirectly by adjusting the federal tax code and imposing mandates. The newly established cap on SALT deductions does not affect state and local tax revenues directly. However, high-tax states and cities may lose some affluent taxpayers and hence part of their tax bases. The overall impact on state and local finances will be small given that more than half of the taxpayers will not be affected by this cap.

Cities vary substantially in their revenue structure, economic condition, and intergovernmental context. The impact of misaligned revenue systems, state control, and federal intrusion is and will be heterogeneous across cities in the American federal system. As a consequence, caution is advised when generalizing the findings presented here to a particular municipal government.

Notes

1. Data from the Federal Reserve Bank of St. Louis, https://fred.stlouisfed.org/series/GDPC1.

2. National Association of State Budget Officers, *Fiscal Survey of the States, Spring 2018*, https://www.nasbo.org/mainsite/reports-data/fiscal-survey-of-states/fiscal-survey-archives.

3. Christy McFarland and Michael A. Pagano, *City Fiscal Conditions in 2017* (Washington, DC: National League of Cities, 2017), http://nlc.org/sites/default/files/2017-09/NLC%20City%20Fiscal%20Conditions%202017.pdf.

4. *South Dakota v. Wayfair, Inc., et al.*, No. 17-494 (Decided June 21, 2018).

5. *South Dakota v. Wayfair, Inc., et al.*, 19.

6. See, for example, John R. Bartle, Kenneth A. Kriz, and Boris Morozov, "Local Government Revenue Structure: Trends and Challenges," *Journal of Public Budgeting, Accounting, and Financial Management* 23, no. 2 (2011): 268–87; and Michael A. Pagano, "Creative Designs of the Patchwork Quilt of Municipal Finance," in *The Changing Landscape of Local Public Revenues*, ed. Gregory K. Ingram and Yu-Hung Hong (Cambridge, MA: Lincoln Institute of Land Policy, 2010), 116–40.

7. Michael A. Pagano et al., "The Fiscal Policy Space of Cities: A Comprehensive Framework for City Fiscal Decision Making," final report, John D. and Catherine T. MacArthur Foundation, 2016; Michael A. Pagano and Christopher W. Hoene, "City Budgets in an Era of Increased Uncertainty: Understanding the Fiscal Policy Space of Cities," Brookings Metropolitan Policy Program, July 2018, www.brookings.edu.

8. Deborah A. Carroll, "Diversifying Municipal Government Revenue Structures: Fiscal Illusion or Instability?," *Public Budgeting & Finance* 29, no. 1 (2009): 27–48; Hal Wolman et al., "Comparing Local Government Autonomy across States," Working Paper 35 (George Washington Institute for Public Policy, 2008).

9. Christopher Hoene and Christiana McFarland, "Cities and State Fiscal Structure, 2015," National League of Cities, 2015, www.nlc.org.

10. Pagano et al., "Fiscal Policy Space of Cities." The one hundred cities are economically representative of the municipal sector using a selection method that crudely approximates the relative economic and fiscal importance of large cities within metropolitan areas. To be included in the sample, a city must be among the largest US central cities and be within the largest metropolitan statistical areas in the United States.

11. Arturo Pérez, "Earmarking State Taxes," National Conference of State Legislatures, 2016, www.ncsl.org/documents/fiscal/earmarking-state-taxes.pdf.

12. James M. Buchanan, "The Economics of Earmarked Taxes," *Journal of Political Economy* 71, no. 5 (1963): 457–69.

13. Elizabeth Deran, "Earmarking and Expenditures: A Survey and a New Test," *National Tax Journal* 18, no. 4 (1965): 354–61; Richard F. Dye and Therese J. McGuire, "The Effect of Earmarked Revenues on the Level and Composition of Expenditures," *Public Finance Quarterly* 20, no. 4 (1992): 543–56.

14. William H. Oakland, "Earmarking and Decentralization," in *Proceedings of the Seventy-Seventh Annual Conference* (Columbus, OH: National Tax Association—Tax Institute of America, 1985), 274–77; Rebecca Hendrick and Shu Wang, "Use of Special Assessments by Municipal Governments in the Chicago Metropolitan Area: Is Leviathan Tamed?," *Public Budgeting and Finance* 38, no. 3 (2018): 32–57.

15. Whitney B. Afonso, "Leviathan or Flypaper: Examining the Fungibility of Earmarked Local Sales Taxes for Transportation," *Public Budgeting & Finance* 35, no. 3 (2015): 1–23.

16. For a detailed description of the sample, see Adam Langley, "Methodology Used to Create Fiscally Standardized Cities Database," Working Paper WP16AL1 (Lincoln Institute of Land Policy, 2016).

17. Jesse J. Richardson Jr., "Dillon's Rule Is from Mars, Home Rule Is from Venus: Local Government Autonomy and the Rules of Statutory Construction," *Publius: The Journal of Federalism* 41, no. 4 (2011): 662–85.

18. Bryan A. Garner, *Black's Law Dictionary* (Eagan, MN: Thomson Reuters, 2014).

19. Richardson, "Dillon's Rule."

20. Jill Welch, "Home Rule Doctrine and State Preemption: The Iowa Supreme Court Resurrects Dillon's Rule and Blurs the Line between Implied Preemption and Inconsistency, *Goodell v. Humboldt County*, 575 NW 2D 486, Iowa 1998," *Rutgers Law Journal* 1548 (1999).

21. Timothy D. Mead, "Federalism and State Law: Legal Factors Constraining and Facilitation Local Initiatives," in *Handbook of Local Government Administration*, ed. John J. Gargan, 31–45 (New York: Marcel Dekker, 1997); Dale Krane, Platon N. Rigos, and Melvin Hill, *Home Rule in America: A Fifty-State Handbook* (Washington, DC: CQ Press, 2001).

22. Welch, "Home Rule Doctrine and State Preemption."

23. Jesse Richardson, Meghan Gough Zimmerman, and Robert Puentes, *Is Home Rule the Answer? Clarifying the Influence of Dillon's Rule on Growth Management* (Washington, DC: Brookings Institution Center on Urban and Metropolitan Research, 2003).

24. Krane, Rigos, and Hill, *Home Rule in America.*

25. Daniel R. Mullins and Bruce A. Wallin, "Tax and Expenditure Limitations: Introduction and Overview," *Public Budgeting & Finance* 24, no. 4 (2004): 2–15.

26. Lincoln Institute of Land Policy and George Washington Institute of Public Policy, "Significant Features of the Property Tax," http://datatoolkits.lincolninst.edu/subcenters/significant-features-property-tax/state-by-state-property-tax-in-detail.

27. Mark Skidmore and Mehmet S. Tosun, "Property Value Assessment Growth Limits, Tax Base Erosion, and Regional In-Migration," *Public Finance Review* 39, no. 2 (2011): 256–87; Shu Wang, "Effects of State-Imposed Tax and Expenditure Limits on Municipal Revenue Reliance: A New Measure of TEL Stringency with Mixed Methods," *Publius: The Journal of Federalism* 48, no. 2 (2018): 292–316.

28. Max Sawicky, "The New American Devolution: Problems and Prospects," in *The End of Welfare? Consequences of Federal Devolution for the Nation*, ed. Max Sawicky, 3–24 (Armonk, NY: M. E. Sharpe, 1999).

29. This represents state and local property tax, general sales, and income tax that are deductible from federal income taxation.

30. www.congress.gov/bill/115th-congress/house-bill/1.

31. www.pewtrusts.org/en/research-and-analysis/articles/2018/04/10/cap-on-the-state-and-local-tax-deduction-likely-to-affect-states-beyond-new-york-and-california.

32. The data is accessible at www.irs.gov/statistics/soi-tax-stats-historic-table-2.

33. While most of the returns filed during the twelve-month period are primarily for tax year 2015, the IRS received a limited number of returns for tax years before 2015, and these have been included within the data.

34. We exclude the filers who chose itemized deductions in 2015 but would switch to standard deductions under the new law.

35. The total SALT deductions would be $474 billion after excluding the taxpayers who would switch to standard deductions.

Exploring Urban Governments' Fiscal Challenges

DAVID MERRIMAN

Elected officials and bureaucrats manage government finances under a constant cloud of suspicion. Taxpayers, who cannot see where their money is going and cannot easily assess the costs to deliver most government goods and services, suspect they are paying too much and getting too little. Those responsible for delivering services may cry poverty, while challengers, hoping to wrest political power, often promise they can deliver government services with less pain and better efficiency. Scholars and analysts can promote good government, constructive debate, and responsive politics by providing clear concepts and solid measurements that promote evidence-based program evaluation and policy analyses. In this chapter, I first discuss some conceptual issues and then provide some empirical evidence about US cities' fiscal condition. The empirical analyses emphasize exploratory description and broad coverage over many years rather than empirical rigor or deep analytics.

With a nod to journalists' essential questions, slightly scrambled, I investigate the following set of issues. What does the term "fiscal health" mean? How can we measure it? Who has bad fiscal health? Where is municipal fiscal health most problematic? When, if at all, should we expect fiscal problems to lead to disruption of government services? Why do fiscal problems emerge, and what can be done about them?

WHAT DOES THE TERM "FISCAL HEALTH" MEAN?

"Fiscal health" is clearly meant to suggest an analogy with biomedical health. The World Health Organization (WHO) has defined health as "a state of complete physical, mental, and social well-being and not merely the absence of disease or infirmity." This definition may be useful as a mission statement, but it is so broad and unspecific that it does not give much direction about how to measure health. Ultimately, scholarly and clinical measures of human health status, health-related quality of life, and quality of life largely rely on patients' essentially subjective evaluations in response to questions posed by medical providers.[1] There is controversy about these measurements, and many different indicators have been developed and applied to assess health status.[2]

Tracy Gordon provides a concise but comprehensive summary of the literature about municipal fiscal health.[3] Her summary of this literature demonstrates that definitions of fiscal health that are both broad enough to capture general concepts and tangible enough to facilitate measurement are equally or perhaps even more elusive than definitions of human health status. For example, Inman's view of this issue is that "the most meaningful definition of urban fiscal health is the ability of a city to affect the welfare of its residents in terms of the basket of consumption opportunities open to them." This broad definition provides little direct guidance about how to assess a particular government's fiscal health. In fact, Inman's definition rejects the idea that urban governments can be separated from their residents. Inman writes that "cities are not people and do not have feelings or desires. . . . [A] . . . way to make city residents better off—one usually absent from political discussion—may be by letting city residents know that the best way to better their lives might be to move out of the city."[4] This seems analogous to the concept, often taught in principles of economics courses, that the optimal choice for a firm that cannot cover all of its costs is to go out of business.

In contrast to Inman, Ladd and Yinger define "*standardized fiscal health* to be the difference between [a city's] revenue-raising capacity and standardized expenditure need." Their approach "isolates the contribution to a city's fiscal health of economic and social factors that are outside the city's control."[5] This definition accepts the city as an entity whose fiscal health is distinct from its residents' welfare. Ladd and Yinger go on to define fiscal health in explicit measurable detail. Their methodology is very practical but provides readers with little guidance about the broad conceptual basis for their measures.

Pagano and Hoene have introduced a separate concept closely related to fiscal health that they call the fiscal policy space.[6] They argue that each city's unique characteristics and history require us to consider each city individually. Their analysis highlights the intergovernmental context—especially state rules that constrain city spending or revenue—of the economic base of the city and the demands and preferences of citizens as it interacts with local political culture.

After surveying this landscape, Richard Bird writes, "Although much has been said recently in many countries about urban fiscal stress, fiscal health, and fiscal sustainability, there is no unique, correct concept of the financial condition of local governments and hence no way to measure fiscal health."[7]

This potentially discouraging conclusion invites readers to reconceptualize urban fiscal health as part of a multidimensional and dynamic process. Hendrick emphasizes the complex nature of government fiscal health and distinguishes between financial "slack" and other environmental factors that influence governments' ability to provide services.[8] Just as human health depends on the condition of the respiratory, cardiovascular, digestive, and other systems, a city's fiscal health depends on the condition of its revenue, service delivery, and political, commercial, and other systems. Just as human physical systems interact (a damaged respiratory system may impair the cardiovascular system), the systems that produce cities' fiscal health are interdependent (poorly functioning political systems may degrade governments' service delivery system). Just as it is difficult to objectively aggregate the many factors that influence human health into a single index, it is difficult to objectively aggregate the many factors that influence fiscal health into a single indicator.

The analogy between human health and cities' fiscal health is imperfect, however. Human health has a natural lower bound since humans have a natural aging process that leads to their eventual demise. Cities have no natural life span and cities rarely "die," so the lower bound on cities' fiscal health may not be particularly relevant. While humans may not have an objective natural upper bound on their health, people seem able to intuit a subjective upper bound operationalized, as in the WHO definition quoted above, as something like "complete well-being." While humans can make subjective judgments about their health status and quality of life, it is not clear how to apply this concept to cities' fiscal health—what questions should be asked, and whose subjective evaluation would be most appropriate?

While these are difficult questions, we can illustrate important ideas while abstracting from the multidimensional nature of fiscal health and focusing on some dynamic salient features. Any assessment of a city's fiscal health almost certainly will depend on the net assets (A_t), that is, assets minus liabilities—essentially the net worth—of the city government. Fiscal health must also depend on the expected future evolution of net assets. The future evolution of net assets will depend on past values and factors such as the economic base, the political system, and legal constraints.

A very simple analytical model presented in appendix 1 and discussed below in more detail illustrates how the long-term (equilibrium) level of fiscal health in the city could be estimated based on past and current observations about net assets and other relevant variables. This way of thinking conceives of fiscal health as being determined by factors like the economic base and the political system as well as the speed at which net assets adjust over time. Using this framework, we can discuss a city's fiscal health at a point in time as well as its long-run fiscal health. The empirical section implements a very simple illustrative version of the model.

This conceptual framework provides a way to think about fiscal health but does not prescribe direct technology for measurement.

HOW CAN WE MEASURE FISCAL HEALTH?

The literature conceives of government fiscal health as multidimensional and ultimately depends on interactions between financial and nonfinancial variables. In practice, most assessments of fiscal health rely on a relatively small number of elements. These include measures of the city's economic base, fiscal resources, and some measure of political and legal constraints and opportunities. Two fundamental approaches have been used.[9] One approach, which we might call the "household-analogy approach," is to objectively assess the cost of providing a basic set of government goods and services and available resources. The premise of this approach seems to be that just as households require a certain minimum level of food, shelter, clothing, and the like, governments of a particular type (city, county, state) are required to provide some basic level of services. Cost is defined as the dollar amount of spending needed to fund a specific bundle of public services, given socioeconomic conditions beyond the direct control of local government. The amount of resources available to the government is assessed separately, and this is labeled as "capacity." Capacity is then subtracted from cost, and this difference is labeled the "cost-capacity gap."[10] The larger the cost-capacity gap, the worse the fiscal condition of the government.

A second approach, which we might call the "credit-worthiness approach," is to look at fiscal indicators of governments. The premise of this approach seems to be that, just as potential lenders use certain indicators to evaluate the credit worthiness of a potential borrower, public policy analysts can use indicators to evaluate a government's fiscal condition. The International City/County Managers Association has been a strong proponent of this approach,[11] and it has been adopted by many cities and adapted for use by other types of governments. For example, the system that the Illinois State Board of Education uses to monitor the fiscal condition of school districts relies on five indicators, including the fund balance–to–revenue ratio (a measure of savings) and the expenditure-to-revenue ratio (a measure of the surplus—or deficit—in the operating budget). Other measures are cash on hand and short-term and long-term borrowing capacity remaining. The five indicators are weighted, and each school district is given a score between one and four, indicating its fiscal condition.[12] The lower the score, the worse the assumed fiscal condition of the school district.

Chernick and Reschovsky discuss the household-analogy approach and identify two methods of measuring need and two separate methods of assessing capacity.[13] The most straightforward method for measuring need—estimation of a cost function—can be used when public-sector output data are measurable and observed and the appropriate level of output is uncontroversial. For example, if the public sector provides school buses to transport children to school, the cost of this activity can be assessed on a relatively objective basis. The necessary inputs—school buses, school bus drivers, fuel, and so on—can be easily discerned, and, if data are available on the locations of students and schools and the prices of inputs, it is straightforward to calculate need by multiplying the cost of each input times the quantity of the input required and summing over each expenditure.

Of course, for many government goods and services, either the quantity of inputs required or the cost of the inputs or both cannot be determined so unambiguously. For example, the appropriate or necessary quantity of input to police services may be subject to dispute. Should police patrols be higher in areas that have historically had higher crime rates? Perhaps other inputs—for example, more publicly funded after-school basketball leagues—would be more appropriate. The appropriate cost of inputs could also be debated. Should police departments offer relatively high salaries and try to attract fewer experienced officers, or should they offer lower salaries and try to attract younger officers who may be more willing to adapt to new policies and procedures?

When it is difficult to obtain reliable estimates of cost functions, Chernick and Reschovsky note that it may be possible to use estimates of "expenditure functions" to estimate need. Ladd and Yinger provide a detailed example of the use of government expenditure function estimates. They conceptualize a city's expenditure need as "the amount it must spend to obtain a standardized level of final outputs."[14] This depends, of course, in part on the cost of inputs, so Ladd and Yinger use statistical controls for cost factors beyond the control of the local government, like wages required to attract private-sector workers to the public sector. The cost of final outputs (say, fire protection) also depends, in part, on environmental factors such as the share of houses that are brick rather than wood, so Ladd and Yinger control for environmental factors as well.

The public services of interest to Ladd and Yinger (general government, police, and fire) are not easily quantified—that is, it is hard to say how many "units" of general government jurisdiction A delivered compared to jurisdiction B. Since Ladd and Yinger do not observe the quantity of each public service, they cannot directly measure the cost per unit. They do observe expenditures on each government service. If they knew the quantity of each service, they could use their statistical controls for the cost of inputs and environmental factors to infer the cost of a unit of services and hence the cost of meeting any level of need.

Ladd and Yinger revert to economic theory to estimate the quantity of each service delivered to each city. They hypothesize, based on economic theory and past research, that the quantity of public services demanded by voters of each city depends on the income of the voter with the median demand and the tax price faced by that voter. With these assumptions, Ladd and Yinger can correlate observed levels of expenditures with controls for voter incomes and prices and data on the costs of delivering services and environmental factors to determine the resources needed by any city.

Having measured "cost," some measure of fiscal capacity is required in order to measure fiscal health. Chernick and Reschovsky identify two basic approaches to measuring fiscal capacity.[15] The "representative tax system" (RTS) approach calculates the level of revenue that would be raised at a standard tax rate common to all governments included in the study. Zhao explains that "by construction, this capacity measure is directly proportional to the size of the municipality's tax base."[16] The main issues when using RTS are what tax bases to include and what the standard tax rate should be. Typically, the included tax bases are those that are used by most or many of the relevant governments, and the standard tax rates are chosen to be near or at the average (mean or median) tax rate chosen by the governments in the study. Skidmore and Scorsone[17] implement a simpler variant designed to measure variation across city governments in Michigan that have little autonomy in determining tax revenue. However, when different governments have different legally available tax bases or different legal political or other limits on the tax rates they can charge, the interpretation of the RTS measure of revenue capacity may suggest misleading interpretations of governments' fiscal positions.[18]

An alternative measure of revenue capacity is promoted by Haughwout and colleagues and focuses on potential maximum revenue, which the authors call the peak of "revenue hills."[19] This approach estimates the long-run tax-rate elasticity of tax revenue—that is, the authors ask how much tax revenue increases with increases in the tax rate. If higher taxes cause a decrease in the quantity of the tax base, demanded tax revenue will be maximized at some finite tax rate. Haughwout and coauthors estimate revenue hills for a total of eight tax bases in four cities (Houston, Minneapolis, New York, and Philadelphia). They interpret the revenue generated at the tax rate that maximizes revenue as the revenue capacity of the city. While this approach is consistent with economic theory, it faces several severe practical obstacles. First, many cities change tax rates only infrequently, so it may be difficult to get sufficient statistical power to precisely estimate rate-revenue curves. Second, if city authorities are well informed and rational and always choose tax rates below the rate that maximizes revenue, estimating the peak of the rate-revenue curve will require extrapolation outside the range of observed data. Doing this means that one cannot use the usual statistical tests to validate estimates.

The most active practitioners of the credit-worthiness approach—the second approach—to measurement of fiscal health are the major bond-rating agencies of Fitch, Moody's, and Standard & Poor's (S&P). Strictly speaking, the ratings issued by these agencies are not designed to assess "fiscal health." Credit-rating agencies assign assets (for example, debt issues like municipal bonds) "ratings" that are designed to reflect the quality of the asset from the point of view of the purchaser. As explained by S&P, assets "rated in each category are intended to be able to withstand the associated level of macroeconomic stress without defaulting." According to S&P, "The scenario associated with the 'AAA' rating [the highest] level is one of extreme macroeconomic stress—on par with the Great Depression of the 1930s. The scenarios associated with the lower rating levels are successively less stressful."[20]

To arrive at their ratings, credit-rating agencies consider a broad range of factors. S&P's methodology considers factors in seven distinct weighted categories. The categories, with weights in parentheses, used by S&P for general obligation debt of US local governments are institutional framework (10 percent), economy (30 percent), management (20 percent), and financial measures, with three subcategories (30 percent) and debt and contingent liabilities (10 percent).[21] No rationale is provided for category weightings.[22]

S&P's methodology relies on a combination of qualitative judgments and quantitative calculations. For example, the management score depends in part on qualitative factors such as whether frequent management turnover inhibits current understanding of the government's financial position. On the other hand, the score for budgetary performance—a subcategory of financial measures—is assessed as a function of the net results (deficits or surpluses) of total government funds and the general fund with scores (from 1 to 5) defined in a simple algorithm.

Overall, municipal bond default probabilities are very low. Cornaggia, Cornaggia, and Hund (2017) present data showing that only about 1 of the 1,862 municipal bonds (0.05 percent) rated AAA by Moody's in their data set defaulted.[23] None of the 2,811 municipal bonds rated AA defaulted, and none of the 715 municipal bonds Moody's rated A defaulted. In contrast, 0.16 percent, 0.34 percent, and 0.51 percent of corporate bonds that Moody's rated AAA, AA, and A, respectively, defaulted. Corporate debt rated below A defaulted at much higher rates, but Moody's did not rate any municipal debt below A, so default rates could not be compared. Spiotto, Acker, and Appleby confirm the very low rate of municipal defaults.[24] In light of the relatively low default rates on municipal debt, credit-rating agencies have been criticized for being too harsh in their ratings, and simple algorithms relying only on objective quantitative accounting and economic indicators have been proposed as an alternative.[25]

Municipal default on a credit obligation—for example, failure to make a bond payment—surely seems a sign of very poor fiscal health. However, a low probability of default may not signal good fiscal health, since governments generally prioritize debt service over virtually all other kinds of spending. While variability in credit ratings may reflect little change in default probabilities, the ratings may carry useful information about fiscal health.

A NEW DATA SOURCE ABOUT CITY GOVERNMENTS' FISCAL HEALTH

I turn next to some exploratory empirical analyses of the fiscal health of US cities. The goal in this section is use a very simple version of the multidimensional dynamic model discussed above and presented mathematically in the appendix to describe the variation across time and space in the long- and short-term fiscal health of US cities.

The empirical analyses uses a previously underexploited data set compiled by the Government Finance Officers Association in the course of their Certificate of Achievement for Excellence in Financial Reporting Program.[26] Under this program, GFOA annually invites governments to submit their comprehensive annual financial report (CAFR) for consideration for the award.[27] CAFRs are reviewed, and some of them are awarded a GFOA certificate of excellence for presentation.

Since at least 1995, the GFOA has collected key data elements from the CAFRs submitted for its award program, compiled them in spreadsheets, and made the information available for purchase.[28] While the data set is neither comprehensive nor necessarily representative, it is large (between 1,343 and 2,039 cities in each year),[29] and, because cities are identified by state and name, the data can be weighted to represent all, or any desired subset, of US cities. The GFOA data set captures only a subset of the information entered into the CAFR, and that subset differs by year.

Since the early 2000s, statement 34 of the Government Accounting Standards Board (GASB) has essentially required that all city governments include a set of government-wide financial indicators based on accrual accounting in their CAFRs.[30] A subset of this data has been consistently included in the GFOA database since 2003 and is employed in the analyses below.

GASB 34 represented a dramatic and controversial rewriting of governmental accounting standards and has been extensively discussed in the governmental accounting literature.[31] GASB presented a concise and nontechnical statement of the most important changes introduced by GASB 34 in its May 2007 "From the Users' Perspective" publication, which read in part:

> GASB Statement No. 34 ... introduced a number of financial reporting innovations, foremost of which may be the government-wide financial statements. These statements—the statement of net assets and the statement of activities—bring together information that previously had been spread among various funds and reported on different accounting bases. ... The government-wide statements ignore the partitions created by the funds, bringing the financial activity together in one place and using just one type of information—accrual-based economic resources. As a result, all assets and liabilities are accounted for, as well as all inflows and outflows of resources. ... Trusts and agency funds are not included in the government-wide statements, because the resources they account for are being held in a fiduciary capacity by the government. ... Additionally, discretely presented component units—legally separate entities for which the primary government is financially accountable—are shown on the face of the government-wide statements. ...
>
> The statement of net assets presents the same information as a balance sheet: It assesses the balance of a government's assets—the resources it can use to provide service and operate the government—against its liabilities—its obligations to turn over resources to other organizations or individuals. The difference between a government's assets and its liabilities is called net assets. The name of the statement reflects its emphasis on what a government would have left over after satisfying its liabilities. Net assets are an indicator of a government's financial position—its financial standing at a given point in time (typically, the

end of the fiscal year). Financial position can be tracked over time to assess whether a government's financial health is improving or deteriorating.[32]

While GASB 34 has been criticized as unnecessarily complex because it requires governments to continue to provide information based at the fund as well as the government-wide level,[33] there is widespread agreement that the requirement for reporting of government-wide assets, liabilities, and net assets on a consistent basis has greatly increased transparency.

Consistent with the earlier discussion and the appendix, these analyses focus on cities' accumulation and decumulation of assets. This analytical strategy conceives of the city as a legal corporation (which it generally is) parallel to a for-profit or nonprofit corporation. The premise is that just as a for-profit (or nonprofit) corporation that accumulates assets becomes economically more valuable, a city corporation that increases its ownership of (real per capita) net assets becomes fiscally healthier. Note that under this conception of fiscal health, a city that is more fiscally healthy does not necessarily serve its residents better. All else being equal, one might expect city residents to prefer that the city provide services with the lowest possible accumulation of assets since as the city accumulates more assets, it has less ability to return assets to residents (or to not take them in the first place). However, this is also true of for-profit corporations. As the corporation accumulates more assets, it has less ability to return assets to shareholders. Despite this, residents and shareholders want their respective corporations to accumulate assets in order that the assets can both be put to use in the service of corporate productive aims and demonstrate the financial worth of the corporation and thereby attract new residents and shareholders, respectively.

GFOA data contain eight particularly relevant variables in relation to city assets:

GAINVCAP	net investment in capital assets of the governmental activities
GARESNET	total restricted net assets of the governmental activities
GAUNRESNET	unrestricted net assets of the governmental activities
GACHANGENET	total change in net assets of the governmental activities
BTAINVCAP	net investment in capital assets of the business-type activities
BTARESNET	total restricted net assets of the business-type activities
BTAUNRESNET	unrestricted net assets of the business-type activities
BTACHANGENET	total change in net assets of the business-type

The first set of variables (prefixed by GA) refers to net assets used in services of governmental activities. These are traditional services of government such as police protection, firefighting, and parks that often are not self-supporting and rely on taxes for their financing. The second set of variables (prefixed by BTA) are business-type activities that charge a fee directly to the people or groups that use their services. Common examples include electric utilities, universities, hospitals, and golf courses.[34]

Total net assets in year t can be defined as

$$A_t = \text{GAINVCAP} + \text{GARESNET} + \text{GAUNRESNET} + \text{BTAINVCAP} + \text{BTARESNET} + \text{BTAUNRESNET}$$

and

$$A_{t-1} = A_t - (\text{GACHANGENET} - \text{BTACHANGENET})$$

We may also be interested separately in assets used for governmental or business-type activities denoted, respectively, as AGA and ABTA:

$$AGA_t = \text{GAINVCAP} + \text{GARESNET} + \text{GAUNRESNET}$$

and

$$ABTA_t = A_t - AGA_t$$

All variables are expressed in real per capita terms.[35]

Before presenting descriptive statistics about government assets, let's look at some background regarding the representativeness of these data. Application for the GFOA award Certificate of Achievement is voluntary, and many cities do not participate. We can learn something about the representativeness of the cities that do participate by comparing them with the universe of cities in the US Department of Census's Census of Governments, which is conducted every five years. Both the GFOA data and the Census of Governments data contain a variable measuring the population of the cities in the data.

Tables 1A and 1B provide information about the number of cities in various population brackets in the two data sets in 2012. About one out of ten US cities' CAFR data is contained in the GFOA database. However, cities are not equally distributed across population categories. Only 97 of the 14,819 cities (0.6 percent) with population below 5,000 submitted applications for the award, but 265 of the 302 cities (87.7 percent) of the cities with populations above 100,000 submitted applications for the award. The percentage of cities submitting applications for the certificate increases steadily with population size. Of course, this pattern by itself does not necessarily tell us the extent to which the GFOA data are representative. The few submissions in the smallest size category could be representative of the vast number that did not submit. Similarly, the 12.3 percent of cities in the largest size category that did not submit could be very different from 87.7 percent of cities that did submit. Thus,

Table 1A. Distribution of city population sizes in Census data in 2012

Population	Frequency	Percentage	Cumulative percentage
<5K	14,819	75.94	75.94
5K to 10K	1,665	8.53	84.47
10K to 25K	1,553	7.96	92.43
25K to 50K	724	3.71	96.14
50K to 100K	451	2.31	98.45
>100K	302	1.55	100.00
Total	19,514	100.00	

Source: Author's calculation based on K. Pierson, M. L. Hand, and F. Thompson, "The Government Finance Database: A Common Resource for Quantitative Research in Public Financial Analysis," *PLoS ONE* 10, no. 6 (2015): e0130119, doi:10.1371/journal.pone.0130119.

Table 1B. Distribution of city population sizes in GFOA data in 2012

Population	Frequency	Percentage	Cumulative percentage
1	97	4.98	4.98
5,000	219	11.24	16.21
10,000	567	29.09	45.31
25,000	472	24.22	69.52
50,000	329	16.88	86.40
100,000	265	13.60	100.00
Total	1,949	100.00	

Source: Author's calculations from the GFOA database.

we should be cautious in interpreting the results found here as representative of the general population, but we do know that at least the results of cities in the largest size categories portray the experience of a large share of big cities.

SOME EXPLORATORY EMPIRICAL INVESTIGATIONS OF FISCAL HEALTH

Who Has Bad Fiscal Health, and When Did It Get Bad?

Figure 1 shows median real per capita net assets by population size group by year. Median net assets vary from more than $8,324 per capita in the smallest cities in 2003 to less than $3,246 per capita in cities with populations of 25,000 to 50,000 in 2003. The data show a large amount of volatility both within and across population groups. Across population groups, there has been a general upward trend in net assets, with a sharp drop in the smallest cities between 2003 and 2004. All size categories except the smallest showed a sharp drop between 2014 (the dashed line) and 2015.[36]

Figure 2 shows the share of cities in each population group with a relatively low level ($1,000) of real per capita net assets. By this measure, these cities

Figure 1. Median city government net assets by population group and year.

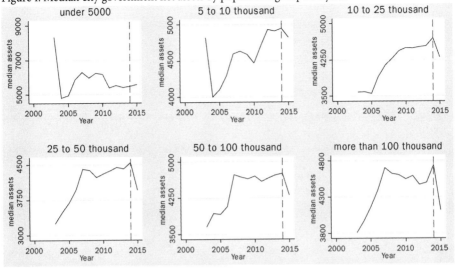

Source: GFOA data and author's calculations. Real per capita assets.

Figure 2. Share of cities with net assets less than $1000 per capita by population group and year.

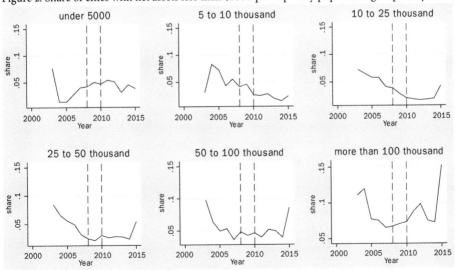

Source: GFOA data and author's calculations. Real 2015 dollars.

Figure 3. Share of cities with growth in net assets by population group and year.

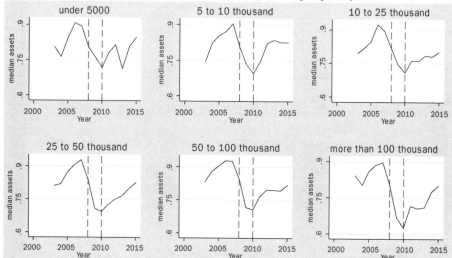

Source: GFOA data and author's calculations. Real per capita assets.

might be considered to be in a somewhat precarious fiscal situation. By 2015 the share of cities in this situation was less than 5 percent for the population groups below 50,000. However, a bigger share of larger cities had this low level of assets, with about 15 percent of the largest cities having assets of less than $1,000 per capita by 2015. Somewhat surprisingly, there is little evidence that the share of cities with this low level of assets rose during the Great Recession.

Using these data, we also can ask what share of cities in each population group saw net assets fall (or rise) in each year. Figure 3 displays this data. In all years and all population groups, net per capita assets have risen in each year in more than 50 percent of cities. Not surprisingly, there is a distinct and noticeable drop in the share of cities whose assets rose during the period of the Great Recession (roughly 2008 to 2010, as marked on the graph) but a notable recovery after that period. Somewhat counterintuitively, despite the marked drop in median assets in 2015, the share of cities whose assets increased did not decline in 2015.

Where Is Municipal Fiscal Health Most Problematic?

Figures 4a and 4b show median real per capita city government assets of cities in the GFOA database by the nine US Census divisions by year. These figures do not adjust for cross-region differences in city population size or other factors that may affect median assets.[37] Nonetheless, to the extent that the type

Figure 4A. Median city government net assets by Census division and year.

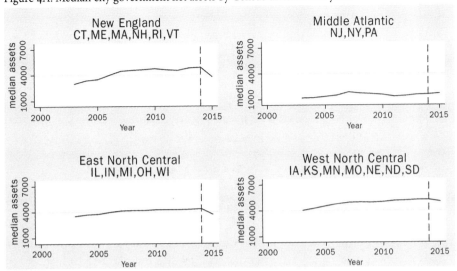

Source: GFOA data and author's calculations. Real per capita assets.

Figure 4B. Median city government net assets by Census division and year.

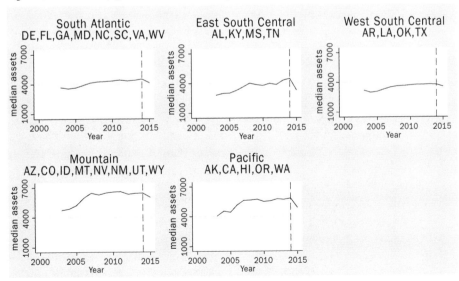

Source: GFOA data and author's calculations. Real per capita assets.

of cities that submit are similar within regions over time or across regions at any point in time, these data reveal underlying trends. Based on these figures, assets are generally lowest in the middle Atlantic region (New Jersey, New York, and Pennsylvania) and highest in the Mountain region (Arizona, Colorado, Idaho, Montana, Nevada, New Mexico, Utah, and Wyoming). This is perhaps surprising since states in the Atlantic region generally have much higher per capita personal incomes than those in the Mountain region. All of the regions had a relatively stable level of assets between 2005 and 2014, with some evidence of decline in several regions between 2014 and 2015.

When, If At All, Should We Expect Fiscal Problems to Lead to Disruption of Government Services?

Some of the discussion of the literature and the discussion in the first section of this chapter together with the mathematical treatment in the appendix conceives of a dynamic process that determines city fiscal health. This conception suggests that poor fiscal health now can lead to further deterioration in the future and a downward spiral leading to fiscal ruin as the tax base abandons the city. On the other hand, good fiscal health now may attract more economic activity and result in an ever-stronger fiscal environment. The simple mathematical model in the appendix suggests an analytical framework to understand these patterns. The basic ideas are illustrated in figures 5A and 5B.

The mathematical model posits a standard first-order linear difference equation that relates current assets to assets in the previous year. Standard mathematical treatments[38] show that such systems reach a stable equilibrium if the adjustment coefficient is positive and less than one so that changes in assets are dampened over time.

This is illustrated in figure 5A, which depicts a 45-degree line along which current and previous years' assets are equal and a deterministic linear *asset adjustment function* with a positive slope of less than one that shows how current assets adjust to assets in the previous year. As depicted in figure 5A, if last year's assets were above the equilibrium level (that is, the level where the two curves cross, which is depicted as 120 in the figure), current year assets will, all else being equal, fall toward equilibrium. If, on the other hand, last year's assets are below the crossing point, this year's assets will be greater than assets in the previous year. This system is stable and self-regulating in the sense that the level of assets neither grows uncontrollably toward infinity nor falls toward negative infinity. Eventually, assets will reach the equilibrium

Figure 5. Dynamic adjustment of assets. Case A: positive slope less than 1; Case B: positive slope greater than 1.

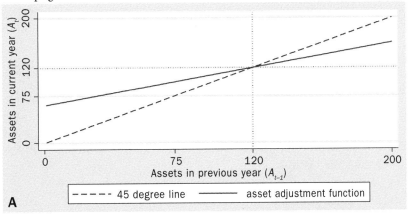

A

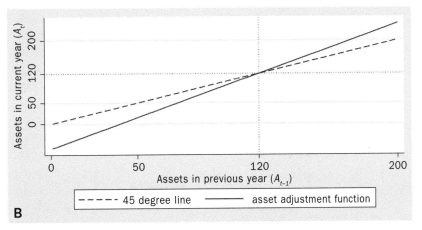

B

Source: Author's illustration. The 45-degree dashed line is a set of points for which current assets (A_t) are exactly equal to a one year lag of assets (A_{t-1}). The 45-degree line has a slope=1. At any point above the 45-degree line $A_t > A_{t-1}$. At any point below the 45-degree line $A_t < A_{t-1}$.

Case A shows the dynamic relationship between A_t and A_{t-1} when the slope of the asset adjustment function is < 1. If $A_{t-1} < 120$ then $A_t > A_{t-1}$ and A_t moves toward the equilibrium level of 120. If $A_{t-1} > 120$ then $A_t < A_{t-1}$ and A_t again moves toward the equilibrium level of 120.

Case B shows the dynamic relationship between A_t and A_{t-1} when the slope of the asset adjustment function is > 1. If $A_{t-1} < 120$ then $A_t < A_{t-1}$ and A_t moves away from the crossing point of 120. If $A_{t-1} > 120$ then $A_t > A_{t-1}$ and A_t again moves away from the crossing point of 120.

point where the current year's assets are equal to the previous year's assets. Once assets reach this equilibrium level, they will remain there as long as other external conditions (represented by the intercept and slope of the asset adjustment function) remain unchanged. A necessary condition for this stability is that the slope of the asset adjustment function has an absolute value less than one.[39]

Figure 5B depicts a 45-degree line and an asset adjustment function that, in contrast to figure 5A, has a positive slope greater than one. For any level of assets below the crossing point (120 in figure 5B), this year's assets will be below last year's assets, and because of that next year's assets will be below this year's assets. This means that once assets fall below the crossing point, there is a tendency toward a *vicious cycle* that will lead to an unsustainable fiscal situation. On the other hand, if last year's assets were above the crossing point in figure 5B, this year's assets will be greater than last year's assets and next year's assets will be greater than this year's assets. This means that once assets are greater than the crossing point, there is a tendency toward a *virtuous cycle* that will lead to an ever-healthier fiscal situation.

Of course, the tendency toward a vicious (or virtuous) cycle can be reversed if the slope or intercept of the asset adjustment function shifts over time. Understanding the fiscal health of a city thus requires understanding the factors that determine the parameters of the asset adjustment function. We can use the GFOA data set to get an initial understanding of some of these factors.

A simple version of this model can be implemented empirically by regressing current year assets on previous year assets and a constant and checking whether the estimated coefficient is greater or less than one and comparing observed assets to the estimated crossing point. Table 2 shows estimated coefficients from such regressions with the GFOA CAFR data pooled over the years 2003 to 2015 and split into several population size groups.

Column 1 simply pools all 23,742 observations in the data set and regresses current assets on the lagged value of assets. This regression explains essentially 100 percent of variation in the dependent variable and shows an estimated slope coefficient of 1.037. This means that, since the coefficient on lagged assets is greater than one, the system is "unstable" in the sense that it will not converge to an equilibrium level of assets. The p statistic (labeled p_lt1) listed in the lower panel of table 2 shows the confidence level at which the data reject the hypothesis that coefficient on lagged assets is equal to one. In this case, because the data fits the model quite well, we can reject that hypothesis with near certainty.

Table 2. Current net assets as a function of lagged net assets by population size

	All cities	<5K	5K–10K	10K–25K	25K–50K	50K–100K	>100K
lagged net assets	1.037***	1.026***	1.050***	1.021***	0.982***	1.122***	1.008***
	(108.37)	(1,997.37)	(789,339.52)	(59,538.24)	(53.24)	(892.55)	(9,845.66)
_cons	31.41	358.30**	–3.806	95.51***	347.30**	–339.10***	181.10***
	(0.50)	(2.76)	(–0.29)	(21.20)	(3.22)	(–8.92)	(4.19)
crossing	–849.40	–14,025.20	76.53	–4,565.60	19,792.50	2,779.50	–23,560.80
p_lt1	0.0000558	3.02e–280	0	0	0.171	0	0
r2	0.999	1.000	1.000	1.000	0.997	0.998	1.000
N	23,742	1,066	2,536	6,956	5,678	4,296	3,210

Data source: GFOA 2003 to 2015.
Notes: No controls.
t statistics in parentheses.
Dependent variable is real per capita net assets.
Row labeled "p_lt1" reports the p statistic from a test of the hypothesis that the coefficient on lagged net assets is less than 1.
Row labeled "crossing" gives the value at which current net assets are predicted to equal lagged net assets. This is the equilibrium asset value if the coefficient on lagged net assets is less than 1.
Each regression restricts sample to cities with a particular range of population as shown at the top of the column.
* p<0.05
** p<0.01
*** p<0.001

Is the fact that the coefficient on lagged assets is greater than one good news or bad news? That depends. If a city's net assets are above the crossing point (–849.40 in column 1), the greater than one slope coefficient suggests that, all else being equal, net assets will continue to grow and a virtuous cycle leading to fiscal sustainability is likely to be established. However, if net assets are below the crossing point, net assets this year will be less (that is, more negative) than assets last year, leading to a vicious cycle and fiscal ruin. In 2015, 24 of the 2,039 cities in the data set had assets below the column 1 crossing threshold of –849.40.

Naturally, different size cities might have different asset adjustment functions. The remaining columns of table 2 report estimates of asset adjustment functions for each population size group. While there is some variation across population size groups, the coefficient on lagged assets is economically and statistically significantly greater than one for all size groups except cities between 25,000 and 50,000. A model-based interpretation of these coefficients suggests that assets tend toward an equilibrium level only in cities in this size group. The equilibrium level of assets in this size group shown in the "crossing" row is $19,792.50 (calculated as [347.30/(1–0.982)]).

Based on this model and empirical estimates, cities in all other size groups are in danger of experiencing a vicious cycle if their assets fall below the critical levels marked in the "crossing" row. Generally, only a few cities fall in this category in each year. For example, none of the 275 cities in the highest population size group had assets below the critical level of -$23,560.80.

One might object that this model is surely too simple to explain the level and adjustment of city assets over time. Surely, the relationship between last year's assets and this year's assets is not constant over time or across space even within population size groups. While it is true that many factors influence city assets and their growth over time, to the extent that omitted variables are uncorrelated with past asset levels, the coefficients reported in table 2 represent unbiased estimates of model parameters.

While time and data limitations preclude full elaboration of the model in table 2, I add important controls for state and year in the estimates reported in table 3. It is not surprising that the estimated coefficients on lagged net assets in table 3 are essentially identical to those reported in table 2 because the models reported in table 2 explained essentially 100 percent of the variation in the dependent variable.

The models estimated for table 3 do, however, have the virtue of allowing us to simulate separate "crossing" points for cities in each size category in each state in each year. Table 4 presents these crossing points for a randomly selected set of twenty cities in 2015. As we saw in table 1, large cities are disproportion-

Table 3. Asset adjustment function current net assets as a function of lagged net assets by population size

	All cities	<5K	5K to 10K	10K to 25K	25K to 50K	50K to 100K	>100K
lagged net assets	1.037***	1.025***	1.050***	1.021***	0.982***	1.122***	1.008***
	(108.56)	(1,999.15)	(232,872.48)	(61,560.29)	(53.39)	(939.92)	(9,896.12)
p_lt1	0.0000558	4.09e−275	0	0	0.169	0	0
r2	0.999	1.000	1.000	1.000	0.997	0.998	1.000
N	23,742	1,066	2,536	6,956	5,678	4,296	3,210

Data source: GFOA 2003 to 2015. Dependent variable is real per capita net assets.
Notes: Controls for year and state.
t statistics in parentheses.
Row labeled "p_lt1" reports the p statistic from a test of the hypothesis that the coefficient on lagged net assets is less than 1.
Each regression restricts sample to cities with a particular range of population as shown at the top of the column.
All regressions include controls for year and state.
* $p<0.05$
** $p<0.01$
*** $p<0.001$

Table 4. Observed real per capita net assets and simulated 2015 "crossing point" (twenty randomly selected cities)

Government	State	Population	At	Crossing
Village of East Dundee	IL	2,860	1,526.5730	4,704.4700
City of LaFayette	GA	7,121	4,370.1730	−599.8899
City of Loveland	OH	12,160	2,657.1550	−744.1316
City of Callaway	FL	14,681	2,204.4820	−1,324.1530
City of Aberdeen	MD	15,434	4,706.2980	4,421.6490
City of Eloy	AZ	16,531	2,413.8890	−5,504.5640
City of Lenoir	NC	17,842	3,672.5140	−40,850.3900
City of Columbia Heights	MN	19,758	3,348.3650	−2,555.9070
Village of Northbrook	IL	33,170	3,910.0390	3,781.2370
City of Wentzville	MO	35,603	5,688.2290	5,425.0050
Town of Blacksburg	VA	43,985	1,944.7770	1,927.5680
City of Southaven	MS	51,824	983.5598	1,131.5040
City of Gilroy	CA	53,000	6,388.4720	5,100.6650
City of Petaluma	CA	59,540	5,288.5290	3,870.8310
City of Edmond	OK	87,877	6,196.6610	3,471.2520
Town of River Bend	NC	105,040	50.8473	−113,186.5000
City of Centennial	CO	107,201	2,167.0130	−23,235.5400
City of Miramar	FL	132,096	2,209.2040	−6,824.6760
City of Orlando	FL	262,949	5,753.0930	−6,689.8590
City of Oakland	CA	410,603	779.3806	−10,526.0200

Note: This table reports observed data on 2015 city population net per capita net assets from GFOA. Data in "crossing" column is calculated as $(\alpha_2 {}^*Q)/(1-\alpha)$ where $\alpha 2^*Q$ equals the predicted value of current net assets when lagged net assets is zero (the intercept in figures 5A or 5B and α_1 is the estimated coefficient on lagged net assets reported in table 3. Crossing is the predicted equilibrium level of net assets in $\alpha_1 < 1$ (e.g., for cities with populations between 25K and 50K). If $\alpha_1 > 1$, crossing is the break point at which fiscal efforts become unsustainable. See appendix model for mathematical justification. If current assets are less than crossing, the model predicts that there will be an unsustainable downward spiral in net assets.

ately likely to submit for the GFOA award program, so it is not surprising that one-quarter (five) of the randomly selected cities have populations above 100,000 and another four have populations between 50,000 and 100,000.

Nineteen of the twenty randomly selected cities had current assets above the crossing point or equilibrium and thus according to the estimated model were on a fiscally sustainable path. Only the City of Southaven, Mississippi, population 51,834, had real per capita net assets of less than its crossing point in this data. I projected Southaven's net assets in the next year (2016) based on the model depicted in Case B of figure 5 (and its algebraic elaboration in the appendix). Because the asset adjustment function for cities in the 50,000 to 100,000 population category has a slope greater than one (1.112 in table 3), the system is predicted to generate vicious (and virtuous) fiscal cycles. Because Southaven has current assets below the crossing point, the model predicts that its finances will be sucked into the vicious cycle of fiscal unsustainability unless external forces change that path. The model projects that Southaven's 2016 net assets will decline from their current level of about $983 to $965.50 (about 1.7 percent) without intervention.[40] Although Southaven's projected net asset decline is small, the model projects a continuous cycle that will eventually lead to fiscal ruin for Southaven.

WHY DO FISCAL PROBLEMS EMERGE, AND WHAT CAN BE DONE ABOUT THEM?

The last, and most difficult, journalist question is why. Why do some cities have large and growing real per capita net assets, while others struggle? Of course, as discussed earlier, the answer to this question is complex and multidimensional, involving historical factors, legal constraints on the city, the city's economic base, its political culture, managerial philosophy, and many other factors.

While full analysis of these factors is surely beyond the scope of this chapter, the data set I use here is well suited to investigate one indicator of city managerial philosophy. Economists distinguish between "private" goods and services like bread, which, when consumed, are used up and cannot be consumed by others, and "public" (or "collective consumption") goods like fireworks displays, for which one person's consumption does not diminish the potential consumption of others.[41] The goods and services provided by city governments can be arrayed along a spectrum from closest to a purely public good or service (for example, a website providing information about child safety) to closest to a purely private good or service (such as municipal parking).

As discussed above, GFOA CAFR data provides information about the amount of city assets in business-type activities and governmental activities. Business-type activities are generally funded by user fees and tend to be closer to the private good and service end of the spectrum, since potential users generally get a discrete good or service when they pay a user fee. Also, potential users can be excluded from consuming that good or service if they do not pay. Government activities could be public (that is, collective consumption) or private goods or services.

One might expect that cities with a more businesslike management philosophy would have a larger share of their assets devoted to business-type activities. Business-type activities (like electricity generation) must be sold to consumers, and the benefits are closely related to payments. Governmental activities (like police protection) are often given away for free and may benefit large, and difficult to identify, groups of people.

I use the GFOA CAFR data to ask whether the ratio of business-type assets to total assets helps to predict the total amount of real per capita net assets across cities. If more "businesslike" cities are better financial managers, we should expect that, all else being equal, the ratio of business-type assets to total assets would be positively correlated with total net assets.

However, we should be aware that causality could also run in the reverse direction—cities facing fiscal struggles and low per capita net assets might be forced to charge more user fees and hence might add more business-type assets. Alternatively, cities with poor fiscal health could find that their citizens were unable or unwilling to pay user fees and might have to limit the accumulation and use of business-type assets.[42] Thus, my empirical results should be interpreted with caution.

Referring to notation defined above the ratio of business-type to total assets is as follows:

$$\text{ratio\_B\_to\_A} = \frac{\text{ABTA}_t}{\text{A}_t}$$

Figure 6 displays data about the mean of this ratio for cities of various population size categories in each year from 2003 to 2015. The mean ratio of business-type to total assets varies from a high of nearly half in small cities at the beginning of the period to a low of one-third in cities of 25,000 to

Figure 6. Mean share of net assets that are business-type assets by population group by year.

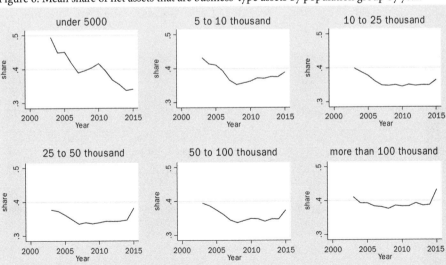

Source: GFOA data and author's calculations. Real per capita assets. 536 city year observations with negative business type or government type assets are dropped.

50,000 in 2007. The mean ratios change somewhat over time and seem to be declining in small cities but have been relatively constant or increasing in other cities since 2006 or so.

Table 5 shows some simple regressions of total real per capita net assets on the ratio of business-type assets to total assets with controls for year and state. The coefficient on this ratio is positive in all population size categories except in cities with populations of 5,000 to 10,000. However, the coefficient is generally estimated quite imprecisely and is statistically significantly different from zero only in the 10,000 to 25,000 population size category. This statistically significant coefficient suggests that a one percentage point increase in the share of assets devoted to business-type activities would increase total real per capita net assets by about $19. This evidence is consistent with the hypothesis that increases in the share of business-type assets increase the overall assets (and therefore the overall fiscal health) of cities. The evidence is inconsistent across city sizes and could explain only a small part of the variation in city assets. This suggests that "running government like a business" will not, by itself, bring fiscal health.

What can be done about fiscal problems? The answer to this question goes beyond the evidentiary base developed in this chapter, but a review of the literature combined with the findings discussed above may provide some insight. The empirical evidence presented here suggests that fiscal "virtuous" and "vicious" cycles are common—the rule rather than the exception. This suggests that preventive measures to head off fiscal problems may be more effective than after-the-fact remedial efforts. Gorina, Maher, and Joffe find

Table 5. Current net assets as a function of ratio of business to total net assets by population size

	(1) All cities	(2) <5K	(3) 5K to 10K	(4) 10K to 25K	(5) 25K to 50K	(6) 50K to 100K	(7) >100K
business-type assets	14,625.4	69,126.7	−1,062.1	1,905.3***	2,149.5	10,824.9	34,459.7
	(1.93)	(1.20)	(−0.09)	(5.26)	(0.37)	(1.00)	(1.03)
r2	0.00636	0.0623	0.0216	0.00853	0.00538	0.0242	0.00606
N	2,3207	1,030	2,497	6,866	5,573	4,198	3,043

Data source: GFOA 2003 to 2015. Dependent variable is real per capita net assets.
Notes: t statistics in parentheses.
Each regression restricts sample to cities with a particular range of population as shown at the top of the column. 536 city year observations with negative business-type or government-type assets are dropped. All regressions include controls for year and state.
* p<0.05
** p<0.01
*** p<0.001

that lagged fiscal indicators like cities' operating balance and total debt help predict fiscal distress, suggesting that systems like the ICMA (International City/County Management Association) financial trends monitoring system may have merit.[43] However, they find that such indictors have weak explanatory power so that a monitoring system may generate many false positives and may miss many cases where local governments are in imminent danger of fiscal distress. In addition, Crosby's study for state monitoring of Illinois school districts finds that state intervention to aid school districts with poor fiscal indicators often does little to improve outcomes.[44]

There is a long tradition of higher-level governments monitoring and limiting explicit debt of subnational governments,[45] but much less effort has focused on monitoring and limiting implicit debt like pension obligations and obligations to fund postemployment benefits of retirees. Poterba as well as Poterba and Reuben provide some evidence that budget rules that restrict governments' fiscal policies do change behavior.[46] This suggest that higher-level governments can contribute to fiscal responsibility by constraining lower levels of government. However, we have very limited information about the relative benefits and costs of such policies compared to alternatives. Some alternative policies might include well-targeted and well-timed intergovernmental aid or programs to allow local governments to pool risk through fiscal insurance.

CONCLUSION AND IMPLICATIONS FOR FUTURE RESEARCH

A clear understanding of city fiscal health holds great promise to improve policies designed to avoid fiscal catastrophes and to provide citizens and analysts with more objective tools to assess government performance. Assessments of fiscal health are difficult for at least two distinct reasons. First, fiscal health, like human health, is multidimensional. For example, fiscal health depends not only the capacity to raise sufficient resources (that is, the revenue system) but also on the ability to use that revenue to effectively deliver services to residents. Second, fiscal health, also like human health, is dynamic. The current state of a government's finances could be fine, but the trend of relevant fiscal variables could lead to ruin in the long run.

The empirical analysis in this chapter abstracts from the multidimensional nature of fiscal health to focus on cities' real per capita net assets. I argue that this measure of fiscal health is analogous to measures often used to assess the economic health of for-profit and nonprofit firms. In future research, this measure should be supplemented by and integrated with other indicators of fiscal health.

In contrast to some accounts that indicate that cities are under substantial and growing fiscal stress,[47] I find a more optimistic picture. Real per capita assets have been growing in the vast majority of cities of every size category. Only a very small share of cities have very low assets (less than $1,000 per capita). Median city government net assets have been somewhat volatile but did not fall in most city size categories between 2003 and 2015.

I estimate simple models of asset adjustment functions that allow me to project future asset trajectories. The empirical evidence suggests that most cities are on course to maintain a *virtuous cycle* that will allow sustained real per capita asset growth in the future. Only a small minority of cities have assets so low that my empirical model predicts a *vicious cycle* of declining assets leading to more declines of asset and eventual fiscal ruin.

I also ask whether, as suggested by some pundits, running government like a business leads to fiscal health. The newly exploited data set that I use has a measure of the share of government assets used in "business-type" activities that are supported by user fees and other charges. I find little evidence that cities with a higher proportion of such assets are in better financial condition than those with a smaller proportion of such assets.

Time and resource constraints preclude a full elaboration of the empirical models employed here. Future research should consider a greater range of variables and many alternative empirical specifications. While the analyses and conclusions presented here should be viewed as tentative and suggestive, I believe they provide important motivation and background for future policy discussions and research.

Future research should explore the benefits and costs of preventive measures that help local governments avoid fiscal distress before it occurs. Policies that do this should be compared with policies that remediate fiscal distress only after the fact.

APPENDIX 1

A simple model of equilibrium fiscal health

$$A_t = f(A_{t-1}, Q_t)$$

Let A = measure net assets and Q = an index of other factors (like the political system and the commercial base) that influence the future evolution of net assets. Let α_1 be parameters and let t index time.

Assume that:

$$A_t = a_1 A_{t-1} + a_2 Q_t \qquad (1)$$

If it exists, the equilibrium level of $A = A^*$ can be found as

$$A^*(1 - a_1) = a_2 Q_t \Rightarrow A^* = \left(\frac{a_2}{1 - a_1}\right) \qquad (2)$$

Note that

$$A_t - A_{t-1} = (a_1 - 1)A_{t-1} + a_2 Q_t \qquad (3)$$

Let

$$A_{t-1} = A^* + X_t = \left(\frac{a_2}{1 - a_1}\right)Q_t + X_t \qquad (4)$$

then

$$A_t - A_{t-1} = (a_1 - 1)\left(\left(\frac{a_2}{1 - a_1}\right)Q_t + X_t\right) + a_2 Q_t \qquad (5)$$

Which simplifies to:

$$A_t - A_{t-1} = (a_1 - 1)(X_t) = (a_1 - 1) X_t \qquad (6)$$

So

$$(a_1 - 1) = \frac{A_t - A_{t-1}}{X_t} \qquad (7)$$

Which means that the share of the difference between observed and equilibrium assets that is closed in any year is equal to $(a_1 - 1)$.

Define equilibrium to occur when

$$\frac{A_t - A_{t-1}}{A_{t-1}} \leq .01$$

If $a_1 = .9$, for example, the change in assets will be equal to 10 percent of the gap between observed and equilibrium assets in each year. In this case, equilibrium (actual assets within 1 percent of equilibrium assets) will be reached in approximately forty-four years if Q does not change over time. If instead $a_1 = .5$, the change in assets will be equal to 50 percent of the gap between observed and equilibrium assets in each year, and equilibrium will be reached in approximately nine years.

Notes

I am grateful to Farhad Kaab Omeyr for many hours of work helping to clean and prepare the GFOA data set and to numerous colleagues at the University of Illinois–

Chicago and elsewhere who provided comments and advice on earlier drafts. Remaining errors and omissions are my own.

1. M. Karimi and J. Brazier, "Health, Health-Related Quality of Life, and Quality of Life: What Is the Difference?," *Pharmacoeconomics* 34, no. 7 (2016): 645–49.

2. See M. Bergner and M. L. Rothman, "Health Status Measures: An Overview and Guide for Selection," *Annual Review of Public Health* 8, no. 1 (1987): 191–210.

3. Tracy Gordon, "Predicting Municipal Fiscal Distress: Aspiration or Reality?," Urban-Brookings Tax Policy Center Working Paper WP18TG1, 2018, www.lincolninst.edu.

4. Robert Inman, "Fiscal Health and Sound City Finance," in *Is Your City Healthy? Measuring Urban Fiscal Health*, ed. Richard Bird and Enid Slack (Toronto: University of Toronto Press, 2015), 201.

5. Helen Ladd and John Yinger, *America's Ailing Cities: Fiscal Health and the Design of Urban Policy* (Baltimore: Johns Hopkins University Press, 1989), 7 (emphasis in the original).

6. See Michael A. Pagano and Christopher W. Hoene, "States and the Fiscal Policy Space of Cities," in *The Property Tax and Local Autonomy*, ed. Michael Bell et al. (Cambridge, MA: Lincoln Institute of Land Policy, 2010).

7. Richard Bird, "Reflections on Measuring Urban Fiscal Health," in *Is Your City Healthy?*, ed. Bird and Slack.

8. R. M. Hendrick, *Managing the Fiscal Metropolis: The Financial Policies, Practices, and Health of Suburban Municipalities* (Washington, DC: Georgetown University Press, 2011).

9. Gorina, Maher, and Joffe provide a useful review of the literature and a third, novel, approach to measuring fiscal distress. They reason that governments with poor fiscal health will undertake observable actions (like employee layoffs or furloughs) that indicate fiscal distress. They search government comprehensive annual reports and media sources to locate such evidence and classify governments based on their findings. E. Gorina, C. Maher, and M. Joffe, "Local Fiscal Distress: Measurement and Prediction," *Public Budgeting and Finance* 38, no. 1 (2018): 72–94.

10. B. Zhao, "From Urban Core to Wealthy Towns: Nonschool Fiscal Disparities across Municipalities," *Public Finance Review* 46, no. 3 (2016): 421–53.

11. See K. Nollenberger, *Evaluating Financial Condition: A Handbook for Local Government* (Washington, DC: International City County Management Association, 2003).

12. See A. W. Crosby, "Intergovernmental Financial Monitoring and Intervention: Does It Make the Grade?" (PhD diss., University of Illinois at Chicago, 2016).

13. H. Chernick and A. Reschovsky, "The Fiscal Health of US Cities," in *Is Your City Healthy?*, ed. Bird and Slack, 83–117.

14. Chernick and Reschovsky, "Fiscal Health of US Cities"; Ladd and Yinger, *America's Ailing Cities*, 81.

15. Chernick and Reschovsky, "Fiscal Health of US Cities."

16. Zhao, "From Urban Core to Wealthy Towns," 437.

17. M. Skidmore and E. Scorsone, "Causes and Consequences of Fiscal Stress in Michigan Cities," *Regional Science and Urban Economics* 41, no. 4 (2011): 360–71.

18. See Pagano and Hoene, "States and the Fiscal Policy Space of Cities."

19. A. Haughwout et al., "Local Revenue Hills: Evidence from Four US Cities," *Review of Economics and Statistics* 86, no. 2 (2004): 570–85.

20. https://www.standardandpoors.com/en_US/web/guest/article/-/view/type/HTML/id/2007013.

21. Standard & Poor's Rating Services, "U.S. Local Governments General Obligation Ratings: Methodology and Assumptions," 2013, www.standardandpoors.com/en_US/web/guest/article/-/view/type/HTML/id/1926879; www.standardandpoors.com/en_US/web/guest/ratings/ratings-criteria.

22. https://www.standardandpoors.com/en_US/web/guest/ratings/ratings-criteria.

23. Jess N. Cornaggia, Kimberly J. Cornaggia, and John E. Hund, "Credit Ratings across Asset Classes: A Long-Term Perspective," *Review of Finance* 21, no. 2 (2017): 465–509, https://doi.org/10.1093/rof/rfx002.

24. J. E. Spiotto, A. E. Acker, and L. E. Appleby, *Municipalities in Distress? How States and Investors Deal with Local Government Financial Emergencies* (Chicago: Chapman and Cutler, 2016).

25. Marc Joffe, "Doubly Bound: The Cost of Credit Ratings," Haas Institute for a Fair and Inclusive Society, University of California, Berkeley, 2017, https://haasinstitute.berkeley.edu.

26. www.gfoa.org/cafr.

27. After this chapter was substantially completed, I became aware of the paper by Gordon ("Predicting Municipal Fiscal Distress") and through that the CAFR data recently compiled by United States Common Sense (see govrank.org). This source may be a supplement or an alternative to the GFOA data. I reran the analysis in table 2 using the govrank data, which covers the years 2009 to 2014 and has a similar sample size for large cities but a larger sample size for small cities. The qualitative results of the analyses were unchanged.

28. www.gfoa.org/financial-indicators-database.

29. The 2012 US Census of Government found almost 36,000 subcounty general-purpose governments (generally cities or towns) in the United States. "Local Governments by Type and State: 2012—United States—States 2012 Census of Governments," https://factfinder.census.gov/.

30. See GASB, "Touring the Financial Report, Part I: The Statement of Net Assets," May 2007, www.gasb.org.

31. For examples, see J. L. Chan, "The Implications of GASB Statement No. 34 for Public Budgeting," *Public Budgeting & Finance* 21, no. 3 (2001): 79–87; W. R. Voorhees and R. S. Kravchuk, "The New Governmental Financial Reporting Model under GASB Statement No. 34: An Emphasis on Accountability," *Public Budgeting and Finance* 21, no. 3 (2001): 1–30; C. P. McCue, J. Gianakis, and H. Frank, "GASB

Statement 34 and the Managerial Accounting Nexus," *Journal of Public Budgeting, Accounting and Financial Management* 19, no. 2 (2007): 153–77; Lu Yi, "Implication of GASB Statement No. 34 for Reporting and Accountability: The Georgia Experience," *Journal of Public Budgeting, Accounting and Financial Management* 19, no. 3 (2007): 317–37, https://doi.org/10.1108/JPBAFM-19-03-2007-B003; T. E. Vermeer, T. K. Patton, and A. J. Styles, "Reporting of General Infrastructure Assets under GASB Statement No. 34," *Accounting Horizons* 25, no. 2 (2011): 381–407; Stewart Jones et al., "Infrastructure Asset Reporting Options: A Stated Preference Experiment," *Accounting Horizons* 26, no. 3 (2012): 465–91; and Rebecca I. Bloch, Justin Marlowe, and Dean Michael Mead, "Infrastructure Asset Reporting and Pricing Uncertainty in the Municipal Bond Market," *Journal of Governmental and Nonprofit Accounting* 5, no. 1 (2016): 53–70.

32. GASB, "Touring the Financial Report."

33. R. N. Anthony and S. M. Newberry, "GASB 34 Should Be Revised," *Journal of Government Financial Management* 49, no. 1 (2000): 36.

34. Dean Michael Mead, *What You Should Know about Your Local Government's Finances: A Guide to Financial Statements*, 3rd ed. (Norwalk, CT: Governmental Accounting Standards Board, 2017), 16.

35. The US Bureau of Labor Statistics does not produce a deflator specifically for government assets covering the years necessary for this study. I use annual data on BLS series WPUFD41312 PPI Commodity data for final demand–private capital equipment, not seasonally adjusted to convert to real quantities, with 2015 as the base year. Per capita values are derived using population estimates included in city CAFR data.

36. Gordon ("Predicting Municipal Fiscal Distress") also incorporates CAFR data on net government assets in her study of municipal fiscal health but uses its lagged value to explain variation in general revenue per capita rather than as a dependent variable. In her most general specifications, she finds a statistically insignificant relationship between debt to asset ratios and per capita own-source revenue.

37. Regression results presented later in the chapter will introduce controls for sample differences over time and across regions. In future research, I plan to introduce additional controls by creating a panel of cities that appear in the data multiple times and by matching city observations in the GFOA data set with other data sets that contain information about additional variables of interest.

38. See Ronald F. Miller, *Dynamic Optimization and Economic Applications* (New York: McGraw-Hill, 1979), appendix C.

39. The system remains stable even if there is an inverse (negative) relationship between current and previous year assets as long as the absolute value of the slope is less than one. The equilibrating process is more complicated than in the positive-slope case, however. (See Miller, *Dynamic Optimization and Economic Applications*, for more detail.) In the empirical work presented below, the slope coefficients are always positive.

40. From the appendix, Southaven's predicted 2016 assets = ($983.55*1.122) + ($\alpha_2$ * Q_t). (α_2 * Q_t) = (1 – α_1) * crossing, so Southaven's predicted 2016 assets = ($983.55*1.122) + (-0.122*1131.504) = $965.500.

41. Economists generally differentiate between public and private goods along two dimensions: the extent to which the goods are *rival* in the sense that one person's consumption precludes the consumption of others and the extent to which the goods are *excludable* in the sense that it is possible to exclude the consumption of unwanted consumers at a reasonable cost. See Ronald Fisher, *State and Local Public Finance*, 3rd ed. (Mason, OH: Thomson South-Western, 2007), 38. Business-type activities are, by definition, excludable since they are paid for with user fees. Goods that are nonrival (like fireworks displays) tend to not be excludable, but some (like cable TV services) may be both nonrival and excludable. Thus, some business-type activities may encompass nonrival goods or services.

42. Ideally, we would study the correlation between "shocks" to business-type assets that were beyond the control of the city and total assets. Standard econometric tools to do this include the use of instrumental variables (such as changes in state laws) that predict changes in business-type assets but do not predict changes in total assets except through the channel of business-type assets. Empirical analyses with instrumental variables are a promising direction for future research but beyond the scope of this chapter.

43. Gorina, Maher, and Joffe, "Local Fiscal Distress."

44. Crosby, "Intergovernmental Financial Monitoring and Intervention."

45. C. Hulbert and C. Vammalle, "Monitoring Sub-central Governments' Debts: Practices and Challenges in OECD Countries," in *Fiscal Federalism 2016: Making Decentralisation Work*, ed. H. Blöchliger and J. Kim (Paris: OECD, 2016).

46. J. M. Poterba, "Balanced Budget Rules and Fiscal Policy: Evidence from the States," *National Tax Journal* 48, no. 3 (1995): 329–36; J. M. Poterba and K. Reuben, "Fiscal News, State Budget Rules, and Tax-Exempt Bond Yields," *Journal of Urban Economics* 50, no. 3 (2001): 537–62.

47. Gorina, Maher, and Joffe, "Local Fiscal Distress"; Chernick and Reschovsky, "Fiscal Health of US Cities."

Linking Resources to Government Services

Is There a Future for Benefit-Based Financing?

REBECCA HENDRICK

In his classic text of public finance, Richard Musgrave describes the field's three fundamental questions or issues.[1] First, what goods and services should governments provide? Second, how much should be spent on these activities? Third, how should governments pay for these activities? Musgrave's questions are normative in the sense that they ask what government should do, but they can be rephrased to ask what governments actually do. This chapter is about both perspectives on the third question more than the other two questions, but answers to the third question have significant relevance for which goods and services government provides and at what levels. More specifically, this chapter examines local governments' use of charges and other benefit-based methods of financing and providing public goods and services relative to other methods that are based on general taxation or ability to pay. It discusses the characteristics and limitations of benefit-based methods from both a theoretical and a practical perspective, and it examines local governments' use of charges relative to other sources of revenue over different time periods using Census of Governments data.[2] It concludes with some assessments of opportunities for and issues with using benefit-based financing to deliver more public goods and services in the future.

Not all methods of paying for local government goods and services can be neatly classified as being based on *benefits received* or *ability to pay*, but general taxes that pay for goods and services that are widely distributed among citizens within the jurisdiction are viewed as closer to the ability-to-pay end of the continuum than the benefits-received end. Similar to a competitive market system, a strict benefit-based financing method levies charges or taxes based on the benefits received by citizens. This method also provides public goods and services only to the citizens who pay for them and at the level citizens are willing to pay for them.

As suggested by the labels of benefits received and ability to pay, the normative implications of financing government activities using revenues on different ends of this continuum are significant. From a normative perspective, benefit-based financing yields more efficient outcomes in terms of citizens receiving the level and bundle of public goods and services that they desire (allocational efficiency). Ability-to-pay financing, such as progressive income taxes, results in a more equitable distribution of the burden of paying for public goods and services, according to the criteria of nonregressive taxation.[3] Although property taxes can be viewed as a benefit-based tax,[4] others disagree on several grounds but, primarily, because it is a general tax that is used to fund many public goods and services for which it is hard to assign unique benefits.[5] By comparison, government user charges, which are considered to be the method of financing that is closest to the ideal of benefit-based financing, provide financing for one service or good only to those who pay for it.[6]

Financial trends show that local governments have reduced their reliance on property taxes greatly since the mid-twentieth century and have increased their reliance on charges and other funding sources.[7] Some also speculate that the severe recessions of 2001 and 2008 have exacerbated these trends and portend the continuation and even intensification of these trends into the future.[8] If true, such trends could represent a significant shift in the basis of local government financing and service provision from general taxation to benefits received in which resources are tied to specific public goods and services are delivered only to the entities that pay for them. This chapter examines the extent to which this is likely to happen and how these methods might be implemented more broadly by local governments. As explained here, these methods work best under some circumstances and will not work under others due to the nature of the public goods and services provided. This, alone, limits the extent to which local governments can effectively use these methods in the future.

CHARACTERISTICS OF BENEFIT-BASED FINANCING RELATIVE TO OTHER METHODS

As a mechanism for providing and paying for public goods and services, charges and other forms of benefit-based financing are levied according to the benefits that each recipient receives. In his theory of government finance,

Buchanan emphasized the advantages of this mechanism that directly links resources to the benefits that governments provide.[9] Theoretically, this linkage allows the government to provide public benefits more efficiently and in a manner that better satisfies citizens' demands compared to a system in which the government or political process determines the level and quality of benefits that citizens should have according to some vague and ill-defined notion of "public utility." Similar to a market system in the private sector, direct-benefit financing provides government with signals about citizens' willingness to pay, which allows public goods and services to be valued or priced at the marginal cost of their production. Acting on this information, government can allocate scarce public resources to their most highly valued uses according to the relative amounts that people, in the aggregate, are prepared to pay.

Benefit-based financing also enhances government accountability by making it more responsive to differing preferences and changes in the demand for publicly provided goods and services and through earmarking of resources for specific uses. Buchanan argues that citizens become more knowledgeable of how much government costs them when the charges or taxes they pay are linked directly to particular benefits that are earmarked for specific purposes.[10] Finally, benefit-based financing can be viewed as a fair method of distributing public goods and services because citizens pay only for the benefits they desire.[11]

Although benefit-based financing seems to be desirable in several dimensions, these methods are not appropriate or workable for government goods and services that are more public than private. On a continuum of pure public to pure private goods, public goods have two primary characteristics that preclude the use of benefit-based financing. One characteristic is nonexclusion, in which all citizens benefit from the good if it is provided and the government cannot exclude people from benefiting that do not pay for the good. In this case, the benefits of nonexcludable goods and services are shared among all citizens, and the benefits to individual citizens cannot be established or determined easily. As with private goods and services, benefit-based financing works only when the benefits to citizens can be clearly established and are not shared.[12]

The second characteristic is nonexhaustion or nonrivalry, which means that the provision of the good to some citizens does not preclude or lessen the provision of the good to other citizens and the costs of providing the good or service to all citizens is the same as providing the good or service to one citizen. This characteristic sets up a problem of free ridership, in which citizens have no incentive to pay for a good or service voluntarily if they receive the benefits of the good or service without paying. In this case, unlike pure private goods, the government cannot rely on citizens' willingness to pay to provide signals about their preferences for or the benefits they receive from public goods and services. Thus, benefit-based financing also does not function well when the goods or services are nonexhaustive.

The classic example of a pure public good is national defense against an external enemy. If a defense system is established, it will cost the same whether it protects one person or many people, although the total costs of national defense will become greater as the population increases beyond a series of fixed levels. More important, citizens who do not pay to support national defense cannot be excluded from benefiting from it, and the costs or price of national defense cannot be used to judge the benefit citizens receive. Examples of pure or almost pure public goods at the local level are public health services to fight contagious diseases; services to handle harmful natural events, such as weather warning systems and storm-water management; and police services.

Although many local public services, such as education and roads, provide significant and unique benefits to citizens that consume it, and are somewhat exhaustive, the goods have significant positive spillovers to citizens who do not use the service. A well-educated population provides well-educated workers to the private sector, and good roads stimulate jobs and economic development. Such spillovers of benefits make it hard to determine and assign charges or levy taxes in a manner that reflects the unique preferences of citizens for these goods and services and the benefits they receive. If consumed voluntarily, goods and services that have positive spillovers will not be provided at the level required to maximize public benefit, and so the good or service will be underprovided. Education is also viewed as a "merit good" by many, which is considered to be so valuable that it should be provided to people regardless of their willingness to pay or benefits received.[13] Health care is another potential merit good that has fewer positive spillovers and public features compared to education but is distributed according to need when provided publicly.

Both merit and public goods are best financed by methods of taxation that are based on the ability to pay or other principle rather than the principle of benefits received. Scholars of public finance recognized early in the field's development that the benefits principle is not an appropriate or workable method of providing and financing for many public goods and services. In such cases, goods and services must be financed with taxes that are levied

more broadly according to a different principle, and the ability-to-pay principle became the equity norm for broad-based tax design.[14]

The ability-to-pay principle is based on the concept of vertical equity (or
regressivity), in which taxpayers pay for public goods and services according
to their ability, which was measured with property values early in our country's history and has been measured with income since the early twentieth
century. According to this concept of fairness, taxpayers with greater income
or other measures of ability to pay should bear a greater burden in paying for
public goods and services. Horizontal equity is a second conceptualization
of fairness, in which taxpayers in similar circumstances should pay similar
amounts of tax. In this case, benefit-based financing has horizontal equity
to the extent that people who receive the same level and quality of public
benefit pay the same amount in charges or taxes, but this method does not
have vertical equity.

Generally speaking, revenues that are collected from citizens according
to their ability to pay, such as progressive income taxes, or other broad-
based taxes, such as retail sales taxes, are usually deposited into a general
fund that finances a bundle of goods and services provided to all citizens.
Based on citizens' preferences expressed at the voting booth, the government determines taxpayers' preferences for all the goods and services being
financed from this fund and the burden that will be placed on taxpayers
to support these benefits. Compared to benefit-based financing, in which
citizens' payments are earmarked for the benefits they receive, the taxes
citizens pay in a broad-based system are diffused over many goods and
services, which obscures the relationship between taxes paid and benefits
received.[15] Because taxpayers and government have less knowledge of how
resources, preferences, and benefits are connected in broad-based financing systems, neither is likely to understand the true costs of the goods and
services provided in this way, and resources are less likely to be allocated
or produced efficiently. Thus, it seems that government should provide and
finance public goods and services using benefit-based methods wherever
it is appropriate.

TYPES OF BENEFIT-BASED FINANCING

Stated simply, it is the ability to exclude people from benefiting from publicly
provided goods and services and to allocate costs and payment according
to individual benefit that makes the provision of some goods and services
amenable to direct-benefit financing.[16] Direct-benefit financing of public

goods and services can take many forms, but the most common is charges or fees for services such as water, sewer, and garbage collection. Although the actual charge may be a flat fee per household rather than a charge that reflects the benefit and level of services received (for example, the amount of garbage collected), it is possible—at least in theory—to identify distinct, nonshared benefits that individual households receive from many services, such as clean water, adequate sewers, and timely garbage pickup.

Scholars also distinguish between user charges that are levied on consumption of a public good or service and benefit taxes that are compulsory and levied on citizens based on their perceived or measured benefit from the public goods and services provided.[17] User charges are more similar to prices for goods and services in a competitive market system than a benefit tax, but few public goods and services that are financed with charges are provided in a competitive market in which consumption is truly voluntary. For instance, most citizens are required by government to dispose of their garbage and wastewater appropriately, so they must pay for these services in some manner. User fees, also called license taxes, are often distinguished from user charges when applied to goods and services that are truly voluntary but where government is the monopoly provider, such as building inspection fees.[18] Other government services for which charges are appropriate, such as higher education, are partially financed with general taxes that are levied based on the ability-to-pay principle. These services are often distributed, in part, according to merit or need because citizens value this outcome over one produced entirely by user charges.[19]

Special assessments are the broadest example of benefit taxes that are not user fees. Special assessments are a method of funding improvements to properties and sometimes services that benefit only property owners within a designated area, called a special assessment district (SAD), rather than all property owners or citizens within the jurisdiction. These districts have many different names across the United States, including community facilities districts (Arizona), assessment districts (California), special service areas (Illinois), special improvement districts (Ohio), and local improvement districts (Washington).[20] Oftentimes, the SADs are residential, but they can be commercial or industrial. Business improvement districts that are used by many local governments to finance economic development projects and other services to commercial and industrial areas within their boundaries are often financed with special assessments. Special assessments are a form of land-secured financing[21] and, similar to SADs, have many other names in different states.[22]

Special assessments usually take the form of additional property taxes that are added to the general property tax levy or bill on each parcel within the SAD. The additional taxes may be ad valorem or based on the physical characteristics of the parcels and, therefore, are non–ad valorem. As a method of benefit-based financing, special assessments are particularly appropriate for property-based goods and services, especially capital improvements, in which the value or benefit of the services or improvements is capitalized into the property values of specific parcels. Although local government has good information on property values, it is often difficult to determine projected increases in property values from improvements and services in SADs that have very dissimilar properties. In such cases, governments tend to use non–ad valorem special assessments that allocate the costs of the improvements based on characteristics such as front footage or the size of the property. In SADs with similar properties where the costs of the improvements are more equal among the parcels, special assessments are more likely to be based on the value of the property.[23]

It should also be noted that general property taxes are sometimes viewed as representative of benefits received from local government services according to several arguments. One is based on Tiebout's claim that households sort themselves into metropolitan jurisdictions such that the marginal benefit of public services to each household equals its marginal cost.[24] Thus, the household will pay the property tax that best reflects the benefits they receive from a broad mix of public goods and services. Another argument, which is more ad hoc, is that the benefits of public goods services are positively associated with the value of one's property and the taxes paid on the property, especially if the good or service is property based, such as capital improvements, sewers, and even police. Indeed, this ad hoc argument that tax paid reflects benefits received might also be applied to income tax, which taxes wealth, but certainly not sales taxes, which are a tax on the value of purchases. Personal wealth, in this case, is a more reasonable measure of benefit from public services than the value of personal purchases.[25]

THE CASE FOR MORE BENEFIT-BASED FINANCING IN THE FUTURE

Research on local government finance has identified three reasons for these governments' migration away from property tax and greater reliance on charges and other funding sources since the mid-twentieth century. First is the public's dislike of the property tax and the visibility of their property tax burden. Governments are constrained from increasing their reliance on property taxes due to the unpopularity of these taxes and pressures from citizens to avoid increasing "the worst tax."[26] Although inelastic and stable, property taxes, which are paid in a lump sum, are very visible to taxpayers[27] compared to sales taxes, in which the burden on taxpayers (as a percentage of income, for instance) is less known.

The public's dislike of property taxes is evident from the nationwide imposition of local tax and expenditure limitations by states beginning with Proposition 13 in California in 1978, which is the second explanation for why local governments have migrated away from the property tax.[28] The TELs implemented by most states target property taxes and take the form of limits on rates, assessed value, or tax levy increases. There is a large body of research on the effect of TELs on local governments that is summarized by Brunori et al. and Maher et al.[29] This research shows that TELs reduce the rate of growth in property taxes[30] and increase reliance on nonproperty taxes and property tax burden.[31] Because special assessments are as visible to taxpayers as general property taxes, compared to user charges and license taxes, it is logical to expect local governments to migrate to the latter financing tools to finance their growth, development, and increased demand or need for local public services.

Fiscal stress is the third reason given for governments migrating away from property taxes and toward direct-benefit financing as a means of recovering the costs of services that are appropriate for such methods.[32] As recessions, declining state aid, and pension obligations threaten local governments' ability to fund services at current levels, they seek to tap more sources of revenue in the past. However, given the advantages of benefit-based financing, as discussed previously, government officials' use of these methods may be motivated as much by these advantages as by the ability to generate additional revenue from them.

Although benefit-based financing has advantages, it has some distinct disadvantages other than it is not appropriate for all public goods and services. It will not result in productive efficiency unless the market is competitive, which is rarely the case with public services. On the other hand, benefit-based financing with earmarking will result in allocative efficiency if the consumption of the good or service can be accurately monitored (or at least satisfactorily approximated) and the marginal costs of providing the good or service can be reliably measured (or satisfactorily approximated). A third condition that is sometimes added as a requirement for the use of benefit-based financing is that the demand for the good or service be responsive to changes in charges and tax levies. But even where this condition does not apply, benefit-based financing can be used for cost recovery, which may be the fairest means of financing this service according to the benefit principle.[33]

Ultimately, all three conditions for applying benefit-based financing are about information gathering and the degree to which the beneficiaries of the public good or service can be identified and their benefits precisely measured. Underlying all conditions is an expectation that government has the capacity to collect and process this information and can allocate costs correctly among those who pay. To the extent that individual governments do not have this capacity and cannot design user charges, user fees, and benefit taxes according to costs and benefits received, these methods should not be used. The less capacity government has to approximate and link benefits, costs, and levies or charges to individual citizens, the more general taxation is a better option for providing public goods and services, even if the good or service is exhaustive and benefits are not shared. Attempting to apply the benefit principle under conditions of poor information will simply distort benefits and costs, and ability to pay may be a more reasonable principle upon which to distribute public resources in such cases. But applying the ability-to-pay principle correctly also requires good information about citizens' financial abilities.

On the other hand, if the individual benefits of the good or service can be reasonably determined and governments have the informational capacity and can design the tools correctly, then governments can be expected to increase reliance on these methods in the future, especially as technology improves their capacity[34] and the motivation for finding alternative and supplemental revenue sources remains high. More than twenty-five years ago, Downing's analysis suggested a potential for increasing charges in many cities by over 200 percent for hospitals and solid waste.[35] Parking, sewerage, and parks and recreation are other areas where he determined that charges could be increased significantly based on an examination of charges collected for city services relative to spending and consideration of the appropriateness of charges for specific services.

Governments should remember, however, that user charges and fees are regressive, meaning that they are a greater burden for the poor, and that earmarking of revenues limits budget flexibility and increases the costs of production relative to financing multiple goods and services from the same pot of resources.[36] In this case, some of the disadvantages of these methods can be mitigated with the use of hybrid methods that merge benefit-based financing and earmarking with traditional financing and adjustments for beneficiaries' ability to pay. Governments' options for designing financing tools are not limited to either direct-benefit financing or general taxation. Rather, there is a continuum of methods between these extremes. Hybrid alternatives can focus on cost recovery rather than marginal-cost pricing. They can be designed to subsidize charges for public enterprises with aid or general taxes and assess charges in a progressive or regulatory manner rather than as a method only for allocating costs according to benefits received.

TRENDS IN THE REVENUE STRUCTURE OF LOCAL GOVERNMENTS

This section uses Census of Governments data on different types of local governments to examine trends in methods of financing all local goods and services and specific services in municipalities.

Trends in Financing All Local Government Services

Prior assessments of revenue trends in local governments show that as a percentage of revenue (counted as total revenue, general revenue, and own-source revenue), property taxes have declined greatly since the mid-twentieth century.[37] By comparison, reliance on charges has increased as a percentage of these governments' revenue, which is particularly evident in municipal and county governments. Table 1 shows these trends a little differently than most other studies by removing significant enterprise charges from the denominator in the own-source revenue ratios.[38] Enterprises are excluded here because financial decisions about these services are made separately from financial decisions about governmental funds and there is an expectation that enterprise services should be supported entirely by charges. Thus, excluding enterprise funds from calculations of trends in reliance on property taxes and other revenue sources presents a more realistic picture of changes in local governments' revenue structure for general operations.

The table shows that property taxes as a percentage of own-source revenue minus enterprise charges have declined since 1972 for municipalities and 1982 for counties, but increased from 2007 to 2012 as a result of the Great Recession's impact on other governmental revenue sources.[39] The table also shows that reliance on governmental charges has steadily increased for municipalities since 1972 and counties since 1982. Reliance on sales taxes have also increased steadily for counties since 1982, but the increase in sales taxes as a percentage of own-source municipal revenues has been somewhat irregular for municipalities since 1972, with the largest increases occurring from 1972 to 1982. The table also shows that enterprise charges as a percent-

Table 1. Local government revenue trends, 1972–2012
Sum of revenues for all governments

| | Municipalities | | | |
| | % Own-source revenue (no enterprise charges)[a] | | | % Enterprise charges of all charges[a] |
	Property taxes	Sales taxes	Charges	
1972	50.4	14.7	9.9	77.9
1977	46.7	17.3	11.1	78.9
1982	36.4	19.0	12.1	80.4
1987	32.7	18.8	11.9	79.4
1992	36.5	18.3	13.7	76.9
1997	33.2	19.7	15.5	74.9
2002	33.1	20.1	15.9	73.8
2007	32.0	18.8	15.3	72.4
2012	37.3	20.1	16.7	73.1

| | Counties | | | |
| | % Own-source revenue (no enterprise charges)[a] | | | % Enterprise charges of all charges[a] |
	Property taxes	Sales taxes	Charges	
1982	53.9	11.2	12.5	61.0
1987	49.0	12.6	12.7	56.3
1992	50.8	12.6	15.2	52.5
1997	46.1	14.8	17.9	51.9
2002	45.5	14.5	18.7	49.4
2007	45.8	14.6	18.0	49.6
2012	51.7	15.0	18.3	53.5

Source: US Census Bureau, Census of Governments, vol. 4, *Governmental Finances*, no. 4, *Finances of Municipal and Township Governments*, 1–2 (72–82), issued September 1984 (Washington, DC: US Government Printing Office, 1982), www2.census.gov/govs/pubs/cog/1982/1982_vol4_no4_fin_muntwp.pdf; US Bureau of the Census, Census of Governments, vol. 4, *Governmental Finances,* no. 4, *Finances of Municipal and Township Governments*, 1–2, issued January 1997 (Washington, DC: US Government Printing Office, 1992), www.census.gov/prod/2/gov/gc92-4/gc924-4.pdf; US Bureau of the Census, Census of Governments, vol. 4, *Governmental Finances*, no. 4, *Finances of Municipal and Township Governments,* 1–2, issued April 2005 (Washington, DC: US Government Printing Office, 2002), www.census.gov/prod/2005pubs/gc024x4.pdf; US Bureau of the Census, Census of Governments, "Local Government Summary Tables by Type of Government," 2007, www.census.gov//govs/local/historical_data_2007.html; US Bureau of the Census, Census of Governments, "Local Government Summary Tables by Type of Government," 2012, www.census.gov//govs/local/historical_data_2012.html.
[a]Enterprise charges are for utility (water, transit, gas, electric), sewerage, and hospital.
[b]Insurance trust is excluded.

age of all charges in these governments have decreased during these time periods. When viewed in conjunction with the increased reliance on charges for nonenterprises, this suggests that governments are charging for more services than in the past and also charging more for services that are funded primarily by general taxes through the general fund.

Based on these trends and those found in prior studies, it seems reasonable to expect governments to increase their reliance on charges and sales taxes and decrease their reliance on property taxes to fund general operations in the future, but there are several caveats to this expectation. First, these trends are likely to vary significantly depending on whether the state allows counties and municipalities to levy sales and or income taxes and the stringency of TELs on these governments. In a working paper, Hendrick shows that trends in reliance on revenue sources, including state aid, revenue diversification, per capita revenue sources, and per capita spending, vary greatly from 1997 to 2012 in municipalities that are in states that allow them to levy a sales or income tax compared to municipalities in states that are limited to a property tax.[40] Specifically, median reliance on property taxes declined more in municipalities in property-tax-only states, but median property taxes per capita in real dollars also increased more in these governments. Median federal and state aid per capita also declines by 34 percent in property-tax-only states but only 13 percent in states that allow a municipal income or sales tax (or both). In this case, the greater loss of aid in property-tax-only states has reduced municipalities' total revenue more than in states with municipal sales and income taxes, which has likely altered the revenue structure of the former indirectly compared to municipalities in other states that have replaced some of the lost revenue through increases in sales taxes.

Recent research by Kim (2017) also shows that reliance on property taxes in 2012 was much less in municipal governments that have a sales or income tax and that have more stringent TELs and that reliance on property taxes is greater in municipalities with more state aid.[41] Reliance on charges is less well explained by Kim's model, but it shows that reliance on charges is less in municipalities that are in states that allow local sales and income taxes and in states that have more stringent TELs. Reliance on charges is also less in municipalities that have higher property taxes per capita. Thus, municipalities seem to prefer general property taxes over charges that are likely to be earmarked for specific purposes, and they prefer other general taxes over property taxes.

The effects of the two recessions on local government finance are the second caveat to predicting greater use of benefit-based financing by these governments in the future. It is clear from Hendrick and others that many local governments increased property taxes but also cut expenditures, especially capital spending, after the Great Recession.[42] It is also important to recognize that the Great Recession lowered property values significantly in many states, which raised property taxes and tax burdens for governments that calculate property taxes by levy and not rate. It is less clear from prior research, however, how the two recessions affected local governments' use of user charges, user fees, and benefit taxes, although one study reports that municipalities raised fees and utility rates to cope with the Great Recession.[43]

Table 2 presents revenue trends for local governments from 1992 to 2012 that show the challenges that governments faced during the two recessions and how they responded. Table 2 shows percentage change in own-source revenues (including utilities), state aid, property taxes, total non–property taxes, and all charges (including utilities), and it shows total spending for all five types of local government during this time period. The table shows that, in real dollars, own-source revenue, state aid, and total spending all declined for most local governments from 2007 to 2012 after the Great Recession. State aid and growth in spending also declined for most local governments from 2002 to 2007 after the 2001 recession and compared to prior years.[44] On the other hand, percentage change in real property taxes continually increased for all governments except school districts from 2007 to 2012. Charges also increased steadily from 1992 to 2012 for most local governments, although the growth slowed from 2002 to 2007 and 2007 to 2012. The surprise here, however, is the relatively high level of growth in other taxes besides property taxes, including license taxes, for all governments during the entire time period, except for general-purpose governments, which show a marked decline in other taxes from 2007 to 2012. These trends suggest that governments prefer to increase taxes, especially other taxes, relative to charges but that other taxes were greatly affected by the Great Recession compared to property taxes and charges.

Trends in Financing of Specific Municipal Services

Table 3 presents trends in per capita charges, operational spending (no capital or construction), and federal and state aid for municipal services that are likely to be separate enterprises or have significant user charges from 1997 to 2012. Because of the skewness of these distributions, the table reports median values for these variables, or means if the median values are all zero, and the per capita values are reported as real dollars. The table also shows the number of municipalities in which spending is greater than zero for all services and the number in which charges are greater than zero for some services. In effect, the table is showing the degree to which each service is covered by charges and intergovernmental aid.

Table 3 shows that per capita charges for water, sewer, gas, electric, and hospitals are greater than per capita operational spending for all years, which may reflect the practice of including capital improvement costs within the

Table 2. Percentage change in real dollars (2002 = 100)

	Counties	Municipalities	Townships	Special Districts	School Districts
Own–source revenue (includes utilities)					
1992–1997	11.1	10.0	10.3	11.8	9.8
1997–2002	11.2	6.8	9.2	11.9	10.4
2002–2007	8.2	9.7	2.6	10.4	8.3
2007–2012	−4.0	−2.0	−0.7	4.0	−7.5
State aid					
1992–1997	12.9	7.6	4.5	50.0	16.6
1997–2002	15.4	16.0	9.8	24.1	18.6
2002–2007	−4.9	−8.6	−4.2	7.8	2.7
2007–2012	−6.1	−5.4	−11.2	−5.1	−7.5
Total spending					
1992–1997	12.0	7.4	6.8	9.8	13.9
1997–2002	14.4	13.8	13.0	17.0	19.6
2002–2007	1.7	2.3	−1.1	12.7	3.0
2007–2012	−1.1	0.5	−1.0	5.4	−7.0
Property taxes					
1992–1997	0.2	−0.4	9.7	23.4	8.5
1997–2002	10.8	7.5	9.0	7.8	9.3
2002–2007	9.2	9.8	1.3	14.5	5.3
2007–2012	5.4	9.1	5.0	7.4	−1.3
All other taxes besides property					
1992–1997	27.9	18.0	21.2	−19.3	33.2
1997–2002	13.5	8.6	22.1	55.2	35.1
2002–2007	14.8	15.8	17.2	33.9	12.8
2007–2012	−10.9	−7.2	−15.9	15.6	7.0
All charges					
1992–1997	28.7	14.2	9.5	15.6	8.4
1997–2002	12.5	6.4	13.2	12.1	17.2
2002–2007	5.6	4.7	1.4	8.9	6.0
2007–2012	3.2	5.8	−0.1	8.8	−7.3
Number of governments					
1992	3,043	19,279	16,656	31,555	14,422
1997	3,043	19,372	16,629	34,683	13,726
2002	3,043	19,429	16,504	35,052	13,506
2007	3,033	19,492	16,519	37,381	13,051
2012	3,031	19,519	16,360	38,266	12,880

charges levied for these services rather than the government "making a profit" from the charges. The high per capita spending and charges for gas, electric, and hospitals are due to the provision of these services beyond the population of the municipality. On the other hand, per capita charges for solid waste and parks and recreation only partly cover operational spending, and per capita charges for highways and transit cover very little operational spending for

Table 3. Mean and median spending, charges, and intergovernmental aid per capita in municipalities
Values are calculated in real dollars (2002 = 100) for governments that spend more than $0.00 for services

Water

	Per capita			
	Median operat'l spending	Median charges	Mean federal & state aid[a]	No. of govts. that spend >$0
1997	103.63	129.83	9.45	13,585
2002	101.95	127.94	12.79	13,785
2007	98.99	125.15	15.31	13,927
2012	99.62	129.13	19.50	13,787

Sewer

	Per capita			
	Median operat'l spending	Median charges	Mean federal & state aid[a]	No. of govts. that spend >$0
1997	70.63	91.12	0.01	12,244
2002	72.45	92.61	0.01	12,948
2007	71.37	92.56	15.36	13,523
2012	73.25	98.87	21.93	13,727

Gas

	Median per capita			
	Operational spending	Charges	Federal & state aid	No. of govts. that spend >$0
1997	301.27	342.26	Not reported	815
2002	312.54	351.25		934
2007	312.97	355.34		961
2012	212.29	234.86		893

Electric

	Median per capita			
	Operational spending	Charges	Federal & state aid	No. of govts. that spend >$0
1997	630.87	756.44	Not reported	1,803
2002	607.22	707.72		1,885
2007	595.78	682.94		2,039
2012	649.52	758.60		1,943

Hospitals

	Median per capita			
	Operational spending	Charges	Federal & state aid	No. of govts. that spend >$0
1997	1,010.01	1,040.49	Not reported	242
2002	1,203.22	1,216.03		208
2007	1,496.81	1,604.15		156
2012	1,854.38	1,942.39		149

Transit

	Median per capita			
	Operational spending	Charges	Mean federal & state aid[a]	No. of govts. that spend >$0
1997	20.78	4.36	40.67	598
2002	20.22	2.21	12.07	670
2007	16.93	1.23	12.24	805
2012	17.59	0.95	18.05	874

Solid Waste[b]

	Median per capita			
	Operational spending	Charges	No. of govts. that charge >$0	No. of govts. that spend >$0
1997	49.55	28.61	7,522	11,573
2002	46.93	29.63	7,792	11,958
2007	43.53	34.37	9,305	12,267
2012	42.96	36.58	9,850	12,321

Highways

	Per capita			
	Median operat'l spending	Median charges	Mean federal & state aid[a]	No. of govts. that spend >$0
1997	63.58	1.56	27.72	17,844
2002	64.63	1.37	27.95	17,587
2007	58.71	2.22	23.70	17,512
2012	57.10	2.38	19.85	17,641

Parking[b]

	Median per capita			
	Operational spending	Charges	No. of govts. that charge >$0	No. of govts. that spend >$0
1997	3.89	3.69	1,273	1,226
2002	4.15	4.16	1,366	1,044
2007	4.21	4.53	1,336	1,008
2012	4.24	4.80	1,300	1,044

Parks and Recreation[b]

	Per capita			
	Median operat'l spending	Mean charges[a]	No. of govts. that charge >$0	No. of govts. that spend >$0
1997	22.16	13.47	5,373	12,244
2002	24.67	15.21	5,838	12,948
2007	23.83	13.52	6,866	13,523
2012	23.09	16.19	7,651	13,727

[a]Means are reported because medians equal $0.
[b]Federal and state aid are not reported.

these services.[45] Thus, of the services reported in this table, charges can be increased to cover more spending only for solid waste, parks and recreation, highways, and transit.

Table 4 shows per capita revenues from various sources, including property and general sales taxes. The table shows an increase in per capita property taxes after the 2001 recession and Great Recession, but a decline in per capita sales taxes. Notice also the decline in per capita miscellaneous commercial charges, special assessments, all license taxes, other taxes (not including property, sales, or personal income tax), and fines after the Great Recession. It is also notable that the number of governments assessing miscellaneous commercial charges increased significantly after the 2001 recession, and per capita license taxes, other taxes, and fines increased also significantly after that recession. Interest earnings per capita also declined precipitously after the Great Recession, which undoubtedly affected these governments' reliance on many revenue sources and increased pressure to raise general taxes and other revenues.

It should also be noted that only non–ad valorem special assessments are reported by the Census of Governments separately from other revenue sources. Ad valorem special assessments are reported as part of general property taxes. Unfortunately, there is very little data on ad valorem special assessments, except in a few states. For instance, Hendrick and Wang show that many suburban municipalities in the Chicago metropolitan area use ad

Table 4. Median per capita revenues and number of municipal governments with values greater than $0, real dollars (2002 = 100)

| | Misc. commercial charges | | License taxes, other taxes,[a] and fines | | Special assessments, non–ad valorem[b] | |
	median	number	median	number	median	number
1997	4.88	392	12.99	14,417	10.76	3,426
2002	3.83	203	15.14	15,034	11.38	3,347
2007	3.86	2423	25.66	15,987	11.49	3,803
2012	3.24	2778	21.07	15,933	9.54	3,728
	Interest earnings		Property tax		General sales tax	
	median	number	median	number	median	number
1997	21.29	16,676	92.45	19,065	93.28	6,083
2002	19.12	17,580	94.15	19,405	92.90	6,150
2007	18.59	16,887	97.72	19,484	90.75	7,100
2012	4.20	14,983	103.39	19,489	88.52	7,677

[a]Other taxes exclude property, sales, and personal income tax
[b]US Bureau of Census, *Classification Manual,* issued October 2006 (Washington, DC: US Government Printing Office), 4–38, www2.census.gov/govs/pubs/classification/2006_classification_manual.pdf?#.

valorem special assessments,[46] but these tools generate little revenue and do not fund many capital improvements or services. They are also used very little in one county where they are not widely understood, and they are not used in the most urban county of the region where non–ad valorem special assessments are more appropriate.

Based on the trends reported here, it is apparent that many local governments are already providing most enterprises primarily through charges, and increases in these charges will not supplement operations elsewhere in the government. It is also apparent that the two recessions diminished the revenue potential of general sales and other taxes, requiring local governments to increase property taxes. However, the trend toward greater use of benefit taxes, user fees, and increased charges in order to cover more of the costs of service delivery for nonenterprise services, such as solid waste and parks and recreation, seems evident.

THE APPLICATION OF BENEFIT-BASED FINANCING IN PRACTICE

There is much written about how governments should design user charges "to get the prices right and impose the correct charges."[47] Textbooks and reports from public economics and financial management describe pricing principles and basic user-charge and -fee designs for government services generally. Publications from professional associations and commissions in specific services areas such as water, transit, libraries, and tollways apply these principles and elaborate on these designs in their service areas. Two basic pricing designs are recognized by this work. In marginal-cost pricing, charges are based on the cost of providing an additional unit of service. In markets where the service provided by governments is competitive, charges will be equal to marginal costs and resources will be allocated optimally. Marginal-cost pricing can be short term, which recognizes only the variable costs in providing the service, or long term, which includes both fixed and variable costs. This method can also be structured to recognize different marginal costs for different service attributes, such as type of user or level of service output.

The second basic user-charge design is average-cost pricing in which all costs or a portion of the costs of providing the service—fixed, variable, operational, and capital—are averaged among all users. Marginal-cost pricing does not work under many conditions for government services, and average-cost pricing is often useful in these cases. But common knowledge suggests that governments often use average-cost pricing when marginal-price costing is possible and will produce efficient outcomes.[48] The goal of government in many cases is cost recovery instead of the efficient allocation of service costs to users (and across services) in the case of marginal-cost pricing. Assessing flat-fee charges across all users is the simplest form of average-cost pricing, but, like marginal-cost pricing, user charges and fees can be assessed at a rate that varies by service attribute, such as type of user or level of service provided. In this case, distributional outcomes of average-cost pricing may approximate those of marginal-cost pricing with respect to allocating costs according to benefits received (or costs incurred), but these two basic designs have somewhat different informational requirements for governments.

Both pricing mechanisms require that governments have good information about service demands (or benefits) and how the number of users will change as fees or charges change. Both mechanisms also require good information about costs, but marginal costs should also take account of opportunity costs in order to allocate costs efficiently. By comparison, average costs take account of accounting costs only.[49] Relatively speaking, obtaining good information on demands and how the number of users of a service change as charges change is more difficult than obtaining good information on unit costs.[50] Additionally, many public services for which benefit-based financing is appropriate have relatively inelastic demand, and demand can be easily estimated by the number of citizens, households, or other widely available indicator of service usage by the public. Marginal-cost pricing will not work using this approach, but estimating demand or benefits in this manner is very useful for producing a flat fee. Although this method is not likely to allocate costs according to benefits, especially if usage varies among users, average-cost pricing is the most frequent method employed by government for many services.[51]

Although governments are likely to have more information on costs than demands, the costs of many public-sector activities can be difficult to define or estimate at the level necessary to allocate accurate average costs using more than a flat-fee approach. In most cases, governments know how much is spent for line items in an agency's budget, but far fewer governments know how much it costs to deliver specific services in that agency or services that are delivered by multiple agencies. Governments may also not assess or allocate indirect costs correctly to services for which they charge or assess fees for the purposes of cost recovery. Looking at different texts and reports on pricing design for specific services shows that much of their content focuses on methods of cost assessment and allocating costs to the cost components of the service.[52] One critical question that arises in this case is whether local governments have the capacity to collect good information on costs or de-termine costs using their accounting and information systems such that they can produce a more accurate and efficient pricing system for services than a flat fee. Even today, many of the properties in Chicago are not metered for water and sewer but are charged for these services based on building size, lot size, and number of sinks and toilets.

To the extent that governments do not have the capacity to determine ac-curate costs and demands or benefits, increasing dependence on user charges and benefit taxes in the future may not constitute a progression toward true benefit-based financing. Rather, it could portend a progression toward ear-marked fees and taxes that have little to do with the benefits citizens receive. For instance, the City of Chicago levies an additional "utility tax" on water and sewer charges to finance mandated pension payments for employees throughout the city. In this case, water and sewer charges are not the most defensible basis for levying a general tax for paying city employees' pensions or a good indicator of the benefits citizens receive from employee pensions.

To the extent that governments do have this capacity, then another im-portant question is whether governments' capacities are likely to improve in the future as technology improves. For instance, the use of smartcards for transit services that record transactions, collect charges, and provide transit agencies with information on the transaction and user has allowed these agencies to improve their pricing structure greatly.[53] More recently, many governments have embraced cloud computing for data collection on service demand and delivery and to provide timely information to the public about service events. Chicago's open data portal is a good example of the use of this tool and its benefits for both the city and its citizens.[54] Blockchain technology also holds promise to record and secure transactions, contracts, and information exchanges of many kinds over a wide range of processes involving both tangible and intangible assets.[55]

Although governments may be motivated to improve their capacity to collect costs and demand information due to improved technology or other pressures, such as greater use of contracting for service production, govern-ments are less likely to incur the costs of such investments when faced with fiscal scarcity, including recessions. But even where governments have the capacity to apply more accurate average-cost pricing or marginal-cost pric-ing, they may not do this for political reasons. Many studies have noted that levels of user charges and fees are often determined by political factors and the budgetary needs of the government for both enterprises and general fund services, rather than being fully grounded in the costs, demands, and objectives for these services.[56] In some cases, increases in charges are vetoed by elected officials or delayed until emergencies occur that require significant increases in charges to resolve.[57] Other studies note that public officials can be risk averse in setting charges, believing that, for instance, flat fees for transit are better than variable rates because they are more worried about the riders they will lose[58] and that high-impact fees, special assessments, and parking fees will dampen economic growth and activity.[59] Thus, many governments underprice their services.

Unfortunately, there is little in-depth investigation of local governments' uses of a broad range of user charges, how they are designed, and whether the application of user charges has improved as a basis for predicting whether governments will increase their use of true benefit-based financing. It is apparent that the Canadian government collects thorough data on charges and fees from its local governments, which has been used by many to conduct investigations of the use of user charges in these governments.[60] There was also investigation of local charges and fees in Great Britain in the 1980s in response to the 1986 green paper *Paying for Local Government* that proposed some radical changes to the way in which UK local government was financed.[61] Some of these changes involved significantly increasing the use of user fees and charges at the local level.[62]

In the United States, by comparison, most investigations of the use of user charges and other direct-benefit financing methods and how they are designed are specific to particular services and take the form of surveys, case studies, or other qualitative methods of gathering information. Examples of such studies that can found within the public administration journals are more descriptive than prescriptive and include the following: a survey of 107 cities nationwide on public parking charges;[63] a survey of municipal and county officials in California about fees and special assessments for building new roads;[64] stormwater fees, special assessments, and hybrid taxing and fee methods in selected cities in the United States;[65] fees for local roads and streets in 34 selected cities;[66] and interviews of transit officials in transit agencies in California and a nationwide survey of transit operators about transit fares.[67] Many more studies of user charges and benefit taxes can be found in journals and reports from associations and groups that target specific government services that rely on charges to deliver services, such as the *Journal of the American Water Resources Association, Journal of Park and Recreation Administration, International Federation of Library Associations Journal*, and Transportation Research Board.

CONCLUSION

Returning to the broader question of whether local governments are likely to increase their reliance on benefit-based financing in the future, this chapter argues that the more precise question is whether local governments are likely to increase their reliance on *effective* benefit-based financing in the future. In other words, are there opportunities for government to increase their use of benefit-based financing in a manner that yields revenues from individual citizens according to benefits received or willingness to pay and that allocates spending efficiently?

Analysis of spending and charges for local governments shows that municipalities are already charging more than what they are spending for the operation of government enterprises, which are the public services that are most appropriate for benefit-based financing. The same is probably true of other local governments that provide enterprise services, such as water, sewer, gas, electric, hospitals, and parking. Thus, charges cannot be dramatically increased by governments for these services. The primary issue for governments in this case is whether they can improve the pricing of these services to produce more efficient outcomes. This chapter has shown that, although technology and techniques for establishing more efficient charges are available, it is not clear whether governments have improved the design of user charges and collection of information to produce accurate pricing of their enterprises. Indeed, there appear to be many governments in which budgetary needs in nonenterprise areas drive charges in enterprise areas higher or where political preference drives enterprise charges lower than what is needed to fully fund operations and capital investment.

With respect to the other service areas that provide exclusive benefits to users—transit, solid waste, airports, water ports, highways, libraries, fire, and parks and recreation—all have characteristics that make charges an undesirable method of financing 100 percent of these services. Solid waste, for instance, has significant positive spillovers in terms of improving the cleanliness of neighborhoods and reducing disease and vermin. The reported figures show that charges for solid waste have increased since 1997 and constituted 86 percent of operational spending in 2012. Thus, there is not much room for increasing charges for this service further, and doing so may reduce the public benefit by encouraging unapproved disposal of solid waste. Similarly, use of charges for parks and recreation, which some view as a merit good, has increased and represented about 65 percent of operational spending in

2012, but half the municipalities shown in table 3 do not charge for these services. On the other hand, charges for transit and highways are very low relative to spending, which suggests that use of benefit-based financing could increase significantly in these areas, although these services have features that make them unsuitable for financing operations and capital spending entirely through charges. Unless user charges are applied thoughtfully and appropriately in these service areas to account for both individual and public benefits, such charges may be no different from a non–ad valorem tax that is earmarked for a specific purpose.

Use of special assessments to finance capital spending is another way in which benefit-based financing could increase in local governments in the near future, especially if the special assessments are ad valorem and administered through the regular property tax system. Ad valorem special assessments are more appropriate for financing public infrastructure in single-use commercial, residential, and industrial areas than urban areas with mixed land use. Ad valorem special assessments have been used to finance new public infrastructure, improvements to existing infrastructure, and ongoing services in business improvement districts, residential subdivisions, shopping centers, and industrial parks. The primary hindrance to their greater use is that many states require voter or property-owner approval to implement them, which is often difficult to obtain, given the public's dislike of property taxes.[68]

Overall, then, it does not appear that the method of financing local government will change dramatically from general taxation deposited into a general fund to accurate and effective benefit-based financing that is earmarked for specific services. Although recent trends show an increase in charges or user fees for nonenterprise public services, this method is inappropriate for pure public goods and does not produce efficient outcomes when used alone to finance goods and services that have distinct individual benefits but significant public or merit value. In fact, implementing numerous charges and fees for these types of services in a manner that is not based on accurate information about economic benefits and costs may be more misleading to both government and citizens than general taxation.

Notes

Paper prepared for 2018 UIC Urban Forum "The People's Money: Pensions, Debt, and Government Services," September 13 and October 25, Chicago; and for delivery at the thirtieth annual conference of the Association for Budgeting and Financial Management, October 4–6, 2018, Denver.

1. Richard Musgrave, *The Theory of Public Finance* (New York: McGraw-Hill, 1959).

2. US Census Bureau, Census of Governments, vol. 4, *Governmental Finances*, no. 4, *Finances of Municipal and Township Governments*, 1–2 (72–82), issued September 1984 (Washington, DC: US Government Printing Office, 1982), www2.census.gov/govs/pubs/cog/1982/1982_vol4_no4_fin_muntwp.pdf; US Bureau of the Census, Census of Governments, vol. 4, *Governmental Finances*, no. 4, *Finances of Municipal and Township Governments*, 1–2, issued January 1997 (Washington, DC: US Government Printing Office, 1992), www.census.gov/prod/2/gov/gc92-4/gc924-4.pdf; US Bureau of the Census, Census of Governments, vol. 4, *Governmental Finances*, no. 4, *Finances of Municipal and Township Governments*, 1–2, issued April 2005 (Washington, DC: US Government Printing Office, 2002), www.census.gov/prod/2005pubs/gc024x4.pdf; US Bureau of the Census, Census of Governments, "Local Government Summary Tables by Type of Government," 2007, www.census.gov//govs/local/historical_data_2007.html; US Bureau of the Census, Census of Governments, "Local Government Summary Tables by Type of Government," 2012, www.census.gov//govs/local/historical_data_2012.html.

3. Richard W. Tresch, *Public Finance: A Normative Theory* (London: Elsevier, 2014), 96–98; Geoffrey Brennan and James M. Buchanan, *The Power to Tax: Analytical Foundations of a Fiscal Constitution* (Cambridge: Cambridge University Press, 1980).

4. William A. Fischel, "Homevoters, Municipal Corporate Governance, and the Benefit View of the Property Tax," *National Tax Journal* 54, no. 1 (2001): 157-74.

5. George R. Zodrow, "The Property Tax as a Capital Tax: A Room with Three Views," *National Tax Journal* 54, no. 1 (2001): 139-56.

6. David G. Duff, "Benefit Taxes and User Fees in Theory and Practice," *University of Toronto Law Journal* 54, no. 4 (2004): 391-447.

7. John R. Bartle, Kenneth A. Kriz, and Boris Morozov, "Local Government Revenue Structure: Trends and Challenges," *Journal of Public Budgeting, Accounting and Financial Management* 23, no. 2 (2011): 268-87; J. Edwin Benton, "Trends in Local Government Revenues: The Old, the New, and the Future," in *Municipal Revenue and Land Policies*, ed. G. Ingram and Y. Hong (Cambridge, MA: Lincoln Institute of Land Policy, 2010).

8. Tracy M. Gordon and Kim Rueben, "The Best of Times or the Worst of Times? How Alternative Revenue Structures Are Changing Local Government," in *Municipal Revenue and Land Policies*, ed. Ingram and Hong, 476-506; Lawrence L. Martin, Richard Levey, and Jenna Cawley, "The 'New Normal' for Local Government," *State and Local Government Review* 44, no. 1-suppl (2012): 17S–28S.

9. James M. Buchanan, "The Pure Theory of Government Finance: A Suggested Approach," *Journal of Political Economy* 57, no. 6 (1949): 496-505.

10. James M. Buchanan, *Public Finance in a Democratic Process: Fiscal Institutions and Individual Choice* (Chapel Hill: University of North Carolina Press, 1967); James M. Buchanan, "The Economics of Earmarked Taxes," *Journal of Political Economy* 71, no. 5 (1963): 457-69.

11. Duff, "Benefit Taxes and User Fees."

12. Paul A. Samuelson, "The Pure Theory of Economics," *Review of Economics and Statistics* 36, no. 4 (1954): 387–89.

13. Musgrave, *Theory of Public Finance*, 13–15.

14. Musgrave, *Theory of Public Finance*, chap. 5; Tresch, *Public Finance*, 173.

15. Wayne R. Thirsk and Richard M. Bird, "Earmarked Taxes in Ontario: Solution or Problem?," in *Taxing and Spending: Issues of Process*, ed. A. Maslove (Toronto: University of Toronto Press in cooperation with the Fair Tax Commission of the Government of Ontario, 1994), 129-84.

16. Louis M. Rea, Glen W. Sparrow, and Dipak K. Gupta, "Direct Benefit Financing: An Opportunity for Local Government," *Public Administration Quarterly* 7, no. 3 (1984): 29-43.

17. Duff, "Benefit Taxes and User Fees."

18. Richard M. Bird and Thomas Tsiopoulos, "User Charges for Public Services: Potentials and Problems," *Canadian Tax Journal* 45, no. 1 (1996): 25-86.

19. Duff, "Benefit Taxes and User Fees."

20. Shu Wang and Rebecca Hendrick, "Financing Urban Infrastructure (and Services) under the New Normal: A Look at Special Assessments," in *The Transformation of the American Local State: Developmental Politics and the Eclipse of Democratic Governance*, ed. E. McKenzie, A. Alexander, and D. Judd (Minneapolis: University of Minnesota Press, forthcoming).

21. Dean J. Misczynski, "Special Assessment in California: 35 Years of Expansion and Restriction," in *Value Capture and Land Policies*, ed. G. K. Ingram and Y. Hong (Cambridge, MA: Lincoln Institute of Land Policy, 2012), 81-112.

22. Marcus T. Allen and Harry C. Newstreet, "Smoothing Wrinkles in the Spread: Special Assessment Issues," *Appraisal Journal* 68, no. 2 (2000): 201-8.

23. Fischel, "Homevoters"; Wang and Hendrick, "Financing Urban Infrastructure."

24. Charles M. Tiebout, "A Pure Theory of Local Expenditure," *Journal of Political Economy* 64, no. 5 (1956): 416-24.

25. David L. Sjoquist and Andrew V. Stephenson, "An Analysis of Alternative Revenue Sources for Local Governments," in *Municipal Revenue and Land Policies*, ed. Ingram and Hong, 433-73.

26. Glenn W. Fisher, *The Worst Tax? A History of the Property Tax in America* (Lawrence: University Press of Kansas, 1996).

27. Wallace E. Oates, "Property Taxation and Local Government Finance," in *Property Taxation and Local Government Finance*, ed. Wallace E. Oates (Cambridge, MA: Lincoln Institute of Land Policy, 2001); Deborah Carroll, "Diversifying Municipal Government Revenue Structures: Fiscal Illusion or Instability?," *Public Budgeting and Finance* 29, no. 1 (2009): 27-48.

28. Christopher Hoene, "Fiscal Structure and the Post–Proposition 13 Fiscal Regime in California's Cities," *Public Budgeting and Finance* 24, no. 4 (2004): 51–72.

29. David Brunori et al., "Tax and Expenditure Limits and Their Effects on Local Finances in Urban Areas," in *Urban and Regional Policy and Its Effects*, ed. Margery Austin Turner, Howard Wial, and Harold Wolman (Washington, DC: Brookings Institution Press, 2008), 1:109-55; Craig S. Maher et al., "The Effects of Tax and Expenditure Limits on State Fiscal Reserves," *Public Policy and Administration* 32, no. 2 (2017): 130–51.

30. Richard F. Dye and Therese J. McGuire, "The Effect of Property Tax Limitation Measures on Local Government Fiscal Behavior," *Journal of Public Economics* 66, no. 3 (1997): 469-87; Richard F. Dye, Therese J. McGuire, and Daniel P. McMillen, "Are Property Tax Limitations More Binding over Time?," *National Tax Journal* 58, no. 2 (2005): 215–25.

31. Rui Sun, "Reevaluating the Effect of Tax and Expenditure Limitations: An Instrumental Variable Approach," *Public Finance Review* 42, no. 1 (2014): 92-116; Mark Skidmore, "Tax and Expenditure Limitations and the Fiscal Relationships between State and Local Governments," *Public Choice* 99, nos. 1–2 (1999): 77–102; Ronald J. Shadbegian, "The Effect of Tax and Expenditure Limitations on the Revenue Structure of Local Governments, 1962-87," *National Tax Journal* 52, no. 2 (1999): 221-37.

32. Jesse Edgerton, Andrew F. Haughwout, and Rae Rosen, "Institutions, Tax Structure and State—Local Fiscal Stress," *National Tax Journal* 57, no. 1 (2004): 147-58.

33. Bird and Tsiopoulos, "User Charges for Public Services."

34. Denvil Duncan et al., "Searching for a Tolerable Tax: Public Attitudes toward Roadway Financing Alternatives," *Public Finance Review* 45, no. 5 (2016): 678-700.

35. Paul B. Downing, "The Revenue Potential of User Charges in Municipal Finance," *Public Finance Quarterly* 20, no. 4 (1992): 512-27.

36. Bird and Tsiopoulos, "User Charges for Public Services."

37. Benton, "Trends in Local Government Revenues"; John R. Bartle, Carol Ebdon, and Dale Krane, "Beyond the Property Tax: Local Government Revenue Diversification," *Journal of Public Budgeting, Accounting and Financial Management* 15, no. 4 (2003): 622-48; Bartle, Kriz, and Morozov, "Local Government Revenue Structure"; Yunji Kim, "Limits of Property Taxes and Charges: City Revenue Structures after the Great Recession," *Urban Affairs Review* 55, no. 1 (2017): 185–209.

38. Enterprise charges are for water, sewer, transit, gas, electric, and hospitals. Airports and water ports are other enterprises that should be removed here, but the sources of data used to construct these tables do not show charges for these enterprises separately. In other studies, general revenue excludes charges for water, transit, gas, and electric but includes other enterprises. Total revenue includes charges for all enterprises, and own-source revenue excludes intergovernmental aid.

39. Rebecca Hendrick, "In the Shadow of State Government: Changes in Municipal Spending after Two Recessions," working paper under review (2018).

40. Hendrick, "In the Shadow of State Government."

41. Kim, "Limits of Property Taxes and Charges."

42. Hendrick, "In the Shadow of State Government"; Richard F. Dye and Andrew Reschovsky, "Property Tax Responses to State Aid Cuts in the Recent Fiscal Crisis," *Public Budgeting and Finance* 28, no. 2 (2008): 87-111; Erich Cromwell and Keith Ihlanfedt, "Local Government Response to Exogenous Shocks in Revenue Sources: Evidence from Florida," *National Tax Journal* 68, no. 2 (2015): 339-76.

43. Kimberly L. Nelson, "Municipal Choices during a Recession: Bounded Rationality and Innovation," *State and Local Government Review* 44, no. 1S (2012): 44–63.

44. The effects of recessions on local governments lag for at least one year after the recession starts.

45. Vehicle license fees are included in highway charges because many governments earmark these licenses for roads and transportation.

46. Rebecca Hendrick and Shu Wang, "Use of Special Assessments by Municipal Governments in the Chicago Metropolitan Area: Is Leviathan Tamed?," *Public Budgeting and Finance* (2017), https://doi-org.proxy.cc.uic.edu/10.1111/pbaf.12190.

47. Bird and Tsiopoulos, "User Charges for Public Services," 51.

48. Bird and Tsiopoulos, "User Charges for Public Services."

49. Duff, "Benefit Taxes and User Fees."

50. Bird and Tsiopoulos, "User Charges for Public Services."

51. Michael E. D. Koenig and Johanna Goforth, "Libraries and the Cost Recovery Imperative: The Emergence of the Issue," *IFLA Journal* 19, no. 3 (1993): 261-79.

52. American Water Works Association, *Principles of Water Rates, Fees and Charges,* 7th ed. (Denver: American Water Works Association, 2017); National Association of Flood and Stormwater Management Agencies, *Guidance for Municipal Stormwater Funding,* 2006, www.epa.gov/sites/production/files/2015-10/documents/guidance-manual-version-2x-2.pdf; Transportation Research Board, *Sharing the Costs of Human Services Transportation,* vol. 1, *The Transportation Services Cost Sharing Toolkit,* Transit Cooperative Research Program (TCRP) Report 144, 2011, www.nap.edu/download/14490.

53. Allison C. Yoh, Brian D. Taylor, and John Gahbauer, "Does Transit Mean Business? Reconciling Economic, Organizational, and Political Perspectives on Variable Transit Fares," *Public Works Management and Policy* 21, no. 2 (2016): 157-72.

54. https://data.cityofchicago.org/.

55. Svein Ølnes, Jolien Ubacht, and Marijn Janssen, "Blockchain in Government: Benefits and Implications of Distributed Ledger Technology for Information Sharing," *Government Information Quarterly* 34, no. 3 (2017): 355-64.

56. Charlie B. Tyer, "Municipal Enterprises and Taxing and Spending Policies: Public Avoidance and Fiscal Illusions," *Public Administration Review* 49, no. 3 (1989): 249-56; Beverly S. Bunch and Robert R. Ducker, "Implications of Using Enterprise Funds to Account for Public Works Services," *Public Works Management and Policy* 7, no. 3 (2003): 216-25; Paul B. Downing and James E. Frank, "Patterns of Impact Fee Usage," in *Development Impact Fees,* ed. A. C. Nelson (Chicago: Planners Press, 1988);

Donald C. Shoup, "The Ideal Source of Local Public Revenue," *Regional Science and Urban Economics* 34, no. 6 (2004): 753-84.

57. Rebecca Hendrick, *Managing the Fiscal Metropolis: The Financial Policies, Practices and Health of Municipalities* (Washington, DC: Georgetown University Press, 2011).

58. Yoh, Taylor, and Gahbauer, "Does Transit Mean Business?"

59. Robert Cervero, "Paying for Off-Site Road Improvements through Fees, Assessments, and Negotiations: Lessons from California," *Public Administration Review* 48, no. 1 (1988): 534-41; Greg Marsden, "The Evidence Base for Parking Policies: A Review," *Transport Policy* 13, no. 6 (2006): 447-57.

60. Duff, "Benefit Taxes and User Fees"; Bird and Tsiopoulos, "User Charges for Public Services."

61. Department of the Environment, *Paying for Local Government*, Green Paper, Cmnd 714 (London: HMSO, 1986).

62. Stephen James Bailey, "Paying for Local Government: Charging for Services," *Public Administration* 64, no. 4 (1986): 401-19; S. R. Smith and D. L. Squire, "The Local Government Green Paper," *Fiscal Studies* 7, no. 2 (1986): 63-71.

63. Amy H. Auchincloss et al., "Public Parking Fees and Fines: A Survey of U.S. Cities," *Public Works Management and Policy* 20, no. 1 (2014): 49-59.

64. Cervero, "Paying for Off-Site Road Improvements."

65. Neil S. Grigg, "Stormwater Programs Organization, Finance, and Prospects," *Public Works Management & Policy* 18, no. 1 (2012): 5-22.

66. Carole Turley Voulgaris, "A TUF Sell: Transportation Utility Fees as User Fees for Local Roads and Streets," *Public Works Management and Policy* 21, no. 4 (2016): 305-23.

67. Yoh, Taylor, and Gahbauer, "Does Transit Mean Business?"

68. Wang and Hendrick, "Financing Urban Infrastructure."

Beyond Political Consolidation

Prospects for Effective Local Governance through Self-Organized Collaborative Networks

JERED B. CARR AND MICHAEL D. SICILIANO

Political authority in America's major metropolitan areas is highly fragmented, often divided among dozens of cities, counties, and special districts. Assessments of the consequences of political fragmentation have changed over time, but the one constant has been criticism. Local government scholars initially attacked political fragmentation as increasing the costs of government; later generations lamented its encouragement of intergovernmental competition for infrastructure and economic development, and more recently, it has been blamed for facilitating the economic and racial segregation prevalent in the United States.[1] Angst about political fragmentation has not been limited to the academy, however. Business and civic organizations commonly express concern about the large number of distinct governments in their states, and state officials periodically launch efforts to encourage mass consolidations.[2]

Much has been written about the "new normal" in the United States in which local governments face environments where revenue growth is severely constrained, demands for services are expanding, and their workforces are shrinking.[3] Many of these governments also have pension obligations and other costs that have accumulated over time and compete with other priorities for funding. These challenges are often highlighted by local media, civic and business organizations, and state officials as a basis for eliminating units of local governments.[4] However, despite the incentives provided by sustained pressure on public budgets, municipal consolidation has not occurred en masse anywhere in the United States.

Empirical research on city-county consolidation, the most common form of large-scale political consolidation, underscores the significant political

challenges to addressing the consequences of fragmentation through elimination of local governments.[5] For instance, distressed communities are un-
attractive mates to more healthy communities because residents often resist
being combined with communities with fewer resources. Research has also
shown residents often fear that consolidation will produce larger and more
powerful jurisdictions that will be empowered to increase taxes and spending.[6] Finally, more politically feasible alternatives to consolidation exist, especially for the small suburban communities most often targeted for elimination
by consolidation advocates.[7] For example, intergovernmental collaboration
permits municipal officials—and ultimately local residents—an option to
address financial challenges while maintaining greater control over the taxes
they pay and the public services they receive.[8]

The term "disarticulated state" was advanced by H. George Frederickson
to describe the challenges confronted by local government officials in confronting the many public problems that transcend jurisdictional lines.[9] He
observed that public problems and local political authority often were not
in alignment, and this issue was particularly acute in urban regions. Political consolidation is one approach for improving this alignment, but Frederickson focused on the strategy of "administrative conjunctions" used to
confront this problem. He described a process whereby municipal officials
create intergovernmental networks in order to work collaboratively across
political boundaries to achieve the scale necessary to develop solutions to
the problems affecting their residents.

Thus, public resistance to political consolidation does not mean that the
landscape of local government service-delivery and policy coordination has
been static over time. Instead, intergovernmental collaboration has been the
process used to address the various challenges political fragmentation creates.[10] Local officials create bilateral and multilateral arrangements to address
a host of issues that do not fit neatly within the borders of the existing set
of political jurisdictions. These networks do not provide the highly visible
changes sought by advocates of consolidation, but the resulting formal and
informal relationships mitigate some of the consequences of political fragmentation and, presumably, also have consequences for municipal budgets.

The existence of these networks is increasingly recognized by local government scholars, but insights about their creation, evolution, and effectiveness
have been produced in disparate research streams. This chapter synthesizes
the research literature examining intergovernmental networks, and the network literature more broadly, to outline four issues critical to understanding
the prospects for effective local governance through networks. First, what
is the rationale for using networks as a tool for delivering public services

instead of traditional structures of in-house production? Second, how are formal and informal mechanisms used to reduce the risks associated with collaborating within networks? Third, what factors influence the selection and establishment of network partners? And fourth, what strategies are used to measure and promote success in the networks? This synthesis also seeks to provide insights about the potential budgetary impacts of increased intergovernmental collaboration and its potential as a solution for municipalities struggling with resource issues.

ISSUE ONE: FACTORS DRIVING THE CREATION OF LOCAL GOVERNMENT SERVICE-DELIVERY NETWORKS

Direct, or in-house, production has essentially been the default position for most local governments in the United States for many public services. However, governments also rely on intergovernmental agreements to produce services for their residents. What does the empirical literature show about the factors explaining when local governments create networks of these agreements to address problems that have transjurisdictional sources and impacts? Cost savings are often highlighted as a potential driver of these relationships, but nonbudgetary factors may also be important.

Network Relations as a Contracting Problem

Much of what we know about the question of network relations comes from research building on the municipal contracting literature depicting other governments as one of several potential partners municipalities might use to produce services to their residents.[11] This research has identified a set of contextual factors that explain when governments will contract for services instead of producing in-house. There is also a smaller case-study literature examining specific collaborations that has produced insights about the importance of differences in priorities among potential partners and how different objectives generate different political challenges for intergovernmental collaboration.[12]

Bel and Warner's meta-analysis of the quantitative analyses in this literature identified the seven most commonly analyzed factors in the empirical literature on interjurisdictional collaboration.[13] Table 1 summarizes their findings for the 49 studies (and 171 estimations) they reviewed. They report that fiscal constraints and cost savings from scale economies were the factors most often analyzed in this literature but that nearly half of the studies reported null findings for these factors. Fiscal constraints are most commonly operationalized as

Table 1. Primary explanatory variables examined in empirical literature

Fiscal Constraints	No. (%)	Community Wealth	No. (%)
Positive	53 (43.8%)	Positive	18 (20.2%)
Negative	16 (13.2%)	Negative	13 (14.6%)
Nonsignificant	52 (43.0%)	Nonsignificant	58 (65.2%)
Total	121	Total	89
Most common measures	Debt burden, own-sources revenues per capita, local taxes and debt	Most common measures	Income per capita

Economies of Scale	No. (%)	Spatial Effects	No. (%)
Positive	20 (16.4%)	Positive	33 (55.0%)
Negative	38 (31.1%)	Negative	4 (6.7%)
Nonsignificant	64 (52.5%)	Nonsignificant	23 (38.3%)
Total	122	Total	60
Most common measures	Jurisdictional population	Most common measures	City in MSA or suburb

Organizational Factors	No. (%)	Racial Homogeneity	No. (%)
Positive	26 (41.9%)	Positive	24 (41.4%)
Negative	5 (8.1%)	Negative	7 (12.0%)
Nonsignificant	31 (50.0%)	Nonsignificant	27 (46.6%)
Total	62	Total	58
Most common measures	Municipal form of government	Most common measures	Percentage racial/ethnic majority in population

Service-Level Transaction Costs	No. (%)
Positive	13 (41.9%)
Negative	6 (19.4%)
Nonsignificant	12 (38.7%)
Total	31
Most common measures	None specified, but likely most often based on measures developed by Brown and Postoski

Source: Redrawn from Germà Bel and Mildred E. Warner, "Factors Explaining Inter-municipal Cooperation in Service Delivery: A Meta-regression Analysis," *Journal of Economic Policy Reform* 19, no. 2 (2016): 91–115, doi:10.1080/17487870.2015.11000842016, table 2.

debt per capita, own-source revenues per capita, and state laws limiting debt. They found that scale economies are typically captured through measures of service and place characteristics and that the population of political jurisdictions is the most common measure used to proxy scale economies used in this literature.

Bel and Warner's study shows that this empirical literature does not provide strong support for the expected role of most of these factors. Table 1 shows that none of the categories of variables has a consistent impact on interjurisdictional collaboration. In half of the categories, nonsignificance was the most frequent finding, and the significant findings showed conflicting directions in another third of the categories. Spatial effects and service-level transaction costs had the most consistent significant findings.

Fiscal Stress and Network Relations among Local Governments

The importance of fiscal stress as a motivator for municipal officials to seek service collaborations is widely presumed,[14] but Bel and Warner also found that expectations about the stimulating effects of fiscal variables on interjurisdictional collaboration were rarely supported by this literature.[15] Given the prominence of fiscal factors in arguments promoting political consolidation, this factor requires further examination. Political consolidation is often advanced as a strategy to relieve fiscal pressure from state austerity or local economic decline, but Bel and Warner's findings suggest that self-organized interjurisdictional collaboration may not spring from these same motivations.

Case analyses provide some insight into this question. Chen and Thurmaier surveyed managers in city and county governments in Iowa about the impetus for agreements their jurisdictions had made with other local governments.[16] The managers reported that the fiscal condition of their local government was a much less important basis for creating these agreements than expectations for improved effectiveness or efficiencies in delivering services to their residents. Research by Hatley and his colleagues illustrates the challenges of collaborations initiated in the context of fiscal stress.[17] This research used the case of a failed effort to create a fire authority to serve several cities to illustrate that efforts to jointly produce services may be hindered by fiscal strain. Hatley found that the fiscal pressures experienced by the five communities increased the difficulty of forming the authority. This surfaced in terms of resistance from the cities' firefighters that led to political losses by several of the elected officials promoting the effort. Another obstacle Hatley reported was that the cities' administrators generally expected to reap long-run savings from the fire authority, but most of the elected officials expected short-run cost savings.[18]

This literature raises important questions about the likelihood that local governments will turn to interjurisdictional agreements as a mechanism to resolve the severe fiscal challenges cited by advocates of governmental consolidation. Table 2 presents data on the interjurisdictional agreements created by Iowa local governments in three key service areas: police, streets and roads, and economic development.[19] The data examines the average number of agreements in each of the service areas a city government has formed at various sizes (population levels) and levels of fiscal capacity (per capita operating expenses and per capita taxable property value). These data show a clear pattern of a greater reliance on these agreements by larger and better-resourced jurisdictions, underscoring the proposition that participation in these self-organized local governance networks is biased toward higher-resource communities.

Table 2. Selected interjurisdictional agreements formed by Iowa governments from 2010 to 2017

Average no. of interjurisdictional agreements by population			
City population	Police protection	Street and road systems	Economic development
First quartile	0.52	0.14	0.02
Second quartile	0.99	0.15	0.01
Third quartile	1.45	0.24	0.03
Fourth quartile	1.43	1.23	0.14

Average no. of interjurisdictional agreements by per capita operating expenses			
Per capita operating expenses	Police protection	Street and road systems	Economic development
First quartile	0.75	0.14	0.01
Second quartile	1.12	0.20	0.03
Third quartile	1.17	0.54	0.08
Fourth quartile	1.35	0.89	0.09

Average no. of interjurisdictional agreements by per capita taxable property value			
Per capita taxable property value	Police protection	Street and road systems	Economic development
First quartile	0.73	0.09	0.02
Second quartile	1.12	0.14	0.03
Third quartile	1.24	0.31	0.03
Fourth quartile	1.3	1.22	0.11

Bel and Warner's meta-analysis focused on self-organized networks, but networks can also be mandated or incentivized by higher authorities focused on resource constraints. Mandated networks may be particularly important in the context of significant collective-action problems brought on by fiscal stress or by a free-rider issue generated by the structure of the problem. Federal and state legislation often encourages intergovernmental collaboration around specific problems, such as transportation, environmental, and public health challenges, through policies for approving grant applications or other requests from local governments for funding. For example, the US Department of Housing and Urban Development requires the use of a continuum-of-care model to access funds through the McKinney-Vento Homeless Assistance Act Supportive Housing Program. The continuum-of-care model requires communities to demonstrate they have a collaborative network in place involving a number of homeless-serving agencies that provide services ranging from emergency care to permanent housing.[20] Similarly, the United Kingdom established Crime and Disorder Reduction Partnerships as part of the Crime and Disorder Act of 1998. The CDRPs were a collaborative network designed to reduce crime and consisted of a number of government agencies that addressed related issues of policing, probation, youth offending, and other local government service organizations.[21]

ISSUE TWO: COLLABORATION RISK AND INSTITUTIONAL MECHANISMS

Local governments that use networks to deliver public services confront three types of risks: coordination, division, and defection. The size of the transaction risks varies from one case to the next, but their existence must be understood and resolved.

Collaboration Risk: Coordination, Division, and Defection Costs

RISKS DUE TO COORDINATION COSTS   The process of bringing together two or more local governments to collaborate is described in the literature as a coordination problem.[22] The factors affecting coordination costs have been extensively studied in the municipal contracting literature, but typically in the context of bilateral agreements. Multilateral agreements are less often studied but are likely to have much higher coordination costs. Agreements typically require approval from each city council, and agreement on terms and conditions may require multiple rounds of negotiation and bargaining.

Heterogeneity among partners is widely presumed to be an important factor in the severity of the coordination problem. Potential partners often bring preferences that will need to be reconciled, and negotiating costs increase costs of coordination, especially if potential joint gains are unclear. Agreements must mitigate these costs by supporting the goals of the group, but also addressing the needs of individual members. In the presence of serious differences among the parties, significant obstacles may arise during negotiations on these agreements.[23]

RISKS DUE TO DIVISION COSTS   Division problems occur when local governments agree on the general goals for the collaboration but encounter difficulty in dividing and distributing the expected benefits among the group. Large gaps between likely returns and participants' ideal levels may prove fatal to the collaboration. Many of the same factors that increase coordination costs are likely to also increase division problems. For instance, heterogeneity is widely presumed to also be an important factor in the severity of division problems.

Differences in political power, policy preferences, resource levels, and demographic composition are likely factors.[24] Hatley's examination of a case involving a multilateral agreement on fire protection found that differences over how future savings would be shared among the participants were a critical element in the collapse of the effort.[25] Power differences may also depend on the activities on the collaboration. Steinacker argued that cities with the largest population have more power in agreements involving capital-intensive services such as water or sewage treatment systems, but that cooperating cities will be on more equal footing when it comes to their own production costs in the case of labor-intensive services.[26]

RISKS DUE TO DEFECTION COSTS   Defection problems emerge when one party does not comply with the agreement.[27] In essence, each participant must be confident that the others have consistent policy preferences, will maintain the underlying goals and objectives of the agreement, and have a commitment to fulfill their obligations.[28] Once again, heterogeneity among the participants in political power, policy preferences, resource levels, and demographic composition is expected to increase problems from defection.

The contacting literature also identifies two production characteristics of public services as shaping the risk of defection: asset specificity and measurement difficulty. The concept of asset specificity refers to whether specialized investments are needed to deliver the good or service. Theoretically, asset specificity creates significant risks for both buyers and sellers and works against the creation of a competitive market for the service. A service is difficult to measure when neither the outcomes to be achieved nor the activities to be performed in delivering the service are easily identifiable. Measurement difficulty is an obstacle to clearly specified performance expectations in contract language.[29] In this context, potential collaborators may choose to maintain the status quo rather than devote scarce resources to intensively monitor and enforce the intergovernmental agreement in an effort to protect against defection by its partners.

Institutional Mechanisms Used to Support Networks

The potential of specific forms of self-organizing institutions to be used to confront problems stemming from the economic and environmental interconnectedness of metropolitan regions is a topic of extensive research.[30] Feiock lists six institutional mechanisms that may be used to support collaborations among local governments.[31] The institutions differ in terms of the autonomy retained by participants and if decisions affecting the partnership are made bilaterally or multilaterally. Self-organizing institutions that permit substantial autonomy to participants reduce coordination costs, but may also encounter significant costs from problems of division and defection. At the other end of the scale, institutional mechanisms that reduce autonomy can mitigate defection and division costs, but may significantly increase coordination costs. The multilateral institutions identified by Feiock include regional authorities, regional organizations, and collaborative groups and councils. This discussion is limited to the three bilateral institutions discussed by Feiock, including managed networks, contract networks, and policy networks.

MANAGED NETWORKS   Managed networks are cooperative agreements among cities that are designed or coordinated by third parties such as state or federal governments to reduce coordination problems and the potential for defection. In these mechanisms, a higher-level government provides funding and mandates the formation of collaborative relations among local governmental actors. Existing institutions or actors, such as the state, a council of government, or a policy entrepreneur, serve as a broker and assume responsibility for helping to craft an agreement.[32] Shrestha concluded that managed networks can be effective mechanisms for collaborations on services for which transaction costs are relatively low.[33]

CONTRACT NETWORKS   Contract networks links individual units through joint ventures, interjurisdictional agreements, and service contracts that require the consent of those involved. This institutional mechanism links local governments in legally binding agreements, but preserves the autonomy of local actors while also providing a formalized shared service-delivery mechanism.[34] Contract networks provide a self-organizing mechanism for local governments to work collaboratively to resolve service-provision problems. Contracts formalizing service delivery and that clearly outline the responsibilities of partners also entail transaction costs related to monitoring the contract and evaluating the performance of the service provider, but, as Wood contends, such interjurisdictional arrangements require less frequent interaction by the participants and thus involve lower transaction costs.[35] These may prove to be more stable and, ultimately, more permanent arrangements. Andrew contends that interjurisdictional agreements can be an effective way to integrate service production in urban regions.[36] Norms of reciprocity among local government actors are important for the maintenance or establishment of new contract networks because these networks often span functional areas.[37] This multiplexity is important to reducing transaction risk, particularly opportunism, because information about defections is shared relatively easily through the network, and noncompliance in one service contract can affect relationships in other service agreements.[38]

POLICY NETWORKS   The third bilateral institution is policy networks. This mechanism uses informal, self-organized exchange relationships between local governments to encourage trust and reciprocity among the members of the network.[39] Andrew argues that an important feature of a policy network is that participants not only pay attention to a potential partner's characteristics,[40] but also consider the relations of the potential partner within the broader network.[41] The repeated interactions among local government actors help to mitigate the transaction costs of forming a shared service agreement.

Policy networks provide the greatest degree of autonomy in decisions to enter and exit agreements, and this autonomy can affect the risk of sharing services. This flexibility can also increase costs of decisions and may limit the situations where policy networks can be effective. These less formal arrangements may still have relatively high transaction costs due to the attention to bargaining, negotiation, consensus building, and conflict resolution required to initiate and maintain the cooperative effort. Feiock points out that policy networks often "complement and reinforce other mechanisms" by providing important support to the more formal authority structures that facilitate service collaboration.[42] The support that the "administrative conjunctions" described by Frederickson is one example of how policy networks may help to mitigate the risks of collaborating through contract networks, regional organizations, and other institutions identified by Feiock.[43]

ISSUE THREE: BASES FOR PARTNER SELECTION IN COLLABORATIVE NETWORKS

Political fragmentation creates a pool of potential partners, but the existence of many different partners also increases uncertainty, informational asymmetries, and, ultimately, collaboration risks.[44] The empirical network literature has shown that the strategies local governments use to select partners fall into two broad categories: homophily-based and network configurations.

Selection Based on Homopohily among Actors

One way local government officials may reduce the risks involved in collaborative agreements is to partner with similar local governing units, a process known as "homophily."[45] Similarity aids in the establishment of trust,[46] reducing the risk of opportunism, lowering monitoring and enforcement costs, and reducing the time required to negotiate agreements.[47] Risks stemming from the selection of partners have long been a focus of the literature on local government contracting, and many studies suggest risk is reduced when governments choose to collaborate with partners with comparable municipal institutions, resident demographics, institutional roles, levels of education and professional training, and the professional affiliations of administrators and elected officials.[48]

The complexity of organizing the potential partners and coordinating the collaboration is expected to be more difficult when the preferences of potential collaborators diverge. Preference divergence is typically operationalized in the empirical literature as differences in terms of demographic characteristics, resource levels, or municipal institutions.[49] Oakerson emphasizes the importance of the homogeneity of residential preferences for services within cities in reducing coordination costs because public officials are more able to "speak with one voice" for the residents when making governing decisions on their behalf.[50] Several studies have focused on this issue. For example, Bae found that differences in demographic composition across jurisdictions have a negative effect on the formation of intergovernmental agreements among governments in Georgia's metropolitan areas.[51] Similarly, respondents to Hawkins's examination of joint-venture formations reported that a lack of agreement among communities on development goals was a significant barrier for local governments seeking to establish an agreement.[52] Finally, Frederickson's concept of administration conjunction suggests that regions with relatively large numbers of professional administrators will have lower coordination costs because these administrators often share a regional perspective and seek to cooperate on public services where possible.[53]

In a study of regional planning networks, Henry, Lubell, and McCoy found homophily effects for local and federal-level actors, indicating local actors tended to interact with other local actors and federal actors tended to more often interact with other federal actors.[54] However, no such homophily effects were found for state-level actors or nongovernmental organizations operating in the same regional planning networks. Research by Siciliano and Wukich on emergency management network formation found strong homophily effects for both organizational sector (public and nonprofit) as well as organizational scale (city, county, state, and national).[55] Other research on economic development organizations[56] and formal contracts among local government organizations[57] produced mixed results.

Findings from research exploring the role of homophily may be mixed due to differences in motivation for collaboration. Some actors may seek to collaborate to gain legitimacy, others to gain needed resources, and others to simply be more efficient.[58] The distance between actors, which can be viewed as geographic homophily, likely plays an important role as well. Reagans found that physical distance moderates the effect of similarity on the frequency and strength of ties between two actors.[59] Distance may also provide additional opportunities for actors to interact and build trust over time. Research by LeRoux, Brandenburger, and Pandey found that local governments were more likely to form interjurisdictional service agreements if their municipal managers were members of the same regional associations or councils of government.[60]

Selection Based on Network Configuration

The configuration of network relationships also influences partner selection. Local governments involved in collaborative service arrangements are part of a broader network of organizations involved in service-production activities. The structure of these networks can shape the types of risks governments confront. The web of relations among organizations can be relatively simple or highly complex, where local governments form multiple relations with one another across a region.[61] Our understanding of how the creation of interjurisdictional service agreements leads to different forms of network structure is limited, but a literature examining different network configurations and how they affect service cooperation among local governments is emerging.[62] One thing that is clear is that the optimal selection of partners also depends on the goods and services involved in the collaboration.

There are many potential network structures that may have implications for the level of transaction costs' association with collaboration, and therefore the structure of the network can strongly influence decisions on with whom to collaborate. The two general types of configurations that have received the most attention in the literature are those associated with "bonding" and "bridging." Bonding and bridging structures vary in the level of connectivity among a set of actors. Bonding structures are dense and characterized by numerous ties connecting actors with each other. Bridging structures, on the other hand, have few ties, resulting in many actors that are not directly connected to one another.

Andrew depicts these two structures as strategic alliances that governments can join when needed. He argues that bridging structures help local governments to reduce risks in collaborative arrangements for services characterized by high asset specificity. Highly asset-specific services are those that are difficult to adapt to other uses, and therefore only a few vendors will likely be willing to provide the service in the local market. Sellers of these services make specialized investments and cannot easily use them to provide other services. Andrew predicts the risks associated with asset-specific problems will lead local governments to enter into service agreements with only a few "high-status" actors: "Establishing contracts with central actors is important for local governments to reduce the costs of crafting and monitoring multiple agreements with other localities independently."[63]

Counties are well positioned to be the central actor in bridging networks among local governments. These sparse networks permit localities with different interests and resources to negotiate in ways that maximize their control over transactions. This type of "bridging" network may allow cities not only to discover a broader set of possible gains from establishing shared service agreements with others inside and outside the region, but also the opportunity to reap the advantage of innovation or visions that are not available within a highly clustered network.[64] Thus, a sparse network structure may provide information advantages and reduce coordination problems across jurisdictions.

A second form of strategic alliance, bonding, occurs when local governments enter into agreements with partners of their current partners to mitigate credible commitment problems. Andrew argues that dense network relationships reduce risks of uncertainty in collaboration on service production, thereby creating social capital.[65] These bonding structures reduce uncertainty by improving the amount and quality of information about the actors in the network and increase the confidence the participants have in the others.[66] This close-knit structure can be particularly useful for collaborations on services with high measurement costs and for confronting policy problems characterized by complex tasks and significant uncertainty over expected outcomes. A highly clustered network reduces the cost of enforcing an agreed set of working rules because any actions taken or not taken by a recipient are easily shared with others in the network. Any threat of collective sanction among the participants in a shared service agreement will enhance the credibility of punishments being imposed. Given this, participation in this kind of structure may signal to the other partners that the local government is willing to take their interests into account.[67]

A related strategy local governments can use to reduce risks in service collaborations is to take part in "multiplex" service-production arrangements.[68] Multiplex relations occur when local governments engage with other units in multiple shared service arrangements simultaneously. In some cases, shared service delivery reflects cooperative arrangements where there are multiple agreements between various city departments between two cities. Multiple service contracts that link more than one service can reduce credible commitment problems and minimize the potential for defection. For example, a city may have a police service contract with a neighboring city in the region, as well as shared service contracts with that same city for fire or emergency medical services. Shrestha and Feiock suggest, "The risks involving contractual arrangements in one service area can be mitigated if these contracts are embedded in broader multiplex service relationships."[69] Multiplexity is important for making decisions in shared service-delivery arrangements because it may signify more trust and, therefore, influence future exchanges and the maintenance or expansion of existing shared service-delivery arrangements. Thus, partner selection in a given service area may be somewhat dependent on prior partnering decisions in other service areas.

We know less about the role that other potential motivations for choosing partners, such as competence and common objectives, play. Collaboration does not occur unless the costs of coordination are overcome, and alignment on these motivations is expected to reduce coordination costs.[70] This aspect of partner selections is understudied but important in light of research by findings reported by Aldag and Warner that cost efficiencies may not provide a sufficient basis to sustain intergovernmental collaborations over time.[71] They reported that their analysis showed that agreement with objectives focused on service-quality improvement lasted longer than those where costs savings were a major objective.

ISSUE FOUR: MEASURING SUCCESS IN NETWORKS

While scholars and practitioners argue for the potential of networks to improve service delivery and address complex policy problems, the evidence of the effectiveness of networks is surprisingly scarce.[72] Analysis of performance in the public sector, even for a single bureaucracy, is a challenge. The goals of a policy or agency often lack clear definition and defy easy measurement.[73] Public organizations also serve a range of stakeholders and constituents who may hold diverse opinions on the appropriate outcomes of a given government program. The inherent challenges of evaluating performance in the public sector become even more pronounced when working within networks. Despite these challenges, a number of scholars have explored the concept of performance in networks.

Measuring Performance in Networks

Networks are multilevel arrangements. As such, measures of performance exist at three distinct levels (see figure 1): the community served by the network, the network itself, and the individual members of the network. "These levels are of concern to three broad categories of network constituents: principals, who monitor and fund the network and its activities; agents, who work in the network both as administrators and service-level professionals; and clients, who actually receive the services provided by the network."[74]

At the highest level, the community served by the network plays an important role in shaping and defining the appropriate outcome measures. Networks often arise to address problems that cross jurisdictional boundaries, giving rise to collaborative arrangements that include actors from a range of municipalities and levels of government.[75] These networks are often tasked with addressing problems associated with public health,[76] crime,[77] economic development,[78] and other policy issues that confront a community or larger region. Reflecting the stakeholders at this level, evaluating performance at the community level entails assessing the public's perception of progress, the overall cost to the community, and aggregate indicators of client well-

Figure 1. Levels of network performance.

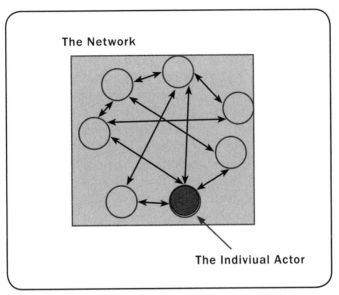

Redrawn from P. Kenis and K. G. Provan, "Towards an Exogenous Theory of Public Network," *Public Administration* 87, no. 3 (2009): 446.

being.[79] For example, in their study of the impact of interagency collaboration networks designed to reduce crime and disorder, Kelman and colleagues measured performance based on changes in the overall crime rate in the communities served by the network.[80]

In addition to considering the broader outcomes for the community and clients served, the network exists as its own functioning entity suitable for evaluation. For networks to be effective in addressing community problems, the network itself must function efficiently and effectively. Evaluating performance at the network level focuses either on the participatory processes that characterize the network or on the direct outputs and outcomes of those processes. Carr, Blöschl, and Loucks provide a list of procedural measures associated with collaborative governance and include accountable discourse, dialogue that supports ideological differences, variety of knowledge sources included in decision making, consensual decision making, and the clarity of the rules and tasks that govern the network.[81] When such desirable participatory processes are in place, networks are more likely to be effective and produce relevant outputs and outcomes.[82] Provan and Milward identify several relevant measures of network effectiveness, including the attraction of new members, retention of existing members, range of services provided, and the strength of relationships among the members.[83]

Last, organizations and local governments enter into collaborative arrangements seeking some direct benefit. These benefits may come in the form of reduced costs, increased resources, greater legitimacy, and better outcomes for their own clients.[84] A related line of research has explored the networking activity of the leaders of organizations. This work demonstrates that leader networking and the establishment of professional relationships with external stakeholders shape organizational performance.[85]

Factors Related to Network Performance

Assuming a local government or organization has chosen to engage in collaborative governance, what variables are associated with the success of the network? There are a range of factors that may influence the potential for networks to perform, grouped into three categories: form of governance, structure and composition of the network, and network management practices and collaborative processes.

FORM OF GOVERNANCE   While networks are often viewed as a distinct form of governance (compared to hierarchies and markets), networks are not monolithic and can be classified into distinct structural forms. Provan and Kenis classified networks into three forms: shared governance, lead organization, and network administrative organization (NAO).[86] These forms of network governance vary along two dimensions. First, networks can be positioned between those that are centered around a single organization that brokers the communication and interaction among the members of a network and those where all organizations share equally in governance and overall connectivity. Second, for those networks that are brokered, the central actor can be a participant of the network or a third-party actor brought in specifically to lead the collaboration. These distinctions are depicted in figure 2.

Based on these varying forms of governance, Provan and Kenis developed a set of theoretical rationales for why certain forms of governance may be more effective than others in producing policy outcomes. These include the level of trust and goal consensus in the networks. Provan and Kenis argue that the level of trust in a network should be reflected in its form of governance.[87] If trust is low, such that few organizations trust one another, shared governance will be limited in its effectiveness, as there is little foundation on

Figure 2. Forms of network governance.

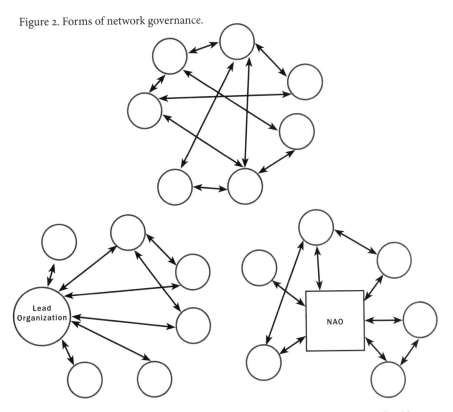

Redrawn from P. Kenis and K. G. Provan, "Towards an Exogenous Theory of Public Network," *Public Administration* 87, no. 3 (2009): 446.

which to build collaboration. Therefore, shared governance structures are most effective when trust is widely distributed among the network members. To be effective when trust is lacking, networks need to be centralized and brokered by a primary actor, whether a lead organization or an NAO. In these brokered networks, trust does not need to be distributed across the members of the network but rather distributed only dyadically between the central organization and each of the other members. Klijn and Koppenjan suggest that institutional design strategies can also be used to enhance trust when it is lacking.[88] Network management strategies, regardless of form of governance, can aim to establish clear rules and standards of action along with specific conflict-management resolutions. These design decisions allow network members to set appropriate expectations for action and recourse and allow actors to engage others with greater certainty and trust.

As noted above, one of the challenges of operating within and measuring the performance of a network is the lack of goal consensus. At the community level, goal consensus concerns the broad objectives of the network. At the network level, consensus focuses more on procedural and network management aspects, such as whether new funding sources should be sought or whether new members should be brought into the network. When goal consensus is relatively low, shared governance forms may not be effective, as it becomes difficult for actors to identify mutual objectives and common tasks. Milward and Provan argue that the joint production of services can lead to "substantial problems regarding resource sharing, political turf battles, regulatory differences, and the like."[89] Indeed, if goal consensus is completely absent, networks may not be an effective form of organization at all. At intermediate levels, lead organizations or NAOs are likely to be more effective. These broker organizations bear responsibility for most strategic and operational decisions and therefore are well positioned to integrate diverse ideas and achieve some level of agreement in order to pursue collective action.

NETWORK STRUCTURE AND COMPOSITION   In addition to the form of governance established to manage a network, the structure and size of the network also influence performance. A straightforward and important dimension of network structure is density. Network density is the ratio of the number of ties present in a network versus the number of possible ties. Ties between organizations can range from formal agreements to informal communication. Some networks may be highly interconnected or densely structured, allowing for information to flow quickly to all members of the network. These networks, termed "closed networks," are often characterized by bonding structures, where actors cluster into tightly connected groups. Several scholars have argued that closed networks help establish trust and set norms of expected behavior.[90] However, closed networks have two limitations. First, the networks can be costly to maintain, as each tie requires time and energy to sustain. Second, closed networks often contain redundant information; because actors are tightly connected with one another, they share similar information and resources.[91]

Given these limitations, open networks, which are less densely structured, are often seen as facilitators of innovation and new ideas.[92] Less dense structures are often full of what Ron Burt terms "structural holes": a gap in the network structure that creates opportunity for actors to bridge disconnected parts of the network. These bridging structures, which provide opportunity to reach out to others with distinct information and ideas, have been shown to produce higher-quality and innovative outcomes.[93]

Likely, the optimal structure of the network, and appropriate level of bonding and bridging, depends on the particular tasks networks are charged with and the level of inherent risk. For less risky forms of collaboration, often referred to as coordination problems, networks can perform effectively if they are less densely structured and more centralized around a key actor who functions as an information broker and primary coordinator. Risk increases when several actors must cooperate and provide resources to address a common problem. Actors involved in more risky collaboration problems may free ride or defect from their obligations, leaving the other network members to provide the needed resources and effort. Closed networks can reduce free riding, as the actions of others are more easily observable and sanctioned by the group.[94] In other words, the advantage of closed networks is in reducing the risk of cooperation, while the advantage of open networks is in increasing the returns that may come from cooperation. Research suggests that both the efficiency and innovation of open networks and the trust and risk reduction that come with closed networks may be needed simultaneously.[95] Yi explored how bridging and bonding patterns in state-level clean-energy governance networks affected green-job growth and renewable-energy capacity. He found that both bridging and bonding had a positive and significant correlation with clean-energy outcomes.[96]

Network size can also influence the performance of networks, but primarily through the effect of size on governance. While larger networks offer the potential for greater resources and political power, they are also more difficult to manage. In smaller networks, members can interact face-to-face and deal with potential problems directly. As the number of network participants increases, so does the complexity of governance. Provan and Kenis argue that while shared governance is often desired by network members, such approaches become highly inefficient as the number of actors grow, and therefore brokered networks become a likely solution.[97]

NETWORK MANAGEMENT AND PROCESSES   Networks, regardless of the form and structure, need to be managed. Agranoff and McGuire argue, "Increasingly, the capacities required to operate successfully in network settings are different from the capacities needed to succeed at managing a single organization."[98] In particular, the traditional hierarchical, command-and-control-style models are unavailable in networks that rely on shared power and decision making.[99] Research suggests that how networks are managed and the processes that define organizational interaction impact overall performance.[100] A key question addressed in the network literature concerns whether leadership behaviors and management strategies needed for high performance in networks differ from those needed for success in single agencies.[101] In their study of county-level emergency managers, Silvia and McGuire classified leadership behaviors into three types: people oriented, task oriented, and organization oriented.[102] They found that leadership behaviors differed between network and single-agency settings. Managers, when operating within their own organizations, tended to focus on task-oriented behaviors (for example, keeping work moving, assigning tasks, scheduling work, setting expectations). But when the same managers operated within the broader emergency management network, their leadership behaviors switched to more relationship-oriented (treating all as equals, freely sharing information, creating trust) and organization-oriented behaviors (identifying resources, establishing a shared vision, identifying stakeholders). In a related study, McGuire and Silvia examined the effect of leadership behavior on perceptions of the performance of emergency management networks.[103] They found that behaviors emphasizing the management of external stakeholders and those that focused on strengthening internal relationships among the network members were correlated with positive performance. Thus, network leaders need to manage both outward and inward when attempting to effectively operate within networks. Kelman and colleagues examined management practices within networks designed to reduce crime.[104] They found that reductions in crime are associated with specific management practices, including the building of trust among network partners and the implementation of performance measures to monitor progress.

Moving from individual leadership practices within networks to the dynamic interactions among the organizations that constitute the networks, two of the major models of collaborative governance stress the importance of deliberative processes. Ansell and Gash highlight five main features that they collectively bundle under the term "collaborative processes": face-to-face dialogue and good-faith negotiation, trust building, commitment to the process by way of shared understanding of interdependence and shared ownership of the process, shared understanding of the mission through identifying common values and developing shared definitions of the problem, and establishing intermediate outcomes through "small wins," such as the formulation of strategic plans and joint fact-finding.[105] Similarly, Emerson and Nabatchi identify three key collaborative dynamics: principled engagement, shared motivation, and joint capacity for action.[106] Empirical research testing these collaborative dynamics demonstrates that face-to-face interaction, developing a common-problem understanding, and awareness of other network actors are all processes associated with network benefits.[107]

Overall, networks can be structured and lead in a variety of ways. Network managers and participants need to consider the existing level of trust and goal consensus when designing the institutions and processes that will govern network interactions. We agree with Kenis and Provan, who state, "Many networks simply lack the functionality to produce certain types of outcomes. This is a matter of design."[108]

CONCLUSION

Political authority in America's major metropolitan areas is highly fragmented. Fragmentation is often criticized as promoting competition among local governments for citizens and resources, encouraging duplication of services, and creating a mismatch between the scale of public problems and local political authority. For states dealing with sustained fiscal stress, political consolidation appears to present a solution. However, the political and legal obstacles to large-scale political consolidation severely undercut the effectiveness of this strategy. The creation of interjurisdictional agreements may represent a more feasible strategy for seeking efficiencies and improvements in effectiveness of local public services. Indeed, the widespread creation of self-organized networks of local governments collaborating on public services is the major structural change to the American local government landscape in recent decades. However, these self-organized networks may be less likely to include the local governments with the most serious financial challenges. If so, these networks may not effectively confront the important resource challenges facing state and local governments often highlighted by advocates of political consolidation.

This is a critical question for state and local policy makers across the United States. These self-organized networks vary considerably in their formality, size, and structure, but much of what we know about networks and their potential for success remains uncertain. Provan and Milward note, "Evaluating network effectiveness is critical for understanding whether networks—and the network form of organizing—are effective in delivering needed services to community members. Evaluation of network effectiveness is especially important for those who formulate public policy at the local, state, and national levels, so that scarce public funding can be allocated to service-delivery mechanisms that are utilizing resources efficiently while adequately serving public needs."[109]

The current empirical literature on the formation, structure, and effectiveness of intergovernmental service agreement networks may best be characterized by its ambiguity and is currently able to provide guidance to policy makers. The mixed empirical findings may be a result of the different risks perceived by local governments as they enter into collaborative relationships and the different goals that actors may seek. More research is needed to help practitioners identify and measure the costs and benefits associated with a given collaboration and the appropriate institutions to best manage risk in hopes of producing positive outcomes for their citizens.

Notes

1. J. B. Carr, "Perspectives on City-County Consolidation and Its Alternatives," in *City-County Consolidation and Its Alternatives*, ed. Jered B. Carr and Richard Feiock (Armonk, NY: M. E. Sharpe, 2004), 3–24.

2. For example, J. B. Carr, E. Gerber, and E. Lupher, "Local Fiscal Capacity and Intergovernmental Contracting: Horizontal and Vertical Cooperation in Michigan," in *Sustaining Michigan: Metropolitan Policies and Strategies*, ed. R. Jelier, S. Adelaja, and G. Sands (East Lansing: Michigan State University Press, 2009), 207–35; Illinois Task Force on Local Government Consolidation and Unfunded Mandates, *Delivering Efficient, Effective, and Streamlined Government to Illinois Taxpayers* (n.p.: State of Illinois, 2015).

3. Lawrence C. Martin, Richard Levey, and Jenna Cawley, "The 'New Normal' for Local Government," *State and Local Government Review* 44, no. 1S (2012): 17S–28S; Richard C. Elling, Kelly Krawczyk, and Jered Carr, "What Should We Do? Public Attitudes about How Local Government Officials Should Confront Fiscal Stress," *Local Government Studies* 40, no. 3 (2013): 380–402.

4. William Hatley, "The Art of Collaboration: Interlocal Collaboration in the Provision of Fire Services in the Detroit Area" (PhD diss., Wayne State University, 2010); Editorial Board, "Illinois, the Government State: How Property Taxes Prop Up Redundant and Useless Bureaucracies," *Chicago Tribune*, January 6, 2016.

5. Richard C. Feiock and Jered B. Carr, "Incentives, Entrepreneurs, and Boundary Change: A Collective Action Framework," *Urban Affairs Review* 36, no. 3 (2001): 382–405; Jered B. Carr and Richard C. Feiock, "Who Becomes Involved in City-County Consolidation? Findings from County Officials in 25 Communities," *State and Local Government Review* 34, no. 2 (2002): 78–95; Carr, "Perspectives on City-County Consolidation."

6. Carr and Feiock, "Who Becomes Involved in City-County Consolidation?"

7. Carr, "City-County Consolidation and Its Alternatives"; Feiock and Carr, "Incentives, Entrepreneurs, and Boundary Change."

8. Feiock and Carr, "Incentives, Entrepreneurs, and Boundary Change."

9. H. George Frederickson, "The Repositioning of American Public Administration," *PS: Political Science and Politics*, no. 32 (1999): 701–11.

10. Austin Aldag and Mildred Warner, "Cooperation, Not Cost Savings: Explaining Duration of Shared Service Agreements," *Local Government Studies* 44, no. 3 (2018): 350–70.

11. Trevor L. Brown and Matthew Potoski, "Transaction Costs and Institutional Explanations for Government Service Production Decisions," *Journal of Public Administration Research and Theory* 13, no. 4 (2003): 441–68; Amir Hefetz and Mildred Warner, "Privatization and Its Reverse: Explaining the Dynamics of the Government Contracting Process," *Journal of Public Administration Research and Theory* 14, no. 2 (2004): 171–90; Jered B. Carr, Kelly LeRoux, and Manoj Shrestha, "Institutional Ties, Transaction Costs, and External Service Production," *Urban Affairs Review* 44, no. 3 (2009): 403–27; Sung-Wook Kwon and Richard C. Feiock, "Overcoming the Barriers to Cooperation: Intergovernmental Service Agreements," *Public Administration Review* 70, no. 6 (2010): 876–84; Manoj K. Shrestha and Richard C. Feiock, "Transaction Cost, Exchange Embeddedness, and Interlocal Cooperation in Local Public Good Supply," *Political Research Quarterly* 64, no. 3 (2011); Amir Hefetz and Mildred Warner, "Contracting or Public Delivery? The Importance of Service, Market and Management Characteristics," *Journal of Public Administration Research and Theory* 22, no. 2 (2012): 289–317; Germà Bel and Mildred E. Warner, "Factors Explaining Inter-municipal Cooperation in Service Delivery: A Meta-regression Analysis," *Journal of Economic Policy Reform* 19, no. 2 (2016): 91–115, doi:10.1080/17 487870.2015.11000842016.

12. Samuel Nunn and Mark S. Rosentraub, "Dimensions of Interjurisdictional Cooperation," *Journal of the American Planning Association* 63, no. 2 (1997): 205–19; W. Hatley, R. Elling, and J. Carr, "Toward Interlocal Collaboration: Lessons from a Failed Attempt to Create a Fire Authority," in *Municipal Shared Services and Consolidation: A Public Solutions Handbook*, ed. A. Henderson (Armonk, NY: M. E. Sharpe, 2014).

13. Bel and Warner, "Factors Explaining Inter-municipal Cooperation in Service Delivery."

14. S. A. Andrew, "Recent Developments in the Study of Interjurisdictional Agreements: An Overview and Assessment," *State and Local Government Review* 41, no. 2 (2009): 133–42.

15. Bel and Warner, "Factors Explaining Inter-municipal Cooperation in Service Delivery."

16. Y.-C. Chen and K. Thurmaier, "Interlocal Agreements as Collaborations: An Empirical Investigation of Impetuses, Norms, and Success," *American Review of Public Administration* 39, no. 5 (2009): 536–52.

17. Hatley, "Art of Collaboration"; Hatley, Elling, and Carr, "Toward Interlocal Collaboration."

18. Hatley, "Art of Collaboration."

19. Jered B. Carr, Michael D. Siciliano, and Victor Hugg, "Understanding Local Government Service Delivery Networks: Initial Findings and a Research Agenda," annual meeting of the Urban Affairs Association, April 4–7, 2018, Toronto.

20. B. L. Lewis, J. Boulahanis, and E. Matheny, "Joined-Up Governance: Mandated Collaboration in US Homeless Services," *International Journal of Public Sector Management* 22, no. 5 (2009): 392–99, doi:10.1108/09513550910972473.

21. S. Kelman, S. Hong, and I. Turbitt, "Are There Managerial Practices Associated with the Outcomes of an Interagency Service Delivery Collaboration? Evidence from British Crime and Disorder Reduction Partnerships," *Journal of Public Administration Research and Theory* 23, no. 3 (2013): 609–30, doi:10.1093/jopart/mus038.

22. Christopher V. Hawkins, "Prospects for and Barriers to Local Government Joint Ventures," *State and Local Government Review* 41, no. 2 (2009): 108–19.

23. Hatley, "Art of Collaboration."

24. Hawkins, "Local Government Joint Ventures"; Annette Steinacker, "Game Theoretic Models of Metropolitan Cooperation," in *Metropolitan Governance: Conflict, Competition, and Cooperation*, ed. Richard Feiock (Washington, DC: Georgetown University Press, 2004), 46–66; Annette Steinacker, "The Institutional Collective Action Perspective on Self-Organizing Mechanisms: Market Failures and Transaction Cost Problems," in *Self-Organizing Federalism: Collaborative Mechanisms to Mitigate Institutional Collective Action*, ed. Richard C. Feiock and John T. Scholz (Cambridge: Cambridge University Press, 2010), 51–72.

25. Hatley, "Art of Collaboration."

26. Steinacker, "Game Theoretic Models of Metropolitan Cooperation."

27. Hawkins, "Local Government Joint Ventures."

28. Hatley, "Art of Collaboration"; Christopher V. Hawkins, "Competition and Cooperation: Local Government Joint Ventures for Economic Development," *Journal of Urban Affairs* 32, no. 2 (2010): 253–75, doi:10.1111/j.1467-9906.2009.00492.x.

29. Carr, LeRoux, and Shrestha, "Institutional Ties."

30. See especially Feiock and Scholz, *Self-Organizing Federalism*; R. C. Feiock, "The Institutional Collective Action Framework," *Policy Studies Journal* 41, no. 3 (2013): 397–425, doi:10.1111/psj.12023.

31. R. C. Feiock, "Metropolitan Governance and Institutional Collective Action," *Urban Affairs Review* 44, no. 3 (2009): 356–77, doi:10.1177/1078087408324000.

32. C. Wood, "Scope and Patterns of Metropolitan Governance in Urban America: Probing the Complexities in the Kansas City Region," *American Review of Public Administration* 36, no. 3 (2006): 337–53, doi:10.1177/0275074005284071.

33. M. K. Shrestha, "Profile of Services Alter Contractual Patterns? A Comparison across Multiple Metropolitan Services," in *Self-Organizing Federalism*, ed. Feiock and Scholz, 114–41.

34. Feiock, "Metropolitan Governance."

35. Wood, "Scope and Patterns of Metropolitan Governance."

36. S. A. Andrew, "Regional Integration through Contracting Networks: An Empirical Analysis of Institutional Collection Action Framework," *Urban Affairs Review* 44, no. 3 (2009): 378–402, doi:10.1177/1078087408323941.

37. M. K. Shrestha and R. C. Feiock, "Governing U.S. Metropolitan Areas: Self-Organizing and Multiplex Service Networks," *American Politics Research* 37, no. 5 (2009): 801–23, doi:10.1177/1532673X09337466; S. A. Andrew, "Adaptive versus Restrictive Contracts: Can They Resolve Different Risk Problems?," in *Self-Organizing Federalism*, ed. Feiock and Scholz, 91–113.

38. Andrew, "Adaptive versus Restrictive Contracts."

39. Andrew, "Regional Integration through Contracting Networks"; Andrew, "Adaptive versus Restrictive Contracts"; Shrestha, "Profile of Services Alter Contractual Patterns?"

40. Andrew, "Adaptive versus Restrictive Contracts."

41. S. A. Andrew and J. B. Carr, "Mitigating Uncertainty and Risk in Planning for Regional Preparedness: The Role of Bonding and Bridging Relationships," *Urban Studies* 50, no. 4 (2013): 709–24, doi:10.1177/0042098012455718.

42. Feiock, "Metropolitan Governance," 365.

43. Frederickson, "Repositioning of American Public Administration."

44. Jered B. Carr, Christopher Hawkins, and Drew Westberg, "An Exploration of Collaboration Risk in Joint Ventures: Perceptions of Risk by Local Economic Development Officials," *Economic Development Quarterly* 31, no. 3 (2017): 210–27.

45. Andrew, "Regional Integration through Contracting Networks"; S. A. Andrew and C. V. Hawkins, "Regional Cooperation and Multilateral Agreements in the Provision of Public Safety," *American Review of Public Administration* 43, no. 4 (2013): 460–75, doi:10.1177/0275074012447676201 3.

46. D. J. Brass, "A Social Network Perspective on Human Resources Management," *Research in Personnel and Human Resources Management* 13, no. 1 (1995): 39–79.

47. Christopher V. Hawkins and Jered B. Carr, "The Costs of Services Cooperation: A Review of the Literature," in *Municipal Shared Services*, ed. Henderson.

48. See especially Feiock, "Institutional Collective Action Framework"; Frederickson, "Repositioning of American Public Administration"; Hawkins and Carr, "Costs of Services Cooperation"; and Kelly LeRoux and Jered B. Carr, "Prospects for Centralizing Services in an Urban County: Evidence from Self-Organized Networks of Eight Local Public Services," *Journal of Urban Affairs* 32, no. 4 (2010): 449–70.

49. J. B. Carr and C. V. Hawkins, "The Costs of Cooperation: What the Research Tells Us about Managing the Risks of Service Collaborations in the U.S.," *State and Local Government Review* 224 (2013): 239.

50. Ronald J. Oakerson, "The Study of Metropolitan Governance," in *Metropolitan Governance*, ed. Feiock, 17–45.

51. Jungah Bae, "Institutional Choices for Local Service Contracting and Collaboration," *International Review of Public Administration* 14, no. 1 (2009): 27–42.

52. Hawkins, "Local Government Joint Ventures."

53. Frederickson, "Repositioning of American Public Administration."

54. A. D. Henry, M. Lubell, and M. McCoy, "Belief Systems and Social Capital as Drivers of Policy Network Structure: The Case of California Regional Planning," *Journal of Public Administration Research and Theory* 21, no. 3 (2011): 419–44, doi:10.1093/jopart/muq042.

55. M. D. Siciliano and C. Wukich, "Network Features and Processes as Determinants of Organizational Interaction during Extreme Events," *Complexity, Governance and Networks* 2, no. 1 (2015): 23–44.

56. Y. Lee, I. W. Lee, and R. C. Feiock, "Interorganizational Collaboration Networks in Economic Development Policy: An Exponential Random Graph Model Analysis," *Policy Studies Journal* 40, no. 3 (2012): 547–73, doi:10.1111/j.1541-0072.2012.00464.x.

57. Andrew, "Adaptive versus Restrictive Contracts."

58. Andrew, "Adaptive versus Restrictive Contracts."

59. R. Reagans, "Close Encounters: Analyzing How Social Similarity and Propinquity Contribute to Strong Network Connections," *Organization Science* 22, no. 4 (2011): 835–49, doi:10.1287/orsc.1100.0587.

60. K. LeRoux, P. W. Brandenburger, and S. K. Pandey, "Interlocal Service Cooperation in U.S. Cities: A Social Network Explanation," *Public Administration Review* 70, no. 2 (2010): 268–78, doi:10.1111/j.1540-6210.2010.02133.x.

61. Shrestha, "Profile of Services Alter Contractual Patterns?"

62. Carr, Siciliano, and Hugg, "Understanding Local Government Service Delivery Networks."

63. Andrew, "Regional Integration through Contracting Networks," 385.

64. Andrew and Carr, "Mitigating Uncertainty and Risk."

65. Andrew, "Adaptive versus Restrictive Contracts."

66. Andrew and Carr, "Mitigating Uncertainty and Risk."

67. Andrew, "Adaptive versus Restrictive Contracts."

68. Shrestha and Feiock, "Governing U.S. Metropolitan Areas"; Carr, Siciliano, and Hugg, "Understanding Local Government Service Delivery Networks."

69. Shrestha and Feiock, "Governing U.S. Metropolitan Areas," 806.

70. Carr and Hawkins, "Costs of Cooperation."

71. Aldag and Warner, "Cooperation, Not Cost Savings."

72. N. Kapucu, Q. Hu, and S. Khosa, "The State of Network Research in Public Administration," *Administration and Society* 49, no. 8 (2014): 1087–1120, doi:10.1177/0095399714555752; T. M. Koontz and C. W. Thomas, "What Do We Know and Need to Know about the Environmental Outcomes of Collaborative Management?," *Public Administration Review* 66, no. s1 (2006): 111–21, doi:10.1111/j.1540-6210.2006.00671.x; R. O'Leary and L. B. Bingham, *The Collaborative Public Manager: New Ideas for the Twenty-First Century* (Washington, DC: Georgetown University Press, 2009).

73. W. N. Dunn, *Public Policy Analysis: An Introduction*, 5th ed. (Boston: Pearson, 2012).

74. K. G. Provan and B. H. Milward, "Do Networks Really Work? A Framework for Evaluating Public-Sector Organizational Networks," *Public Administration Review* 61, no. 4 (2001): 416, doi:10.1111/0033-3352.00045.

75. Feiock, "Metropolitan Governance."

76. K. G. Provan and B. H. Milward, "A Preliminary Theory of Interorganizational Network Effectiveness: A Comparative Study of Four Community Mental Health Systems," *Administrative Science Quarterly* 40, no. 1 (1995): 1–33.

77. Kelman, Hong, and Turbitt, "Outcomes of an Interagency Service Delivery Collaboration."

78. R. C. Feiock, A. Steinacker, and H. J. Park, "Institutional Collective Action and Economic Development Joint Ventures," *Public Administration Review* 69, no. 2 (2009): 256–70, doi:10.1111/j.1540-6210.2008.01972.x.

79. Provan and Milward, "Do Networks Really Work?"

80. Kelman, Hong, and Turbitt, "Outcomes of an Interagency Service Delivery Collaboration."

81. G. Carr, G. Blöschl, and D. P. Loucks, "Evaluating Participation in Water Resource Management: A Review," *Water Resources Research* 48, no. 11 (2012), doi:doi:10.1029/2011WR011662.

82. C. Ansell and A. Gash, "Collaborative Governance in Theory and Practice," *Journal of Public Administration Research and Theory* 18, no. 4 (2008): 543–71, doi:10.1093/jopart/mum032; K. Emerson and T. Nabatchi, *Collaborative Governance Regimes* (Washington, DC: Georgetown University Press, 2015).

83. Provan and Milward, "Do Networks Really Work?"

84. Provan and Milward, "Do Networks Really Work?"

85. K. J. Meier and L. J. O'Toole Jr., "Managerial Strategies and Behavior in Networks: A Model with Evidence from U.S. Public Education," *Journal of Public Administration Research and Theory* 11, no. 3 (2001): 271–94: K. J. Meier and L. J. O'Toole Jr., "Public Management and Educational Performance: The Impact of Managerial Networking," *Public Administration Review* 63, no. 6 (2003): 689–99, doi:10.1111/1540-6210.00332.

86. K. G. Provan and P. Kenis, "Modes of Network Governance: Structure, Management, and Effectiveness," *Journal of Public Administration Research and Theory* 18, no. 2 (2008): 229–52.

87. Provan and Kenis, "Modes of Network Governance."

88. Klijn and Koppenjan, *Governance Networks*, 201.

89. Provan and Milward, "Do Networks Really Work?," 415.

90. P. Bourdieu, "The Forms of Capital," in *Handbook of Theory and Research for the Sociology of Education*, ed. J. G. Richardson (Westport, CT: Greenwood Press, 1986), 241–58; R. D. Putnam, *Bowling Alone: The Collapse and Revival of American Community* (New York: Simon and Schuster, 2000).

91. R. S. Burt, *Structural Holes: The Social Structure of Competition* (Cambridge, MA: Harvard University Press, 1992); R. S. Burt, "The Network Structure of Social Capital," *Research in Organizational Behavior* 22 (2000): 345–423.

92. R. S. Burt, "Structural Holes and Good Ideas," *American Journal of Sociology* 110, no. 2 (2004): 349–99, doi:10.1086/421787.

93. Burt, "Structural Holes and Good Ideas"; M. D. Siciliano, E. W. Welch, and M. K. Feeney, "Network Exploration and Exploitation: Professional Network Churn and Scientific Production," *Social Networks* 52 (2018): 167–79, doi:https://doi.org/10.1016/j.socnet.2017.07.003.

94. R. Berardo and J. T. Scholz, "Self-Organizing Policy Networks: Risk, Partner Selection, and Cooperation in Estuaries," *American Journal of Political Science* 54, no. 3 (2010): 632–49, doi:10.1111/j.1540-5907.2010.00451.x 2010; M. Lubell, "Familiarity Breeds Trust: Collective Action in a Policy Domain," *Journal of Politics* 69, no. 1 (2007): 237–50, doi:10.1111/j.1468-2508.2007.00507.x.

95. R. S. Burt, *Brokerage and Closure: An Introduction to Social Capital* (Oxford: Oxford University Press, 2005).

96. H. Yi, "Network Structure and Governance Performance: What Makes a Difference?," *Public Administration Review* 78, no. 2 (2018): 195–205, doi:10.1111/puar.12886.

97. Provan and Kenis, "Modes of Network Governance."

98. R. Agranoff and M. McGuire, "Big Questions in Public Network Management Research," *Journal of Public Administration Research and Theory* 11, no. 3 (2001): 296.

99. C. Koliba, J. W. Meek, and A. Zia, *Governance Networks in Public Administration and Public Policy* (Boca Raton, FL: CRC Press, 2011).

100. Emerson and Nabatchi, *Collaborative Governance Regimes;* M. McGuire and C. Silvia, "Does Leadership in Networks Matter?," *Public Performance and Management Review* 33, no. 1 (2009): 34–62, doi:10.2753/PMR1530-9576330102.

101. C. Silvia and M. McGuire, "Leading Public Sector Networks: An Empirical Examination of Integrative Leadership Behaviors," *Leadership Quarterly* 21, no. 2 (2010): 264–77, doi:http://dx.doi.org/10.1016/j.leaqua.2010.01.006.

102. Silvia and McGuire, "Leading Public Sector Networks."

103. McGuire and Silvia, "Does Leadership in Networks Matter?"

104. Kelman, Hong, and Turbitt, "Outcomes of an Interagency Service Delivery Collaboration."

105. Ansell and Gash, "Collaborative Governance."

106. Emerson and Nabatchi, *Collaborative Governance Regimes.*

107. T. A. Scott and C. W. Thomas, "Winners and Losers in the Ecology of Games: Network Position, Connectivity, and the Benefits of Collaborative Governance Regimes," *Journal of Public Administration Research and Theory* 27, no. 4 (2017): 647–60.

108. P. Kenis and K. G. Provan, "Towards an Exogenous Theory of Public Network," *Public Administration* 87, no. 3 (2009): 446.

109. Provan and Milward, "Do Networks Really Work?," 414–15.

When Public Pension Reforms Fail or Appear to Be Impossible

Are Unbalanced Budgets, Deficits, and Government Collapse the Only Answer?

JAMES E. SPIOTTO

A number of state and local governments in the United States confront the problem of underfunded public pensions. In the past, numerous public employers in the United States have agreed to pension benefits that now appear challenging to afford, given current revenues and the increased cost of providing governmental services. Further, this challenge has been exacerbated by past failures to set aside sufficient moneys to meet the pension benefit obligations incurred to date. All of this is occurring on the heels of the Great Recession of 2007, followed by an anemic recovery, and at a time when many state and local governments face an aging infrastructure that must be attended to and increased demands for basic public services (sanitation, water, streets, schools, food inspection, fire department, police, ambulance, health, and transportation) that must be met. Because the public pension underfunding problem pits the requirement of meeting pension obligations against the need to provide for essential public services, all citizens have an interest in the fair and equitable solution to the dilemma.

Unfortunately, a just and effective method of resolving unaffordable public pension obligations has been elusive for some public governmental employers and employees. This is due in part to promised pension benefits costs exceeding the government's ability to pay and the failure to fund promptly the incurred obligations. In some cases, solving the problem has been complicated by the lack of any ability to adjust or modify pension benefits to those that are sustainable and affordable to the fullest extent possible without adversely affecting the funding of essential public services. This chapter reviews some legal and practical obstacles that have been making needed pension reform and balancing the budget difficult, if not impossible, and suggests possible new approaches to the problem that have not yet been tried.

COMPETING INTERESTS

Just as the federal government was created to establish justice, provide for the common defense, and promote the general welfare,[1] the states as co-sovereigns[2] and municipalities pursuant to state law are expected to serve the citizenry by providing necessary public services in exchange for the payment of taxes. Generally, public employees, often union members, have performed the public services expected of state and local governments. Those public employees are entitled to be the recipients of pensions upon retirement payable by their public employer. Prior to the mid-1900s, most public pensions in the United States were treated as gratuities, namely, a pay-as-you-go-if-you-desire obligation, which could be modified or eliminated at any time.

It is widely accepted today that public pensions are in the nature of a contract[3] and thus entitled to the benefits of the Contract Clause of the United States, which provides that "[n]o [s]tate shall . . . pass any . . . [l]aw impairing the [o]bligation of [c]ontracts."[4] Despite significant United States Supreme Court jurisprudence that the Contract Clause is qualified by the authority the state possesses to serve the health, safety, and welfare of its citizens, an important public purpose,[5] resolution of the competing interests of public pensions and the police power of state and local governments has proved challenging. This is true regardless of arguments that the public safety and welfare require that unaffordable and unsustainable public pension benefits must be addressed successfully.

To the extent a public employer has the ability to meet promised pension benefits, even if it means raising taxes, it should do so. But if raising taxes ultimately will have a negative effect on the financial health of the employer, with a flight of business and individual taxpayers resulting in loss of revenues and less ability to pay pension benefits, raising taxes can result in the dreaded "death spiral." A balance must be struck so that the public employer can pay public pension obligations to the fullest extent financially possible and ensure full funding of necessary services to attract new businesses and increased new good jobs, thereby creating new tax revenue sources to solve the pension funding issue.[6] Actually, the interests of taxpayers, public employees, retirees, and creditors of the public employer should be aligned in supporting the provision of adequate public services to ensure all parties receive what they need. Unfortunately, in the past, some public employers have been unable to strike the necessary balance because of the practical inability of the parties to negotiate needed pension adjustments, the legal obstacles of state constitutional and statutory provisions, as well as court rulings that prevent needed pension reform from being enacted and enforced.

SHORTCOMINGS OF CURRENT METHODS

In the best of all possible worlds, when essential services of a government cannot be appropriately funded due to unaffordable public pension benefits despite raising taxes and reducing unnecessary expenses voluntarily, effective pension reform would occur. Specifically, the beneficiaries of pensions and other postemployment benefits would agree with public employers to voluntary adjustments to maximize the ultimate benefit to all. Some states have successfully implemented constructive pension reform.[7] Since 2009 nearly every state has made meaningful changes to its pension plan benefits structure, financing arrangements, or both.[8] However, some of those efforts have faced obstacles in carrying out their goals, and a number of state and local governments have been unable to make sufficient modification or changes to public pension benefits to ensure that they are sustainable, are affordable, and do not threaten funding of needed governmental services and infrastructure.[9]

Legislation Imposing Pension Adjustment

The state or municipality by legislation or executive order can enact an adjustment to pension benefits and defend it as an important public purpose and an exercise of police power in order to preserve its essential function of providing governmental services that are affordable and sustainable at an acceptable level. Such pension adjustments must be justified as necessary to make the pensions sustainable and affordable and the least drastic action available.[10] As noted, since the crisis of 2008, many states have enacted meaningful reform to pension plans.[11]

Further, since 2009, there have been more than twenty-six major state court decisions dealing with pension reforms by state and local governments.[12] Over 75 percent (20 out of 26) of those decisions affirmed the pension reform, which covered reduction of benefits, including cost-of-living adjustments, or increase of employee contributions, as well as plan conversion and other necessary reforms.[13] Many times, those decisions cited the higher public purpose of ensuring funding for essential governmental services and infrastructure. Many of the cases where pension reform was approved cited United States Supreme Court decisions that contracts can be impaired by state and local governments for a higher public purpose of the health, safety, and welfare of their citizens that outweighs any legal argument that the contracts are sacrosanct.[14] In a government contractual relationship, the government does not surrender its essential governmental power such as the police power to protect the health, safety, and welfare of its citizens.[15]

However, the ability of state legislation modifying pension obligations to withstand legal challenges is by no means ensured. This is particularly true in states that have constitutional provisions that prohibit the state from reducing pension benefits. The State of New York's Constitution provides that "membership in any pension or retirement systems of the state or of a work division thereof shall be a contractual relationship, the benefits of which shall not be diminished or impaired."[16] The highest court of that state has found that legislation that reduced benefits payable upon the death of employees violated the state constitution.[17]

The Illinois Constitution contains similar language: "Membership in any pension or retirement system of the State, any unit of local government or school district, or any agency or instrumentality thereof, shall be an enforceable contractual relationship, the benefits of which shall not be diminished or impaired."[18] The history of the application of that pension protection clause by the Illinois courts demonstrates the challenge that pension reform legislation may face.

In 2013 Illinois enacted pension reform legislation that provided an estimated $160 billion in savings over a thirty-year period. The legislation was struck down by the Illinois Supreme Court as unconstitutional.[19] The state supreme court held the reform legislation was unconstitutional under the pension protection clause of the Illinois Constitution, Article XIII, Section 5, whereby, according to the court, benefits accrue to the public worker once an individual begins work and becomes a member of a public retirement system, and those contractual provisions cannot be impaired or diminished even in the face of an important public-purpose argument. The court held that there could be no exercise of police power to disregard the express provision of the pension protection clause, and the failure of the legislature to act consistent with the pension protection clause in the face of the well-known need for funding of the unfunded pension obligations undermines the police-power argument.

The state had argued as an affirmative defense the police power of the state, namely, that funding for the pension systems and state finances in general have become so dire that the Illinois General Assembly is authorized, even compelled, to invoke the state's "reserved sovereign powers," that is, its police powers, to override the rights and protections set forth in the pension protection clause of the Illinois Constitution in the interests of the greater public good. In dismissing this affirmative defense, the Illinois Supreme Court found that the funding problems were clearly foreseeable and due in large part to the prior actions of the Illinois General Assembly. The Illinois Supreme Court appeared to be preoccupied with the failure of the Illinois legislature to raise taxes and address the pension underfunding issue as opposed to the adverse effect to citizens due to the crowding out of funding for essential governmental services caused by paying unaffordable pension benefits.[20]

The following year, the Illinois Supreme Court invalidated the City of Chicago Labor Pension Reform.[21] The court, consistent with its earlier decision, ruled that the annuity-reducing provisions of a public act, which amended the Illinois Pension Code as it pertains to certain City of Chicago pension funds, contravened the pension protection clause and that exigent circumstances were no justification for such reduction. The argument that the public act contained a number of provisions that in sum provided a net benefit to employees by strengthening the system was rejected.[22] The court found that there can be no net benefit when the legislation was only offering what the employees were already guaranteed.

Efforts to legislate pension reform in California are restricted by the so-called California Rule, a court-imposed principle that limits the ability to modify pension obligations. The California Rule provides that while pensions may be modified in "reasonable" ways, to be sustained as reasonable, "alterations of employees' pension rights must bear some material relation to the theory of a pension system and its successful operation, and changes in a pension plan which result in disadvantage to employees should be accompanied by comparable new advantages."[23] The California Public Employee Pension Reform Act of 2012 (PEPRA) has been estimated to save between $42 billion and $55 billion for the California Public Employees' Retirement System (CalPERS) and $27.7 billion for the California State Teachers' Retirement System (CalSTRS). PEPRA is now being attacked in the CalFire, Marin County, and Alameda County litigation regarding PEPRA's prohibition on pension spiking.[24] The application of the California Rule, that any change in pension benefits that results in a disadvantage cannot be made without an accompanying advantage, was rejected by the California Appellate Court in several recent decisions,[25] and appeals to the California Supreme Court raise the issue of reversal or modification of the California Rule that creates an obstacle to prospective modification of pension benefits. The appellate court in the Marin County case, explaining the *Allen* decision, declared: "There is nothing in the opinion linking the reduction to provision of some new compensating benefit. . . . In the light of the foregoing, we cannot conclude that *Allen v. Board of Administration* in 1983 was meant to introduce an inflexible hardening of the traditional formula for public employee pension modification."[26] The appellate court in the *Marin* County case also declared that "while a public employee does have a 'vested right' to a pension, that right is only to a 'reasonable' pension—not an immutable entitlement to the most optimal formula of calculating the pension. And the Legislature may, prior to the employee's retirement, alter the formula, thereby reducing the anticipated pension. So long as the Legislature's modifications do not deprive the employee of a 'reasonable' pension, there is no constitutional violation."[27] This Marin County litigation has been pending for a number of years with no prompt resolution in sight. The *CalFire* appeal to the California Supreme Court is now fully briefed and ready for oral arguments and ruling.

Illinois and California are not the only states that have struggled post-2008 to validate public pension reform. Oregon and Montana courts cited the failure of the proponents of reform to prove a balancing of equities in favor of reform for a higher public purpose.[28] Another state, Arizona, included state court judges in the reform that increased employee contributions and reduced cost-of-living increases, which was found to have violated the Contract Clause and another of that state's constitutional provisions about improper influence over judicial officers during service.[29] The Arizona Supreme Court ruled the "needed" reform unconstitutional. Recently, police and firefighters in Arizona recognized the need for a sustainable and affordable pension fund, in the best interest of both themselves as the employees and their government employers, and agreed to pension adjustments with a onetime constitutional amendment setting forth the sustainable and needed pension reform.[30] However, the Arizona Supreme Court decision still stands as a possible obstacle to any future public employer public pension reform efforts other than as accomplished by the Proposition 124 method. The Illinois Supreme Court rulings on state and local government pension reform efforts appear to stand strongly against pension reform even for a higher public purpose or as a reasonable effort to save an insolvent public employer and its pension system.

What is clear from the foregoing discussion of legislation to impose pension reform is that, depending on the legal and political climate in the state, this path is time-consuming, subject to lengthy and expensive litigation, and not the most effective forum to resolve the competing interests. Does the use of Chapter 9 municipal bankruptcy provide an acceptable solution?

The Unplanned, Free-Fall Chapter 9 Problem

While the case law emerging from recent Chapter 9 cases has reinforced the ability to modify pension obligations in the proceeding, political pressure has diluted the chapter's effectiveness. Chapter 9 of the United States Bankruptcy Code[31] governs the adjustment of debt of municipalities.[32] Only the municipality itself can initiate a Chapter 9 proceeding; there can be no involuntary case.[33] In order to be able to institute a Chapter 9 proceeding, the municipality must be specifically authorized by state law, and fewer than half of states have generally authorized their municipalities to file Chapter 9.[34] While Chapter 9 cases are rare (only 680 cases since 1937), some municipalities, faced with debt obligations, including public pensions that dwarf their resources, have resorted to Chapter 9 protection without any prior extensive planning or effort to resolve their financial difficulties or agreement with creditor constituencies as to the resolution of debts. In bankruptcy parlance, such a filing is deemed "free-fall," since the fate of the municipality and its competing creditors is played out in the unscripted drama of the bankruptcy court without any prior agreement or preplanning of the intended result and subject to the uncertainty of court rulings and the aggressive arguments of various stakeholders. As a result, a free-fall Chapter 9 case by a city of any size is likely to be lengthy and costly. Interestingly, the legal treatment of the ability to adjust public pensions by the courts in Chapter 9 cases has been fairly consistent.

Treatment of Public Pension Obligations in Chapter 9

The bankruptcy proceedings involving the City of Stockton, California, and the City of Detroit, Michigan, have brought to the forefront the treatment of municipal pensions as a matter of law in a Chapter 9 bankruptcy proceeding. In these proceedings, the bankruptcy courts determined that the pension agreements were executory contracts, and thus a municipality could alter its pension obligations in a Chapter 9 proceeding, even if a constitutional provision existed providing that such contractual obligations could not be altered.[35] These cases have shown that, absent a settlement, pension obligations of a municipality, as a matter of law, can be treated equally with other unsecured debt with limited recovery. An earlier case set the stage for this result.

THE VALLEJO EXPERIENCE   The City of Vallejo, California, filed for Chapter 9 in 2008. The principal causes of the filing were unsustainable public employee compensation and pension packages. In the Vallejo case, the debtor filed a motion to reject collective bargaining agreements, which was met by protracted litigation and ultimately with the unions agreeing to certain modifications of benefits, given the court's ruling that the agreements could be rejected. However, Vallejo chose not to adjust the pension payments for current retirees because of the penalties CalPERS would impose in the event of failure to make the originally scheduled payments. This policy prohibited altering benefits of those already in the system, even though benefit reduction was a part of the rationale for the bankruptcy filing. Current employees were asked to pay an increasing cost of their medical coverage. Further, for current employees, Vallejo was able to do away with such contractual obligations as binding arbitration and minimum manning for the fire department. The city also eliminated a contract provision that required the city to pay firefighters an average of what their peers made in ten area cities, including major cities like Sacramento, the state capital. There were dramatic cuts in public safety, with the budgets of the police and fire departments slashed by almost 50 percent and resulting response times by first responders rivaling the worst anywhere.[36] Interest payments to bondholders were to be suspended for three and a half years. The city spent about $10 million in legal fees in the process.[37] Unfortunately, the austerity required by the plan of adjustment did not lead to prompt economic recovery or even a balanced budget. By 2014 Vallejo had a budget deficit, and there were claims that municipal services were less than during the crisis.[38] Thus, in Vallejo, even where the court held that public pensions could be impaired, the bargaining power by CalPERS to increase required pension payments if reduction was attempted by the public employer debtor essentially precluded any resolution of the pension crisis through Chapter 9. After Vallejo confirmed a plan of debt adjustment with changes to labor costs but no impairment of pension benefits, it still could not provide essential services at an acceptable level and there was talk of a second bankruptcy filing.[39]

THE STOCKTON EXPERIENCE   In the Vallejo case, at issue was the collective bargaining agreement affecting current employees. The pension benefits that were the subject of *Stockton* and *Detroit* Chapter 9s included accrued benefits. The *Stockton* court's initial opinion ruled that the bankruptcy court had no power to require the debtor to keep paying for retirees' health benefits in Chapter 9.[40] In the decision confirming the plan of debt adjustment, the *Stockton* bankruptcy court held that, as a matter of law, the city's pension administration contract with CalPERS, as well as the city-sponsored pensions themselves, may be adjusted as part of a Chapter 9 plan.[41] Stockton chose to adjust health care payments but not to impair or adjust pension payments to retirees, despite the court's recognition that both could be impaired. The purported reasoning of the city was that, under the terms of contractual arrangements with CalPERS, penalties imposed on any modification of pension benefits were too severe to justify impairment. Despite protests from a large debt holder, the court found that employees and retirees were sharing the pain with capital market creditors at least as to the treatment of claims for health care benefits. At the same time, pensions received more than certain other unsecured creditor groups due to the municipality's fear that, as a practical matter, no modification could be made because failure to make CalPERS's required payment on the originally scheduled unadjusted pension benefit would subject the municipal pension fund to a penalty for changes or termination of the old pension plan, namely, a very unfavorable discounted value of pension assets is used for a reevaluation of pension assets, thereby significantly increasing unfunded liabilities.[42] A similar result was achieved in the *San Bernardino* Chapter 9,[43] where the court confirmed a plan in which retiree pension benefits were not modified and where the court found that the city was unable to maintain a sustainable workforce without providing CalPERS pension benefits.

THE DETROIT EXPERIENCE   Citing *Stockton*, the bankruptcy court in the Detroit, Michigan, Chapter 9 proceeding specifically held that, in Chapter 9, the bankruptcy court had the power "to impair contracts and to impair contractual rights relating to accrued vested pension benefits. Impairing contracts is what the bankruptcy process does."[44] Nonetheless, under the negotiated compromise plan of debt adjustment in Detroit, certain unsecured creditor groups received less than the beneficiaries of the pension plans.

In Detroit's bankruptcy, as a part of a settlement with the city, pensioners recovered an initial 82 percent of the amount that they had been promised by the city before its bankruptcy proceeding.[45] With respect to the City of Stockton, although Stockton's bankruptcy plan of adjustment did not impair the city's pension obligations, as a part of a settlement with the city, the lifetime health care that had been promised to certain retirees was eliminated in exchange for a onetime payment of $5.1 million into a retirees' health care trust. As indicated above, the court in *Stockton* repeatedly noted that the obligation to CalPERS could be impaired if necessary to have a viable plan, but because the cost to Stockton in failing to make original unadjusted scheduled pension payments would result in a "penalty" discount to the valuation of pension assets and increased future costs, Stockton chose in its plan of debt adjustment not to impair the prepetition obligation to CalPERS.[46]

The *Detroit* case in particular demonstrates the inefficiency of a free-fall Chapter 9 as a vehicle to resolve the pension problems of major cities. The *Detroit* bankruptcy proceedings were contentious and ultimately resulted in settlements among the various constituencies, providing little in guidance for future Chapter 9 proceedings by similar-size municipalities, should such filings occur. Indeed, professional fees of more than $170 million were paid by the city or by the state of Michigan in connection with the *Detroit* bankruptcy.[47] This figure should and has provided pause to both municipalities and creditors and evidence that if they can, the various constituencies with respect to a municipal restructuring should attempt to reach a consensus on pension issues outside of the free-fall Chapter 9 process.[48]

Neither a resort to legislation imposing pension adjustments nor the institution of a free-fall Chapter 9 proceeding to impose adjustment on inflexible public pension rights has proven particularly suited to resolving the complex problem of dealing with promised pensions that simply are unaffordable. Ultimately, these methods are less than successful because they do not focus on or do not mitigate the real source of the problem.

THE PUBLIC PENSION PROBLEM AS AN INABILITY TO PAY

While failure of a state or local government to fully fund its annual actuarially determined contribution (ADC) should never be condoned, it many times can be explained. Efforts to offset the effects of economic downturns; lack of economic growth; losses of population, jobs, and related business; and increased costs of services, infrastructure improvements, and repairs have resulted in budget crises and deficits and accompanying underfunded pension obligations. The saga of Detroit and many other cities has demonstrated that raising taxes and lowering services do not produce more tax revenues and a balanced budget. In fact, this process causes citizens and businesses to flee, with the resulting reduction in tax revenues collected due to the loss of taxpayers and a corresponding loss of economic growth. The resulting practical reality is state and local governments cannot pay what they do not have funds to pay. Demanding full payment of unaffordable pension benefits many times means shorting the funding of essential services and needed infrastructure improvements. This results in the economic meltdown of the government employer and continuing decreasing funds available to pay employees and pension obligations. The only real solution to economic meltdown of a state or local government is economic development and growth through reinvestment in the government and providing the services and infrastructure at an acceptable level to attract new businesses, jobs, and residents with the resulting increase in taxpayers and tax revenues. The inability to enact needed public pension reform can be fatal to this needed economic recovery that would benefit workers, retirees, taxpayers, and creditors.

If reform efforts fail or necessary constructive reform appears to be legally impossible (such as in Illinois given the state supreme court decisions and in California due to CalPERS's required contributions, the California Rule, and so on),[49] what can be done? The reality of public pension reform is that the problem has been percolating for so long, there may well be situations where voluntary reform is not possible, any actual reforms on a prospective basis or on what appears to be within the restrictions of state laws are not sufficient to be sustainable or affordable, and even the higher public-purpose argument (calling for reduction of pension benefits that crowd out funding for essential services and needed infrastructure) is not effective or practically possible. In such situations, new approaches to modifying unaffordable pension benefits on a prospective basis should be considered as a last resort to prevent government service meltdown. This chapter proposes four possible alternatives to public employers who face this serious problem. These alternatives assume that all traditional pension reform efforts have been explored, including raising taxes and reducing expenditures to the extent possible, and more needed pension plan adjustments and modifications appear to be impossible legally or on a consensual basis. The four alternatives to be considered by the state or local government employees are as follows:

1. prepackaged Chapter 9 plan of debt adjustment
2. creation of a special federal bankruptcy court for insolvent public pension funds
3. Government Oversight, Refinance, and Debt Adjustment Commission (GORDAC) to assist where public pension reform is otherwise legally or practically impossible
4. Model Guidelines for a state constitutional amendment or legislative public pension funding policy for a higher public good: the necessity of pension benefits adjustment for the public safety and welfare in those situations where state constitutions, statutes, or case law appears to prohibit any impairment or reduction of pension benefits

POSSIBLE APPROACHES WHEN PENSION REFORM EFFORTS FAIL OR APPEAR TO BE LEGALLY IMPOSSIBLE

Prepackaged Chapter 9

As corporations confronted the time and cost of the traditional Chapter 11 case, troubled businesses and their counsel considered the use of a prepackaged plan of reorganization to reduce the time and expense of bankruptcy.[50] Section 1126(b) of the Bankruptcy Code provides an expedited process by which a debtor may propose and confirm a Chapter 11 plan. Under this provision, a prospective debtor may solicit consents for a proposed plan from its major creditor constituencies prior to filing a petition under Chapter 11. After filing for Chapter 11, the debtor schedules a single bankruptcy court hearing to pass on the adequacy of its prepetition disclosure materials and confirmation of its proposed plan. A "prepackaged" bankruptcy reorganization is one method of binding all of the security holders and other creditors to a restructuring.

A summary of steps involved in a prepackaged reorganization include the following:

1. Negotiate a plan with major creditor constituencies.
2. Prepare and disseminate a proposed plan, disclosure statement, and voting ballot to solicit creditor votes.
3. All parties with impaired interests under the reorganization plan are entitled to vote. In order for a class to accept the plan, at least two-thirds in amount and more than one-half in number of the class voting must vote to accept the plan. Only claims actually voted are computed in determining creditor acceptance.
4. After the development of the prepackaged plan, the solicitation of votes with full disclosure and the vote tally (ideally showing at least one class of creditors voted to accept the plan), the bankruptcy petition is filed, together with the prepackaged plan and creditor acceptances thereof.
5. The bankruptcy court holds a hearing to consider whether the prepetition disclosure materials meet the requirements for adequate disclosure as set forth in the Bankruptcy Code and any applicable rules of the Securities and Exchange Commission. If disclosure is found adequate, as well as compliance with the requirements of the Bankruptcy Code for confirmation of a plan, the debtor presents a certification of creditor acceptances, and the court considers whether the proposed plan can be confirmed under the requirements of the Bankruptcy Code.

Prepackaged plans are particularly suited to situations in which a debtor public employer intends to leave many creditor classes virtually untouched or with the consideration negotiated prefiling but desires to modify the terms of judgments, contractual relationships, public debt, or pension obligations that adversely affect the public safety and welfare of its citizens and the full funding and provision of essential governmental services and infrastructure improvements. A principal benefit of a prepackaged plan is the speed of the proceeding, which necessarily reduces costs, uncertainly, and anxiety. In addition, the relatively brief time in bankruptcy (often less than three months) minimizes disruption of the debtor's operations and relationships with needed creditor constituencies. Of course, the prepetition negotiation and solicitation may take substantial time.

Section 1126(b) of the Bankruptcy Code is applicable in a Chapter 9 municipal bankruptcy.[51] Municipalities authorized by their states to file Chapter 9 should consider using such an approach to provide effective pension reforms where efforts at voluntary reform fail and state courts are hostile to reform efforts. This prepackaged Chapter 9 municipal debt adjustment plan can provide the needed pension obligation reform to save the municipality, its taxpayers, public workers, retirees, and creditors. As previously noted, courts hearing Chapter 9 municipal debt–adjustment cases have unanimously ruled that the labor and pension contract obligations can be impaired where impairing pension benefits was necessary to save the municipality's financial and operational future.[52] Although a prepackaged Chapter 9 will not resolve the threat that CalPERS may not accept the reduced pension obligation modified public pension plan in its calculation of pension obligations due without a "penalty" reduction in the present value of assets from prior present values, this issue can be addressed as to the binding effect of the court's order on CalPERS or other pension fund administrators. It is clear that a prepackaged plan will greatly reduce costs, delay, and uncertainty of results to the municipality.

Since 2013 and the *Detroit* Chapter 9 filing, no city, town, village, or county has filed for Chapter 9 relief (except Hillview, Kentucky). Some of the reasons for this are the stigma of Chapter 9, its cost and expense, the uncertainty of the process and results, and the general delay of years before a resolution is reached. The expense of Chapter 9 is a problem, as demonstrated by the fact that, as previously noted, the professional fees incurred in Chapter 9 for Detroit were more than $170 million, for Jefferson County were over $30 million,[53] and for even smaller Vallejo were more than $10 million.[54] The benefit of the brevity of a prepackaged Chapter 9 should reduce any stigma, resolve any uncertainty as to the result, reduce if not eliminate strain on operations and key relationships, and drastically reduce costs and expenses to the municipality. Further, the savings of time, effort, and costs all can aid in the financial recovery of the municipality. There should be further development of the use of a prepackaged Chapter 9 for municipalities suffering from such an impossible situation in order to save the municipality, its taxpayers, public workers, retirees, and creditors. However, since fewer than half the states authorize their municipalities to file a Chapter 9 proceeding and states cannot file Chapter 9, other alternatives should be explored.

Creation of a Special Federal Bankruptcy Court

The United States Congress has the exclusive power under the US Constitution to establish uniform laws on the subject of bankruptcy.[55] The notion of a consistent bankruptcy law throughout the United States was part of the drafters' goal to establish the framework for a successful commercial republic. The rationale was summarized by James Madison in *The Federalist*, No. 42: "The power of establishing uniform laws on bankruptcy is so intimately connected with the regulation of commerce, and will prevent so many frauds where the parties or their property may lie or be removed into different States, that the expediency of it seems not likely to be drawn into question."[56]

The Chapter 9 cases involving public pension issues have been filed in various courts throughout the United States. Judges with an extensive background in corporate restructuring many times face a once-in-a-lifetime experience in municipal and public employee benefit law and have been forced to deal with the complicated issues of analyzing what constitutes unaffordable and unsustainable pensions when municipal services are maintained at an acceptable level and when they are not. While these judges have done an admirable job educating themselves in these relatively specialized, and for them untraveled, areas of expertise, the results have not always been uniform and the burden on the courts has been challenging. Further, the filing of a Chapter 9 for the entire municipality, plunging a whole city into crisis when the principal problem is a pension obligation that cannot be met, can be inefficient and more complicated than necessary. In furtherance of the uniform bankruptcy law ideal to strengthen the economy of the United States and the goal of limited disruption of the government and affairs of the municipality,[57] the creation of a new separate federal court to hear public pension fund bankruptcy is appropriate. Public pension funds are separate and distinct legal entities, and the assets they hold in trust are not part of the government employer's assets.

A separate federal bankruptcy court could be established for public pension funds (Public Pension Fund Bankruptcy Court) that are deemed insolvent as determined by a specified ratio of funding or demonstrated inability by the public employer to be able to fully fund the pension obligations or to pay benefits as they become due. The inability to pay the actuarially required payments due to lack of revenues sufficient to fully fund the cost of essential government services and needed infrastructure improvements and also fully fund the required pension benefits would qualify as insolvency. It could be a separate title of the United States Code or a new separate chapter of the Bankruptcy Code.[58] The specialized court could be located in Washington, DC, or in several locations across the country.

Federal legislation would preempt any other laws and would give exclusive jurisdiction to the Pension Fund Bankruptcy Court to deal with pension fund insolvency. Just like a municipality's ability to use Chapter 9, states would have to specifically authorize local government pension funds or state pension funds to file for relief before the Public Pension Fund Bankruptcy Court. This court would be composed of judges who understand principles of municipal finance and the relationship between a well-functioning municipality and funding public pension obligations. To avoid jurisdictional issues, the judges for the separate court could be Article III judges selected like federal district court judges and not an adjunct to the federal district court, like the current Article I bankruptcy judges in the bankruptcy court that are subject to federal district court delegation or approval of their actions.[59]

A plan of adjustment for the pension obligations would be proposed by the employer governmental body based on what is affordable while permitting the adequate funding of governmental services and infrastructure.[60] The pension fund and other parties in interest would be able to comment on or object to the proposed plan. The Public Pension Fund Bankruptcy Court would determine if the plan is sustainable, affordable, and in the best interest of the pension fund and its beneficiaries (workers and retirees), as well as other parties in interest such as creditors, taxpayers, and businesses of the governmental body and employer. The statute could also provide for a mediation process with court supervision if the pension fund and the governmental body reasonably believe they can reach agreement on the plan of adjustment. If agreement cannot be reached between the parties, the court would ultimately decide on the plan of recovery for the government employer and pension fund with such modifications and adjustments to the plan as required by the court.

The use of prepackaged plan of debt adjustment would be incorporated so that the bankruptcy plan for the pension fund could be confirmed in forty-five to ninety days and be a good last resort that is efficient and more affordable. State authorization would be necessary for state and local government pension funds to file before the Public Pension Fund Bankruptcy Court, since states cannot file for Chapter 9 bankruptcy and municipalities need to be authorized by their state to file for a Chapter 9 proceeding. The Public

Pension Fund Bankruptcy Court would allow financially troubled state and local government pension funds that also need a last resort to have one if so authorized by the state. Also, a Public Pension Fund Bankruptcy Court is a means of avoiding a prepackaged Chapter 9 bankruptcy of the municipality itself when the only or significant obligation that needs to be addressed is the public pension cost that cannot be controlled or fully funded. The focus is where pension obligations are the issue, and other relationships of the governmental body do not need to be disrupted or adversely affected. Further, the exclusive jurisdiction of the Public Pension Fund Bankruptcy Court over the insolvent public pension fund should successfully cure the California situation as in Vallejo, Stockton, and San Bernardino, where threats by CalPERS of penalties for terminating the original pension plan or reducing payment from the full original pension benefit liabilities unadjusted by bankruptcy court and plan of recovery result in reevaluation of pension fund assets at an unfavorable discount rate. This result can be avoided by the Public Pension Fund Bankruptcy Court ordering adjusted pension payments that would be binding on all parties. This court would determine what obligation the government employer and pension fund must pay to the pension administration entity as an obligation of the government employer and the payments to be received by the debtor pension fund in bankruptcy and upon confirmation of the plan of debt adjustment as well as the appropriate valuation of pension assets. Such a determination, based on traditional bankruptcy case law, would be binding on the pension fund administrator, such as CalPERS, just as any prepetition obligation of the debtor pension fund to pay or to perform could be modified by the confirmed plan and binding on the parties in interest.

Government Oversight, Refinance, and Debt Adjustment Commission

A variation on the two approaches above, a prepackaged Chapter 9 and the Federal Public Pension Fund Bankruptcy Court, is the creation by state legislation of a state commission that would help facilitate voluntary agreement but would have the ability to bind all parties to an affordable and sustainable recovery plan through a prepackaged Chapter 9 filing. GORDAC would be composed of a panel of at least three commissioners and a professional staff with experience in finance, government, accounting, employee benefits, and financial restructuring. The commission would be independent of the government. GORDAC would be created by state legislation as a quasi-judicial commission initiated through either voluntary petition by affected parties (municipalities, pension funds or requisite percentage of taxpayers, creditors, or employees) or the use of triggering criteria requiring mandatory review of financially troubled situations.[61]

The first phase of the process is mediation and consensual agreement by the municipality and the affected creditor constituencies. The negotiations and discussions of positions as part of the GORDAC process should be confidential. Accordingly, the state law establishing the commission should contain an exception to the state's open-meeting and freedom-of-information laws to allow for open discussion of any sensitive and confidential topics. If the consensual agreement requests additional tax revenues, loans, or grants from the state, the commission will make recommendations to the state and determine the prudence and feasibility of such actions.

If the voluntary process is not successful, a second phase of the process may be requested or may be mandatory if the commission so requires. At this stage, the commission functions as a quasi-judicial panel. The municipality sets forth the actions proposed to be taken to address the specific financial problems (recovery plan) for the commission's approval. GORDAC will bring its expertise to bear on the proposed recovery plan. GORDAC would determine, after hearing and input from all parties, the projected future revenues, the cost of essential governmental services and infrastructure, what pension obligations are sustainable and affordable for the municipality, and whether the recovery plan should be approved or modified.

The first determination is whether the specific situation involves an ability-to-pay problem or a willingness-to-pay issue. Should taxes be increased to fund pensions if it is a willingness problem? Should a referendum be sought? Should an adjustment to wages or pension benefits be necessary in order to ensure essential governmental services will be provided at an acceptable level? This independent objective expert commission will determine from the input of the parties the realistic projection of revenues compared to the amount of dollars required to pay for essential governmental services and necessary infrastructure improvements with the remaining funds available to pay wages and pensions benefits and whether taxes should be raised or debt, including for pension obligations, refinanced or restructured.

However, simply raising taxes to pay pension benefits is unwise at certain times when the raising of taxes and the lowering of services (reducing expenditures) bring about an exit of both business and individual taxpayers, which reduces tax revenues and frustrates the ability to pay workers and pensions and also to provide essential governmental services. Pension underfunding is adverse to young workers and transforms pension benefits into a game of musical chairs. GORDAC will take such factors into consideration as it determines what unfunded pension obligations can be paid and are affordable and what are not versus what funds are needed to provide essential governmental services and infrastructure and must be funded. GORDAC will determine the elements of a recovery plan. If, following this quasi-judicial process, needed pension reform is possible voluntarily, this approach would include a sustainable and affordable pension benefit obligation as part of a recovery plan. If, however, a voluntary and binding resolution on all parties is not possible on a consensual basis, then the parties will be bound by the recovery plan approved by GORDAC (with such modifications and adjustments to the recovery plan as GORDAC determines necessary for its approval). The approved recovery plan would be enforced by having the municipality file a prepackaged Chapter 9 using the recovery plan, vote of creditors, and the proceeding before GORDAC as the basis for the bankruptcy court's confirmation of the recovery plan as a prepackaged plan in a Chapter 9 (Prepackaged Plan Option).

Further, as part of GORDAC or as a separate entity, the state could establish an agency to foster best practices in pension fund management, to police against fraud, abuse, and waste in any pension system within the state and to determine for any new proposed pension benefit whether it is in good faith, consistent with fair dealing, and affordable (Pension Policing). This state agency would be charged with looking into recommended best practices as well as any instances of fraud, waste, and abuse in the granting and administration of pensions. While governments should pay their contractual obligations to the fullest degree possible, pension underfunding due to losses attributed to fraud, waste, and abuse by investment advisers or others uninvolved in pension administration should not be tolerated. The purpose of this agency is to provide an objective, independent entity to police against such practices as pension spiking in the last years of employment by significant raises in the pensionable salary, which creates unjustifiable increases in pension benefits; unjustified disability findings and awards; failure to work a full day for a full day's pay; politically connected or otherwise incompetent financial advisers when significant losses are suffered; and other wrongful, abusive, or wasteful actions. This approach recognizes there is a quid pro quo for every contract, as most state laws describe the relationship between the public worker and the government as contractual. Failure to perform in good faith on the part of a public worker should lead to an adjustment or elimination of pension benefits. Failure by the pension fund to properly administer or collect pension benefit payments in the appropriate amount can be reviewed and corrective administrative efforts can be instituted so that as much as possible can be collected by such policy and review. Failure to raise taxes or contributions can be reviewed and determined when additional tax revenues or contributions by the government employer are necessary and appropriate. Having such an agency on the books may be the best deterrent to prevent fraud, abuse, and waste and to encourage best practices and full funding of public pension obligations.

Model Guidelines Where Pension Reform Appears Prohibited

As previously noted, some states have constitutional provisions that appear to prohibit the state from reducing pension benefits.[62] While each state constitution has varying requirements for amending its terms, given the mounting crisis caused by unaffordable, unsustainable pensions and the demands of cities for increased funding for governmental services and infrastructure, consideration may be given to providing some relief from inflexible interpretation of constitutional or statutory restrictions on modification and reduction of benefits. Instead, a more balanced approach of specific legislative findings is to be made by the government as to the necessity and extent of any adjustments of pension benefits before modification or adjustment to pension benefits could be made. If the health, safety, and welfare of citizens mandate funding of services or needed infrastructure improvements at an acceptable level, required pension obligation funding should not and must not crowd out the funding of governmental services, as defined below. Obviously, unalterable pension benefits for unaffordable and unsustainable pension benefits can create an intolerable situation for citizens, taxpayers, workers, retirees, and the business community, where everyone fails to obtain what they should receive. A safety valve is needed to resolve the conflict if there is too little revenue and too many demands for payment. Accordingly, there is need for either an amendment to constitutions or statutory provisions that solve this funding gridlock or a legislative policy for the least drastic and most appropriate adjustment of pension benefits for the higher public purpose of the health, safety, and welfare of citizens and for the ultimate benefit of all concerned.

PROPOSED MODEL GUIDELINES TO DEAL WITH PENSION PROTECTION   It is possible to develop an amendment to a state constitution or statute containing a pension protection clause (Pension Protection Clause) that protects the general welfare of citizens while funding to the fullest extent possible the public pension obligations. Any such amendment should include balancing tests and conditions the United States Supreme Court has articulated that would justify modifications and reductions of contractual benefits previously granted. While the actual language of a constitutional or statutory amendment may vary, as well as the language of legislation for public pension funding policy, the following guidelines should be the tonic for any constitutional amendment or legislative funding policy appropriately amending state statutes to prevent a public pension crisis (Model Guidelines):

MODEL GUIDELINES FOR A CONSTITUTIONAL AMENDMENT OR LEGISLATIVE FUNDING POLICY TO PREVENT A PUBLIC PENSION CRISIS

1. *Balanced Budget.* Balanced Operating Budget for Governmental Entity for the fiscal year where all expenses and liabilities that are due and payable do not exceed anticipated revenues of the Governmental Entity.

2. *Pay Annually the ADC.* The Governmental Entity shall pay in each and every fiscal year the actuarially determined contribution (ADC) it is liable for under its pension or retirement system for that fiscal year, provided the effect of any modification or reduction of pension benefits required by these Model Guidelines or determined by its legislative body is included in such calculations. The state may from time to time enact standards and accepted reasonable assumptions to be used in calculating the ADC.

3. *Reasonable and Necessary Modification Permitted.* Reasonable modification and reduction of Pension Benefits of the Governmental Entity shall be permitted that are necessary for a higher important public purpose of fully funding and providing for the essential governmental services at an acceptable level, including needed infrastructure and capital improvements as determined in good faith by the Governmental Entity's legislative body or its equivalent. Again, the states may from time to time enact standards or further Model Guidelines for what is a sustainable, affordable, and acceptable level of Governmental Services.

4. *Fully Funding of Governmental Services at Acceptable Level.* The Governmental Entity's Legislative Body shall in good faith determine the amount of full funding of Governmental Services at the acceptable level required for the welfare of its citizens and the appropriate operation of its government.

5. *Reasonableness of Modification of Public Pension Benefits in Relation to Governmental Entity's Ability to Fully Fund and Afford Governmen-*

tal Services and Pension Benefits. The Governmental Entity's Legislative Body shall make a good-faith determination of the reasonableness of any modification or reduction of Pension Benefits in relation to the Governmental Entity's ability to fully fund and provide Governmental Services and afford and fund actuarially determined Pension Benefits as well as maintain a Balanced Budget for the current fiscal year and the foreseeable future. The inability to do so requires the reasonable modification or reduction of Pension Benefits to that which is affordable and sustainable in the good-faith determination of the Legislative Body consistent with these Model Guidelines.

6. *Priority of Public Pension Modifications So That to the Extent Possible Any Modification Will Be Made First to Unearned Future Benefits and Any Impairment of Vested Rights Would Be Subject to a Court Validation Process.* Any required modification or reduction of Public Pension Benefits may be for Pension Benefits to be earned prior to or after the effective date of the modification or reduction with the priority that any modification or reduction first be made to the extent reasonably possible to Pension Benefits to be earned in the future. Any modification or reduction of Pension Benefits earned shall be effective only after a court validation proceeding that confirms the need for the modification or reduction of Pension Benefits in accordance with the Model Guidelines and permitted impairment of contractual rights for a higher public purpose. The Government Entity may also seek a court validation of any reduction or modification of Pension Benefits, including Pension Benefits to be earned in the future. This court validation process would follow a statutory procedure similar to bond validation proceedings where the court will validate the reduction or modification after a petition by the Governmental Entity. A hearing with notice to affected parties who have an opportunity to appear determining the modifications and reductions is permitted for a higher public purpose pursuant to these Model Guidelines and once all required action and legislative funding thereunder have been made.

7. *Public Pension Benefits Should Be Affordable and Sustainable by the Governmental Entity.* Public Pension Benefits granted or to be granted by a Governmental Entity should be affordable and sustainable by the Governmental Entity and specifically state that such benefits are subject to reasonable modification or reduction as necessary to accomplish affordability and sustainability as determined by the exercise of the good-faith judgment of the Legislative Body.

8. *Additional Legislative Findings for Any Modification of Pension Benefits.* These legislative findings, in addition to those legislative findings and determination as noted above, would generally consist of: (1) the existence of a government function emergency requiring modification of Pension Benefits (Governmental Emergency); (2) modification necessary for provision of Governmental Services at an acceptable level, reasonable in relation to the Governmental Emergency, and paying public Pension Benefits to the fullest extent possible consistent with these Model Guidelines; (3) the balancing of harm caused to beneficiaries is outweighed by the harm to the public; and (4) the modification of Pension Benefits is necessary for the financial stability of the Governmental Entity and is the least drastic. A further explanation of these findings is to be made in the legislation or pension reform. In addition to the Legislative Body's determination and findings noted above, the Legislative Body for the Governmental Entity shall make the following findings in connection with any modification or reduction of Pension Benefits found to be reasonable and necessary under these Model Guidelines:

(A) *Existence of Governmental Emergency.* A Governmental Emergency exists or will occur in the foreseeable future that will adversely affect the health, safety, and welfare of its citizens and the Governmental Entity's ability to fully fund and provide Governmental Services. Any further increase in taxes and any further reduction in expenditures are in the good-faith judgment of the Legislative Body unreasonable and contrary to the interest of citizens and taxpayers as well as contrary to financially responsible government.

(B) *Modifications Are Mandated for the Public Good.* Any modification or reduction of Pension Benefits by the Legislative Body is required in the exercise of its governmental powers in order for the Governmental Entity to be able to fund and provide Governmental Services for the other higher public purpose of the health, safety, and welfare of its citizens.

(C) *Any Modification Is Reasonable in Relation to the Governmental Emergency and Extent of Any Impairment with Pension Benefits Paid to the Fullest Extent Possible.* A modification or reduction of Pension Benefits is appropriate and reasonable both (1) in relation to the Governmental Emergency and adverse effects set forth in the legislative finding under sub-paragraph (A) above and (2) to the extent of any impairment of Pension Benefits.

Pension Benefits are be funded to the fullest extent possible and paid without modification or reduction so long as no Governmental Emergency exists and there is full funding of and provision for Governmental Services as mandated by the enactment of the Model Guidelines.

(D)   *The Harm to Pension Beneficiaries Due to a Modification Is Outweighed by the Harm Suffered by the Governmental Entity and the Citizens.* The harm caused by any modification or reduction of Pension Benefits to the beneficiaries pursuant to these Model Guidelines is, in the reasonable judgment of the Legislative Body, the least required under the requirements of these Model Guidelines and is outweighed by the harm to be suffered by the Governmental Entity and its citizens if such modification and reduction of Pension Benefits required hereunder are not made to address the Governmental Emergency and the lack of funding for providing Governmental Services to its citizens.

(E)   *The Financial Creditability of the Governmental Entity Is Preserved.* In the reasonable judgment of the Legislative Body, its financial credibility and access to the credit markets are encouraged by any Legislative Body's action hereunder and are not adversely affected or limited by any modification and reduction to such Pension Benefits required hereunder.

9. *Any Modification or Reduction of Pension Benefits Pursuant to These Principles Is Not Considered an Impairment or Diminishment.* Any modification or reduction of Pension Benefits in compliance with these Model Guidelines hereunder shall not be considered under applicable state constitution, statutes, and court rulings to be an impairment or diminishment of the contractual right to Pension Benefits because such Pension Benefits could not realistically be paid by the Governmental Entity due to limited financial resources and the Governmental Entity could not at the same time pay the Pension Benefits without such modification or reduction and fulfill its primary mission of fully funding provisions for Governmental Services along with its financial survival.

JUSTIFICATION FOR THE PROPOSED MODEL GUIDELINES   *Governmental emergency.* Any legislative action for reduction or modification of pension benefits under the amendment should provide that there is a determination of a governmental emergency caused by the cost of pension benefits without modification or reduction that crowds out funding and provision of essential governmental services and necessary infrastructure improvements at an acceptable level, thereby adversely affecting the health, safety, and welfare of the government's citizens. A governmental emergency exists when funding for governmental services at an acceptable level is insufficient and the ability to raise taxes is practically or legally impossible, as determined in good faith by the legislative body, and any further reduction of services and costs would be hazardous to the proper function of government. Waiting until infrastructure collapses or a significant percentage of taxpayers and businesses have exited is too late and the threat of a death spiral too great. Further, the legislative body should in good faith determine that there is no further reduction of expenses or services that can be justified without impairing the health, safety, and welfare of its citizens. Accordingly, all that can be done to address the governmental emergency practically has been done before modification and reduction of pension benefits.

Current pension obligations are not sustainable and affordable. The essential purpose of government is to provide for the health, safety, and welfare of its citizens. Given the significant and increasing percentage of revenues needed for fully funding the actuarially required contribution (ARC) and actuarially determined contribution (ADC), many state and many local governments are facing a funding crisis where funding of essential services and needed infrastructure improvements is deferred or services reduced to permit larger contributions for unfunded pension obligations that, based on the ability to pay, are generally unaffordable and unsustainable. This again is due to the fact that revenues have decreased to a level to be insufficient to pay now and in the foreseeable future all obligations due on time, and further tax increases and projected increased revenues are practically or legally impossible and further reductions of costs not possible or prudent.

The Model Guidelines for a constitutional amendment or legislation funding policy for public pensions address the important public purpose of ensuring that essential governmental services at an acceptable level (including needed infrastructure and capital improvements) are fully funded and provided for and that obligations for pension benefits are funded to the fullest extent possible given the cost of governmental services so that pension benefits are affordable and sustainable. The governmental entity is required to have balanced financial budgets providing full funding of governmental services at an acceptable level with the only modification or reduction of pension benefits due to that which is required by the governmental entity's legislative body in a good-faith determination to balance the financial budget for each fiscal year for the foreseeable future. The legislative body for the governmental entity in determining whether any reduction or modification of such pension benefits is reasonably necessary should take into consideration the following: such pension benefits should, to the fullest extent possible, be funded and paid without modification or reduction so long as there is full funding of and provision for governmental services (including raising taxes to the extent feasible, legal, and practicable and reducing expenses to the extent possible and prudent); and the credit markets' perception of the financial credibility of the governmental entity as indicated by access to the credit markets and actual borrowing costs is encouraged by the legislative body's actions and not adversely affected or limited by the failure to make modification and reduction to such pension benefits.

Any modifications or reductions in pension benefits pursuant to these Model Guidelines would serve the legitimate and important public purpose of preventing the crowding out of the funding of governmental services by unaffordable and unsustainable pension benefits. While such reductions and modifications are to be reasonably determined by the legislative body in good faith for the public good and welfare of the citizens of the governmental entity, they should not be considered an impairment or diminishment of the pension benefits since the limited resources of the governmental entity realistically are not sufficient to pay such. The payment of the amounts that are the subject of the modification or reduction is a cost that threaten and impair the welfare of the citizens and cannot, given the limited resources of government, be paid in reality.[63] The payment of such unaffordable and unsustainable pension benefits leads not only to impairment of the health, safety, and welfare of citizens but also, in the long term, to the death spiral of the government entity, where everyone receives less.

The examples of Detroit, Bridgeport (Connecticut), and other financially distressed governments have demonstrated that if the government raises taxes and reduces services to pay for unaffordable and unsustainable costs, the result will be that individual and corporate taxpayers will leave and less revenue will actually be collected, to the detriment of all. In effect, there are no issues of impairment of pension benefits or inappropriate reductions or modifications of pension benefits since all that realistically can be paid will be paid and that which cannot be paid without harm to all is not paid and cannot be paid. Accordingly, there is no impairment of contract or inappropriate diminishment of pension benefits.

Preventing harm to public health, safety, and welfare. The Model Guidelines are focused only on reasonable modifications or reductions of pension benefits to the extent necessary to avoid a governmental emergency due to the failure to fully fund and provide governmental services. This requires the respective legislative body to determine in good faith the necessity of any reduction or modification of pension benefits and only to the extent necessary to ensure a balanced financial budget and the operation of government for the general welfare of its citizens. The legislative body, as the representative of the people's will, makes those determinations within the parameters of the Model Guidelines. If proposed modifications or reductions of pension benefits are too much or too little to balance the budget and provide governmental services at an acceptable level, the modifications or reductions would not meet the required test of the Model Guidelines. There must be a good-faith determination of what is necessary for the funding of such pension benefits to the fullest extent possible while not crowding out governmental services needed for the welfare and survival of the government and its people. The Model Guidelines are intended to address the governmental emergency through the necessary modification or reduction of pension benefits for the welfare of citizens and appropriate operation of government.

Any modification must balance citizen welfare with harm to pension beneficiaries. As noted, the Model Guidelines deal with modifications and reductions to pension benefits only to the degree necessary to allow appropriate operation of the government for the health, safety, and welfare of its citizens. The crowding out of funding of vital governmental services by unaffordable and unsustainable pension benefits is to be avoided. As part of a determination of a modification or reduction in pension benefits, the Model Guidelines require the legislative body to fund such pension benefits to the fullest extent possible so long as the fiscal year budget is balanced and governmental services are fully funded and provided for an acceptable level (as determined by the legislative body). The Model Guidelines leave to the legislative body the determination of what specific modifications or reductions should be made.

Modification or reduction of pension benefits of a prospective nature as of the effective date as opposed to those already in effect for past services, in the exercise of good faith, should be considered first. The unaffordability and unsustainability of the pension benefits may be so great that full funding of essential governmental services and appropriate operation of government may require pension benefits for past services earned to be modified or reduced so the government can continue to survive and fund the remaining pension benefits rather than face a financial meltdown, providing for less to all concerned. Further, the Model Guidelines provide for a validation process of any modification or reduction in earned pension benefits that are vested contractual rights. This process would be similar to a bond validation procedure where the governmental body, pursuant to a state statute, petitions a court to validate that the proposed modification or reduction in pension benefits meets the requirements of the Model Guidelines and that all required actions and legislative findings thereunder have been made so that, under applicable case law, any impairment of contractual rights is permitted for a higher public purpose. The process would provide for a public hearing with notice to all affected parties and an opportunity for them to be heard on an expedited basis with direct appeal to the highest court of the state and, if necessary, to the US Supreme Court based on the civil rights of citizens under the US Constitution to have their health, safety, and welfare protected by state and local governments and the Guarantee Clause of the US Constitution relating to a republican form of government.[64]

Further, the simple answer of not paying public debt and defaulting on those obligations is not only shortsighted but more likely in the long term fatal to the financial future of the government. Defaulting on public debt securities brings not only a financial stigma but also increased costs for borrowings necessary for needed infrastructure improvements as well as providing liquidity to governments given uneven and sometimes delayed tax payments. Being a weak credit due to unaffordable and unsustainable debt such as pension benefits (even without a default on public debt) can bring low credit ratings and high borrowing costs of an additional 2 percent to 3 percent additional interest cost per year.[65] An additional two hundred basis points (2 percent) annual interest cost on a twenty-year borrowing with a bullet maturity at 5 percent discount rate equals a present-value additional cost of borrowing of about 25 percent of the principal amount borrowed (namely, on a $1 billion principal borrowing, the additional present-value cost is about $250 million). Certainly, this additional significant cost could be better used to pay pension benefits or other governmental costs. For this reason, the Model Guidelines encourage financial credibility by the governmental entity.

The Model Guidelines are intended to balance the needs of an important public purpose (the general welfare of its citizens) with the least harm possible to beneficiaries of public pension funds, recognizing that if there are not funds sufficient to fund fully all reasonable costs, adjustments must be made. After exhausting tax increases and expenditure reduction, the legislative body balances the general health, safety, and welfare of citizens due to lack of funds to pay for necessary and needed governmental services against the harm suffered by pension beneficiaries due to implementation of proposed reduction or modification of pension benefits under the Model Guidelines. Further, the Model Guidelines, as part of balancing the interest of the general welfare of citizens and taxpayers against the harm suffered by public pension beneficiaries, provide that the annual actuarially determined contribution, or ADC, will be funded and paid by the government entity subject to such modification and reduction of pension benefits as provided for by the legislative body pursuant to the Model Guidelines.

The Model Guidelines do not allow governmental entities and legislative bodies to fail to make necessary modifications and reductions of pension benefits and still avoid the pain of unaffordable and unsustainable grants of pension benefits by requiring the payment of ADC each and every year. The difficult and troubling questions and possible litigation regarding whether unaffordable and unattainable grants of pension benefits were ultra vires and voidable acts by government officials (contrary to various balanced budget mandates contained in state constitutions and statutes)[66] can be avoided by the enactment of the Model Guidelines. Under the Model Guidelines, modification and reduction should be enacted by the legislative body promptly in good faith. Any unaffordable obligation that remains will be subject to clear pain of full funding of the ADC each year and the requirement of a balanced budget. Pursuant to the Model Guidelines, the legislative body is required to make specific legislative findings that justify the need for such modifications and reductions of benefits under the police power for a higher public good.[67]

Indeed, where the legislature has made an *express* determination that a statute is constitutional in the face of arguments that it is not, the statute should be upheld "unless it is clear beyond reasonable doubt that it is violative of the fundamental law." *Ala. State Fed'n of Labor v. McAdory*, 18 So.2d 810, 815 (Ala. 1944), *cert. dismissed*, 325 U.S. 450 (1945); *see also Huber v. Colorado Mining Ass'n*, 264 P.3d 884, 889 (Colo. 2011) ("We presume legislative enactments * * * to be constitutional. Overcoming this presumption requires a showing of unconstitutionality beyond reasonable doubt"); *Nelson*, 170 F.3d at 651 (under Michigan law, "a statute should not be declared unconstitutional unless the conflict between the Constitution and the statute is *palpable and free from reasonable doubt*") (emphasis original); *State v. Muhammad*, 678 A.2d 164, 173 (N.J. 1996) ("whenever a challenge is raised to the constitutionality of a statute, there is a strong presumption that the statute is constitutional. * * * Thus, any act of the Legislature will not be ruled void unless its repugnancy to the Constitution is clear beyond a reasonable doubt"); *Sch. Dists' Alliance for Adequate Funding of Special Educ. v. State*, 244 P.3d 1, 5 (Wash. 2010) ("the legislature is entitled to great deference and * * * a party challenging a statute's constitutionality must therefore prove the statute unconstitutional beyond a reasonable doubt"); *Chappy v. Labor & Indus. Review Comm'n*, 401 N.W.2d 568, 573–574 (Wis. 1987) ("there is a strong presumption that a legislative enactment is constitutional. * * * [T]he party challenging the statute carries a heavy burden of persuasion [and] must prove beyond a reasonable doubt that the act is unconstitutional"). In this context, "beyond a reasonable doubt" does not refer to an evidentiary standard, but rather emphasizes the court's "respect for the legislature" and the importance of conducting a "searching legal analysis" before determining that a statute violates the constitution. *Sch. Dists' Alliance*, 244 P.3d at 5. Courts, held that this deferential standard of review is prudent because "declaring a statute * * * to be unconstitutional is one of the gravest duties impressed upon the courts," *Huber*, 264 P.3d at 889, and because courts "do not act as a super-legislature." *Muhammad*, 678 A.2d at 173.

MODEL GUIDELINES AS A LEGISLATIVE STATEMENT OF PUBLIC PENSION FUNDING POLICY   If the political obstacles to enacting a constitutional amendment pursuant to the Model Guidelines are insurmountable or are not necessary as there is no state constitution pension protection clause, then the alternative approach is adopting the Model Guidelines as a legislative pronouncement of the governmental entity's public pension funding policy. Such legislative enactment may well draw significant litigation by representatives of current public employees and retirees. The response may be to take objections to public pension reforms head-on, based on the important public purpose of the government to first and foremost provide for the health, safety, and welfare of its citizens by fully funding governmental services and preventing anything, including pension benefits, from crowding out the fully funding of essential and needed services necessary for the general welfare of citizens. Such litigation of the exercise by the legislature of the public pension funding policy as pronounced in the Model Guidelines could lead to a test case. If such a test case is properly presented to the court, it could ease the way for pension reform to be enacted and implemented or the legislative public pension funding policy to be followed by the state and local governmental bodies.

The legislative enactment should be supported by factual analysis and finding of the governmental emergency and the crowding out of fully funding of needed governmental services by unaffordable and unsustainable pension benefits. In addition, public education and support of civic groups, taxpayers, workers, retirees, and citizens are essential, and the information developed in that effort should also be considered for inclusion in legislative findings. In addition, the governmental entity may proceed after public education efforts by referendum or survey of its citizens to determine the support for the public pension funding policy as set forth in the proposed Model Guidelines, which is to be incorporated into a legislative enactment. This developed record of the critical need and public support for the public pension funding policy contained in the Model Guidelines will provide the evidentiary and legislative support combined with the expression of the will of the people. As noted, the balancing of interests of the beneficiaries of pension benefits with the mission of government and the welfare of citizens is embodied in the Model Guidelines and public pension funding policy to be adopted by governmental entities.

To say that the government and the welfare of its citizens should fail or go lacking so that unaffordable pension benefits imprudently granted can be paid in full only leads to the failure and demise of government. As a result, the beneficiaries of pension benefits receive far less than that provided by the Model Guidelines and the legislative public pension funding policy related thereto.

LEGAL JUSTIFICATION FOR THE GUIDELINES' IMPAIRMENT OF CONTRACTUAL PUBLIC PENSION RIGHTS

The Contract Clause of the US Constitution Does Not Prevent the Exercise of Police Power

The mandate of state government and its reason for being are to provide essential governmental services at an acceptable level for the health, safety, and welfare of citizens so the state and its citizens may prosper and grow.[68] Legally, the assessment of a state's ability to adjust pension benefits begins with the Contract Clause in the US Constitution and the mission of the state to provide mandated public services at an acceptable level. Currently, it is widely accepted that public pensions are in the nature of a contract and therefore entitled to the protection of the Contract Clause.[69] Public pension protection is generally classified as a contractual right, whether the "right" is attributable to a constitutional provision or a state statute or judicially created by a court ruling.[70]

In a Government Contractual Relationship, the Government Does Not Surrender Essential Governmental Powers

The Contract Clause of the US Constitution provides that "no State shall pass any Law impairing the Obligation of Contracts" (Article I, Section 10,

Clause 1). The question raised is whether public pension obligations must be observed to the financial ruin of the state or local government or whether the obligations can be adjusted, modified, or reduced so that the government can fulfill its duty of providing essential public services at an acceptable level for its citizens.

For nearly two hundred years, courts have held that legislatures lack the power to "surrende[r] an essential attribute of [their] sovereignty" or "bargain away the police power of a State" *U.S. Trust Co. of N.Y. v. New Jersey*, 431 U.S. 1, 23 (1977) (quoting *Stone v. Mississippi*, 101 U.S. 814, 817 [1880]). As the US Supreme Court explained in *Butchers' Union Slaughter-House & Live-Stock Landing Co. v. Crescent City Live-Stock Landing & Slaughter-House Co.*, 111 U.S. 746, 751 (1884), "The preservation of [the public health and morals] is so necessary to the best interests of social organization, that a wise policy forbids the legislative body to divest itself of the power to enact laws for the preservation of health and the repression of crime." See also *Home Bldg. & Loan Ass'n v. Blaisdell*, 290 U.S. 398, 436–437 (1934) (collecting Supreme Court authority). This has been generally referred to as the exercise of police powers for a higher public purpose.

An early case holding that the US Contract Clause does not require a state to adhere to a contract that surrenders an essential governmental power was *Stone v. Mississippi*, 101 U.S. 814 (1879). In that case, the state had granted a charter to a lottery company for twenty-five years but subsequently adopted a constitutional provision banning lotteries. In upholding the constitutional ban, the court noted that supervision by the state of this issue needed to be dealt with "as the special exigencies of the moment require." *Id.* at 819. This limitation on the Contract Clause thus found its source in the police power, that is, in the capacity of the states to regulate behavior and enforce order within their territory in the interest of the health, safety, morals, and general welfare of the inhabitants.

THE POLICE POWER IS PARAMOUNT TO ANY CONTRACTUAL RIGHTS AND THE IMPLIED RESERVATION OF THE RIGHTS OF GOVERNMENT   This principle that a state may not alienate the basic police power that "is one of the great purposes for which the State government was brought into existence" has been generally recognized by state courts.[71] As these authorities demonstrate, the "national Constitution[al]" problem with alienating police power is that such power is an "essential"—indeed the "inherent" and defining—characteristic of a sovereign state. Cooley, Treatise, at 283. The very "maintenance of a government" *at all* requires that a state "retai[n] adequate authority to secure the peace and good order of society": the "necessary residuum of state power" is that "the state * * * continues to possess authority to safeguard the vital interests of its people." *Home Bldg. & Loan Ass'n*, 290 U.S. 398, 434–35 (1934). And those vital interests extend to the economic well-being of the state as well as to public order and safety. As the Supreme Court has said, "The economic interests of the state may justify the exercise of its continuing and dominant protective power * * *." *Id.* at 437.[72] The nation's federalist structure depends on "every State in this Union" in fact governing, exercising its police powers so as to maintain the conditions for commerce and prevent the need for the United States to make good on its Article IV, Section 4, "guarantee" to backstop a failure to govern with federal power.[73]

In another early case, parties who had contracted with the state for clear passage through a creek objected to subsequent legislation providing for the installation of a dam across it. *Manigault v. Springs*, 199 U.S. 473, 473 (1905). The US Supreme Court noted that police power is *paramount* to any contractual right, and the principle against the impairment of contracts does not prevent the state from exercising such powers as are vested in it for the promotion of the common good. *Id.* at 480.

Similarly, in *Chicago and Alton Railroad Company v. Tranbarger*, the plaintiff argued that subsequent legislation requiring railroads to construct ditches and drains interfered with its operation. *Chicago & Alton R.R. Co. v. Tranbarger*, 238 U.S. 67, 74 (1915). The Supreme Court found that no person has a vested right in any policy of legislation entitling him to insist that it shall remain unchanged, nor is such right implied in any express contract. *Id.* at 76. There is an implied reservation of rights that cannot be abrogated, surrendered, or bargained away by contractual provisions. In an extension of this view, the Supreme Court in *Stephenson v. Binford* rejected the complaint of private carriers to provisions of highway legislation; it noted that contracts are to be regarded as having been made subject to the future exercise of the constitutional police power of the state. *See Phillips Petroleum Co. v. Jenkins*, 297 U.S. 629 (1936).

There is no doubt that the principles described above prohibit a state by contract conferring special immunities from its power to advance the public welfare. As Justice Holmes explained, "One whose rights * * * are subject to state restriction, cannot remove them from the power of the state by making a contract about them. The contract will carry with it the infirmity of the subject-matter." *Hudson Cnty. Water Co. v. McCarter*, 209 U.S. 549, 357 (1908). Allowing alienation of the police power would permit states to delegate too much authority to a private person, who may not act for the best interests of the community. Courts have adopted two rules to implement this prohibition. First, where a contract is silent on alienating the state's reserved powers, the contract will be understood as reserving them to the Stats. *Home Bldg. & Loan Ass'n*, 290 U.S. at 435 ("the reservation of essential attributes of sovereign power is * * * read into contracts as a postulate of the legal order"). Second, clear and express contractual promises to alienate the state's reserved power are void and unenforceable. *Butchers' Union Slaughter-House & Live-Stock Landing Co. v. Crescent City Live-Stock Landing & Slaughter-House Co.*, 111 U.S. 746 at 751 (1884); *Stone v. Mississippi*, 101 U.S. 814 at 817–819 (1880).[74]

The United States Supreme Court Recognizes Balancing of Interests as Applied to the Contract Clause

Over time the Supreme Court's stated reasoning in determining the propriety of alleged impairment of contract rights has become more nuanced. In *Homebuilding & Loan Ass'n v. Blaisdell*, the Minnesota Mortgage Moratorium Law (which provided that, during a declared emergency, relief could be had with respect to mortgage foreclosures and execution sales) was challenged as being repugnant to the Contract Clause. *Homebuilding & Loan Ass'n v. Blaisdell*, 290 U.S. 398 (1934). The United States Supreme Court upheld the statute as a valid exercise of the police power, noting that the constitutional protection against the abrogation of contracts was qualified by the authority the state possesses to safeguard the vital interests of its people and that the legislature cannot bargain away the public health or the public morals. Further, the economic interests of the state may justify the exercise of its continuing and dominant protective power, notwithstanding any interference with contracts. Importantly for this analysis, the *Blaisdell* court noted that there needs to be a *rational compromise* between individual rights and the public welfare. It articulated the conditions that justify interference with contractual rights, including the following: an emergency is present, the legislation is addressed to a legitimate end, the relief afforded is of a character appropriate to the emergency, and the conditions do not appear to be unreasonable. *Id.* at 444.

CONTRACTUAL RIGHTS ARE NOT ABSOLUTE   The US Supreme Court applied these principles in an instance of governmental distress. In *Asbury Park*, the Supreme Court upheld a challenge by the unsecured bondholders of Asbury Park to a New Jersey law that provided for a plan of adjustment in which they received refunding bonds that represented a haircut from their original securities. The Supreme Court specifically rejected the bondholders' claims that the original bonds "constituted contracts, the obligation of which was impaired by the denial of their right to recovery thereon and by the transmutation without their consent into the securities authorized by the plan of adjustment." 316 U.S. 502, 509. The Supreme Court also rejected the view that the Contract Clause barred "the only proven way for sure payment of unsecured municipal obligations." *Id.* at 512–13. According to the *Asbury Park* Court, the state retains police power for the maintenance of its political subdivisions and for the protection of all citizens. *Id.* at 513–14. The Court specifically noted that its holding did not apply to secured claims, claims secured by property (revenues) dedicated or pledged for the obligation by statute or contract, such as revenue bonds. *Id.* at 516. Further, the Court commented that, in view of the slump of the collections from the exercise of the city's taxing power, the original bonds had little value. *Id.* at 513. The *Asbury Park* Court noted that, under the circumstances, the modification of contract obligations was not an impairment but a recognition of limited resources, and the paper rights of the contract did not alter the duties of government to provide essential services.[75] The Court in *El Paso v. Simmons,* 379 U.S. 497 (1965), cited these cases when summarizing that not every modification of a contractual promise impairs the obligation of a contract under the Contract Clause. The Court cited *Blaisdell* for the proposition that the prohibition against impairment of contract "is not . . . absolute . . . and is not to be read with literal exactness like a mathematical formula." *Id.* at 509.

Many view the *U.S. Trust* decision as the case in which the Supreme Court refined its analysis of the ability to impair public contracts. The trustee and holder of port authority bonds brought suit, claiming that a New Jersey statute impaired the obligations of the state's contract with bondholders in violation of the Contract Clause. 431 U.S. 1, 3. Citing *Blaisdell,* the Supreme Court confirmed that the Contract Clause was not absolute. *Id.* at 21. However, the Court noted that the New Jersey statute, in fact, *totally eliminated* an important security provision for the bonds. *Id.* at 19. The Court specified that when a state impairs the obligations of its own contract, the "reserved-powers doctrine has a different basis." *Id.* at 23. Impairment may be constitutional if it is reasonable and necessary to serve an important public purpose. *Id.* The court found that the *extent* of impairment is a relevant factor in determining its reasonableness. *Id.* at 27.

The following year, in *Allied Structural Steel Co. v. Spannaus,* the Supreme Court quoted *U.S. Trust* for the proposition that the Contract Clause does not obliterate the police power of the statute but does impose some limits upon the power of the state to abridge existing contractual relationships. *Al-*

lied Structural Steel Co. v. Spannaus, 438 U.S. 234 (1978). Legislation adjusting the rights and responsibilities of contracting parties must be based on reasonable conditions and of a character appropriate to the public purpose justifying its adoption. *See Id.* at 242.

The wisdom of the above-cited US Supreme Court cases should reinforce the appropriate interpretation of the Model Guidelines that unaffordable pension benefits whose funding would interfere with the appropriate funding of governmental services and infrastructure must be reasonably adjusted for the sake of all concerned.[76]

CONCLUSION

If pension reform efforts under current state law have failed and state constitutional and statutory provisions are obstacles to any needed pension reform efforts, the answer should not and cannot be that the government reduces funding for essential governmental services, services decline to unacceptable levels, the government melts down financially, and corporate and individual taxpayers leave. As horrific and unacceptable as that result would be, it is the probable reality state and local governments face if needed pension reform is not capable of being implemented. This is not the case of unwillingness to pay, which is never an acceptable excuse for not funding public pension obligations. Rather, this is the financial and practical inability to pay and still provide the services that are mandated by the vital mission of government. This chapter provides four possible alternatives to prevent the financial ruin of the government and the resulting human suffering of its citizens, taxpayers, workers, and retirees.

First, effect restructuring of obligations and priorities through an expedited and efficient prepackaged Chapter 9 plan of municipal debt adjustment that is negotiated and agreed upon before jumping into a Chapter 9 proceeding.

Second, create a new federal bankruptcy court for public pension funds that find themselves insolvent. The government employer and pension fund with the help of a specialized court designed to balance the best interests of the workers and retirees, and the best interest of taxpayers, citizens, and local business interests, resolve the insolvency and government function emergency. The goal will be to pay as much as can be paid on pension obligations while ensuring full funding of essential governmental services at an acceptable level. Again, the purpose of the new federal bankruptcy court is to provide a fair and just resolution of the pension fund insolvency with an objective independent determination of what is sustainable and affordable;

whether there should be an increase in contributions or taxes or both, if necessary; and what is the best method of adjusting pension obligations to a level that is feasible and affordable for the benefit of all.

Third, use a Government Oversight, Refinance, and Debt Adjustment Commission as supervisor and overseer of the government to facilitate consensual resolution and, if necessary, determine what can be paid and what cannot. The local government would propose a recovery plan with the ability to comment or object by interested parties, including workers and retirees, followed by a hearing before GORDAC. If agreement on the recovery plan is not reached, then GORDAC would rule on the recovery plan and enforce it, thereby using the approved recovery plan (possibly modified by GORDAC) as a prepackaged Chapter 9 plan of debt adjustment.

Fourth, if none of the above alternatives is possible or desirable, there can be a resort to a constitutional amendment or statutory public pension funding policy that follows the Model Guidelines and US Supreme Court precedent for modification or adjustment of contractual rights for a higher public purpose to protect the health, safety, and welfare of citizens. This constitutional amendment or legislative policy would provide for legislative findings to support the need and justification for the modification or adjustment of pension benefits, consistent with the Model Guidelines, developed case law, and the purported rights of workers and retirees, while assuring taxpayers, citizens, and business interests that governmental services will be fully funded and provided at an acceptable level. The public pension obligation, as mandated by the amendment and public policy, would be paid to the fullest extent possible without crowding out full funding for needed essential services and infrastructure. Also, the actuarially determined contribution for the annual pension fund payment would be calculated and mandated to be paid each year to assure the public workers and retirees that past underfunding practices will not be repeated and appropriate funding will be made.

These alternatives are conceptual proposals to be further refined and developed by the constructive dialogue of interested parties. While voluntary resolution of unfunded pension problems is the preferred and most appropriate approach, when all else fails, these four methods provide a realistic and practical way of resolving pension underfunding and preventing a government service and financial meltdown. The answer should never be that the needed public pension reforms have failed or appear impossible so the government itself fails and all parties suffer the worst outcome possible.

Notes

1. U.S. Constit. pmbl.

2. McQuillin, The Law of Municipal Corporations, §§ 1.20, 1.40 (3d ed. 2013).

3. Amy B. Monahan, *Public Pension Plan Reform, The Legal Framework*, 5 Educ. fin. & Pol'y 617 (2010).

4. U.S. Const. art. I, § 10, cl. 1, and similar provisions in state constitutions.

5. *See* discussion in James E. Spiotto, *How Municipalities in Financial Distress Should Deal with Unfunded Pension Obligations and Appropriate Funding of Essential Services*, 50 Willamette L. Rev. 515 (2014) (hereafter cited as *Willamette*).

6. While the National Conference on Public Employee Retirement Systems has released a study purporting to demonstrate that public pensions are net contributors to state and local economies through the investment of pension fund assets, the study goes only so far. www.businesswire.com/news/home/20180516005930/en/NCPERS -Study-Shows-Public-Pensions-Net-Contributors. Further analysis must be conducted as to the adverse effect on those economies of failure to fund infrastructure improvements and essential services as a result of funding public pensions.

In its 2016 economic study, *Failure to Act: Closing the Infrastructure Investment Gap for America's Economic Future,* www.infrastructurereportcard.org/the-impact/ failure-to-act-report/, the American Society of Civil Engineers has predicted that if we do not do $4.9 trillion of needed infrastructure improvements by 2025 (of which at least $2 trillion presently has no source of funding), it will cost the country $3.9 trillion in losses to the US gross domestic product, $7 trillion in lost business sales, and 2.5 million lost American jobs. There needs to be a balancing of interests and costs, and it appears that if services and infrastructure improvements are shorted, the adverse effect is far more significant to all as opposed to shorting payments to public pensions that are truly unaffordable.

7. *See* Jean-Pierre Aubry and Caroline V. Crawford, *State and Local Pension Reform Since the Financial Crisis*, 54 Center for Retirement Research at Boston College (January 2017).

8. *Pension Reforms Continue Since 2016*, National Association of State Retirement Administrators, www.NASRA.org/pensionreform.

9. While some state and local governments have made progress and have solved, for the most part, any pension underfunding issue that may exist, there still remain a considerable number of about four thousand public pension plans on behalf of 19.5 million active and former employees that are still troubled by significant underfunding of public pension liabilities. *State and Local Government Pensions at a Crossroads*, the CPA Journal (April 2017) www.cpajournal.com/2017/05/08/state-local-government-pensions -crossroads/; Urban Institute, *State and Local Government Pensions*, www.urban.org/ policy-centers/cross-center-initiatives/state-local-finance-initiative/projects/state -and-local-backgrounders/state-and-local-government-pensions.

As Bloomberg has reported:

According to *Hidden Debt, Hidden Deficits*, a 2017 data-rich study of US pension systems by Hoover Institution Senior Fellow Joshua Rauh, almost every state or local government has an unbalanced budget—due to runaway pension fund costs that are continually chipping away at already inadequate budgets.

In 2016, Rauh stated, "while state and local governments across the US largely claimed they ran balanced budgets, in fact they ran deficits through their pension systems of $167 billion." That amounts to 189.2% of state and local governments' total tax revenue.

According to the 2017 report, total unfunded pension liabilities have reached $3.85 trillion. That's 434 billion more than last year. Amazingly, of that $3.85 trillion, only $1.38 trillion was recognized by state and local governments.

Laurie Meisler, *Pension Fund Problems Worsen in 43 States*, Bloomberg (August 29, 2017), https://Bloomberg.com/graphics/2017-state-pension-funding-ratio/ at page 2.

According to Bloomberg, as of 2016, five states have pension funding levels of less than 50 percent (New Jersey, Kentucky, Illinois, Connecticut, and Colorado), and six additional states had public pension funding below 60 percent and above 50 percent (Pennsylvania, Minnesota, South Carolina, Rhode Island, Massachusetts, and New Hampshire). Another nine states had pension funding below 70 percent and above 60 percent (Louisiana, Indiana, Michigan, Vermont, Maryland, Kansas, New Mexico, North Dakota, and Alabama). Twenty-two states have public pension funding of less than 70 percent of liabilities as of 2016. *Id.*

See Olivier Garret, *The Disturbing Trend That Will End in a Full Fledged Pension Crisis*, Forbes (June 9, 2017), www.forbes.com/sites/oliviergarret/2017/06/09/the-disturbing-trend-that-will-end-in-a-full-fuledged-pension-crisis/#4530896a6620.

10. *See U.S. Trust Co. of N.Y. v. N.J.*, 431 U.S. 1 (1977).

11. Keith Brainard and Alex Brown, *Spotlight on Significant Reforms to State Retirement Systems*, National Association of State Retirement Administrators (June 2016), www.nasra.org/files/spotlight/ significant%20reforms.pdf.

12. *See Id., Willamette*, fn. 29.

13. Between 2009 and 2016, there were twenty states with courts that ruled in favor of pension reform out of more than twenty-six states that had courts that ruled on pension reform issues. These decisions dealt with increased employee contributions, suspended or reduced cost-of-living adjustments, elimination of spiking, plan conversion, elimination of early retirement incentives, changes in final salary calculation, and elimination of gainsharing. Some of the states that ruled favorably on some form of pension reform were Alabama, California, Colorado, Florida, Georgia, Idaho, Kentucky, Maine, Massachusetts, Michigan, New Hampshire, New Jersey, New Mexico, Ohio, Rhode Island, South Dakota, Tennessee, Texas, Washington, and Wisconsin. Also, the territory of Puerto Rico had a favorable ruling on pension reform. *Hernandez v. Commonwealth*, 188 D.P.R. 828 (2013) (translation).

14. For nearly two hundred years, courts have held that legislatures lack the power to "surrende[r] an essential attribute of [their] sovereignty" or "bargain away the police power of a State" *U.S. Trust Co. of N.Y. v. N.J.*, 431 U.S. 1, 23 (1977) (quoting *Stone v. Miss.*, 101 U.S. 814, 817 [1880]). As the US Supreme Court explained in *Butchers'*

Union Slaughter-House & Live-Stock Landing Co. v. Crescent City Live-Stock Landing & Slaughter-House Co., 111 U.S. 746, 751 (1884), "The preservation of [the public health and morals] is so necessary to the best interests of social organization, that a wise policy forbids the legislative body to divest itself of the power to enact laws for the preservation of health and the repression of crime." *See also Home Bldg. & Loan Ass'n v. Blaisdell*, 290 U.S. 398, 436–437 (1934) (collecting Supreme Court authority). This has been recognized by recent state court rulings. *See, e.g., Justus v. State of Colo.*, 336 P.3d 202 (Colo. 2014) (distinguishing true contract obligations from public policy to be changed by the legislature). *Hernandez v. Commonwealth*, 188 D.P.R. 828 (2013) (translation) (recognizing US Supreme Court precedent for impairing pension contractual rights for a higher public purpose).

15. This principle that a state may not alienate the basic police power "is one of the great purposes for which the State government was brought into existence" and has been recognized by the courts of various states. *E.g., Chicago, R. I. & P. Ry. Co. v. Taylor*, 192 P. 349,356 (Okla. 1920) ("As neither the state nor the municipality can surrender by contract the [police] power * * *, a contract purporting to do so is void ab initio, and, being void, it is impossible to speak of laws in conflict with its terms as impairing the obligations of a contract"); *Brick Presbyterian Church v. City of N.Y.*, 5 Cow. 538, 542 (N.Y. Sup. Ct. 1826). It has been described in leading treatises. *E.g.,* Thomas M. Cooley, A Treatise on the Constitutional Limitations which Rest upon the Legislative Power of the States of the American Union 283 (1868) ("the prevailing opinion" is "that the state could not barter away, or in any manner abridge or weaken, any of those essential powers which are inherent in all governments" and "that any contracts to that end cannot be enforced under the provision of the national Constitution now under consideration"); Christopher G. Tiedman, A Treatise on the Limitations of Police Power in the United States 580–581 (1886) (it has "been often decided, in the American courts, federal and state, that the state cannot * * * in any way curtail its exercise of any of those powers, which are essential attributes of sovereignty, and particularly the police power"). The very "maintenance of a government" *at all* requires that a state "retai[n] adequate authority to secure the peace and good order of society": the "necessary residuum of state power" is that "the state * * * continues to possess authority to safeguard the vital interests of its people." *Home Bldg. & Loan Ass'n*, 290 U.S. 398, 434–435 (1934). And those vital interests extend to the economic well-being of the state as well as to public order and safety. As the Supreme Court has said, "The economic interests of the state may justify the exercise of its continuing and dominant protective power * * *." *Id.* at 437.

16. N.Y. Constit. art. V, sec. 7. Other states with constitutional protections for public-sector retirement benefits include Alaska (Alaska Constit., Article XII, § 7), Arizona (Ariz. Constit., Article XXIX, § 1), Hawaii (Haw. Constit., Article XVI, § 2), Illinois (Ill. Constit., Article XIII, § 5), Louisiana (La. Constit., Article X, §29), Michigan (Mich. Constit., Article IX, § 19), and Texas (Tex. Constit., Article XVI, § 66(d).

17. *Public Employees Federation v. Cuomo*, 62 N.Y.2d 450 (1984).

18. Ill. Constit. 1970, Art. XIII, § 5.

19. *In re Pension Reform Litg.*, 2015 IL 118585 (2015). In this state pension reform case, more than ten separate amicus curiae briefs, in support of the state reforms, were filed with the court, but, in an unusual move by the Illinois Supreme Court, each of these amicus curiae briefs was stricken and not considered due to the objection of the labor representatives that it would take too much time for the labor representatives to respond to the amici curiae arguments. Some of the arguments and footnotes herein are taken from those amici curiae briefs. We may wonder if the result or language of the court's opinion would have changed if the amici curiae arguments were considered by the court.

20. From the State of Illinois's perspective, pension contributions from general funds more than quadrupled to $6.9 billion in fiscal year 2017 from $1.6 billion in FY 2008 and are expected to increase to $7 billion in FY 2018 or approaching 23 percent of the general fund revenues in FY 2018. The State of Illinois's unpaid bills reached $6.997 billion by FY 2016 and were, as of the end of FY 2017, approximately $14.7 billion. According to the Civic Federation, by the end of FY 2016, the State of Illinois unfunded liability had grown to $129.1 billion, based on the market value of assets and funded ratio about 40 percent, which is one of the lowest among the states.

In 1995, when the state enacted previous pension reform legislation, the unfunded pension obligation for the State of Illinois was $19.8 billion. There has been a 650 percent increase in the unfunded pension obligations over the past twenty years to $129.1 billion. The unfunded pension fund liability for the state's pension plans of $129.1 billion as of FY 2016 is approximately 333 percent of the State of Illinois's general fund revenues for FY 2016. Pension obligations being underfunded by 100 percent to 200 percent of annual revenues collected by government is a very difficult challenge, but underfunding exceeding 300 percent of a government's annual revenues collected is fatal to government services and clearly unaffordable and unsustainable. *See* Civic Federation, *State of Illinois FY2019 Budget Roadmap* (February 9, 2018), https://civicfed.org/sites/default/files/fy2019reportroadmap_0.pdf.

Michael Cembalest of J. P. Morgan Asset Management, in his 2014 Report (www .jpmorgan.com/jpmpdf/1320668288866.pdf) and 2016 Report (www.jpmorgan.com/jpmpdf/1320702681156.pdf), calculated that approximately 40 percent of Illinois's state revenue collected over the next thirty-year period would be required to pay interest on bonded debt and the state's share of defined-benefit plan actuarially required contributions, retiree health care costs, and defined-contribution plan expenses with level payments and a 6 percent pension investment return. This is a clear demonstration of crowding out needed funding of governmental services. Only eleven other states are above 15 percent of state revenues collected, and only three states, including Illinois, are above 25 percent. Illinois had the highest percentage of revenues collected required to pay pension underfunding obligations at approximately 40 percent of state revenues collected over a thirty-year period.

21. *Jones v. Mun. Emp. Annuity and Benefit Fund of Chi.*, 2016 Il. 119618 (2016).

22. The city had interesting and appealing arguments that it had offered new consideration in increased pension payments above those required by statutes and that,

under Illinois law, the city was not liable to pay more than the statutory formula required, which they had fully complied with each year. See Section 22-403 of the Illinois Pension Code. The State of Illinois in legislation has set forth for Chicago a statutory formula for the annual funding payment for pension liability. The city had dutifully paid what the state statute mandated. However, the legislative formula bore no practical relationship to the actual pension liabilities incurred in that year or prior years, so this mismatch created a significant amount of underfunding over the years. The city in its proposed pension reform offered to make payments significantly in excess of the statutory formula amount that were not required by statute to be made. This was a real benefit to the public workers since state court rulings prohibited courts from ordering public employers to make additional payments absent the insolvency of the pension fund. *See McNamee v. The State of Ill.*, 173 Ill. 2d 433 (1996), *People ex rel. Sklodowski v. State of Ill.*, 182 Ill. 2d 220 (1998).

23. *Allen v. City of Long Beach*, 287 P.2d 765, 767 (Cal. 1955).

24. *Cal Fire Local 288 1 v. CalPERS*, 7 Cal. App. 5th 115 (1st Dist. 2016), *review granted*, 391 P.3d (Cal. Apr. 12, 2017); *Marin Assoc. of Public Emp. v. Marin Cnty. Emp. Retirement Assoc.*, 2 Cal. App. 5th 674 (1st Dist. 2016), *review granted*, 383 P.3d 1105 (Cal. Nov. 22, 2016); *Alameda Cnty. Deputy Sheriff's Association, et al. v. Alameda Cnty. Emp. Retirement Assn.*, 19 Cal. App. 5th 61 (1st Dist. 2018), *review granted*, 413 P.3d 1132 (Cal. Mar. 28, 2018).

25. *Marin Assoc. of Public Emp. v. Marin Cnty. Emp. Retirement Assoc.*, 2 Cal. App. 5th 674 (1st Dist. 2016), *review granted*, 383 P.3d 1105 (Cal. Nov. 22, 2016); *Cal. Fire Local 2881 v. Cal. Public Emp. Retirement System*, 7 Cal. App. 5th 115 (2016) *review granted*, 391 P.3d (Cal. Apr. 12, 2017).

26. *Marin Assoc. of Public Emp. v. Marin Cnty. Emp. Retirement Assoc.*, 2 Cal. App. 5th at 699. The need in California for reasonable flexibility for needed public pension modification was demonstrated in a recent study examining fourteen California jurisdictions. This study found that, from 2002–3 to 2017–18, these jurisdictions were forced to increase pension contributions by more than 400 percent on average. Joe Nation, *Pension Math: Public Pension Spending and Service Crowd Out in California, 2003–2030*, at x (2018) (hereafter cited as *Nation Report*), available at https://siepr.stanford.edu/research/publications/pension-math-public-spending-and-service-crowd-out-california-2003/. The result of such drastic increased pension contribution was that these local governments were forced to cut important programs, such as "social, welfare and educational services, as well as . . . libraries, recreation, and community services." *Id.* at xi. Some local governments were forced to threaten public safety such as the City of Vallejo experienced, in large part because of rising pension costs. The City of Vallejo was forced to slash employment in its police department from 221 to 143 and in its fire department from 133 to 94. *Id.* at 60. These drastic measures were not enough to keep pension costs under control. Between 2008 and 2015, debt for these fourteen local government pension systems soared from $11.8 billion to nearly $120 billion—an increase of more than 900 percent. *Id.* at 84.

27. *Id.* at 680.

28. *Moro v. St. of Or.*, 351 P.3d 1 (Or. 2015); *Byrne, et al. v. St. of Mont., et al.*, No. ADV-2013-738, (Mont. First Judicial Dist. Ct., Lewis and Clark Cnty., June 30, 2015) (order granting summary judgment), appeal dismissed on stip., DA 15-0140 (Mont. July 23, 2015).

29. *See Fields v. Elected Officials' Retirement* Plan, 234 Ariz. 214 (2014); *Hall v. Elected Officials' Retirement Plan*, 241 Ariz. 33 (2016).

30. Thom Reilly, *Prop 124—Changes to the Public Safety Personnel Retirement System (PSRS)*, Ariz. St. University, Morrison Institute for Public Policy (April 2016), https://morrisoninstitute.asu.edu/products/undersanding-arizonas-propositions-2016. In 2017 two Arizona legislators raised the issue of the need for additional reform and constitutional amendment since municipalities were financially challenged to pay the required payments under Proposition 124 and many face filing for Chapter 9 municipal adjustment. Craig Harris, *Amend Arizona's Constitution to Alter Police and Fire Pensions? 2 GOP Lawmakers Say Yes*, Arizona Republic (August 2, 2017), www.azcentral.com/story/news/politics/arizona/2017/08/02/2-gop-lawmakers-seek-amend-arizona-constitution-tackle-public-safety-pension-costs/527009001/.

31. 11 U.S.C. § 901 *et seq.*

32. For a detailed discussion of Chapter 9 and its unique characteristics, particularly regarding secured claims, see James E. Spiotto, *Municipalities in Distress* (2d ed.) (Chapman and Cutler, 2016), available at Amazon.

33. 11 U.S.C. § 109(c).

34. Twelve states have statutory provisions specifically authorizing the filing of a Chapter 9 petition by an in-state municipality: Alabama, Arizona, Arkansas, Idaho, Minnesota, Missouri, Montana, Nebraska, Oklahoma, South Carolina, Texas, and Washington. Another twelve states authorizing a filing conditioned on a further act of the state, an elected official or a state entity, or through some other required process like use of a neutral evaluator mechanism: California, Connecticut, Florida, Kentucky, Louisiana, Michigan, New Jersey, New York, North Carolina, Ohio, Pennsylvania, and Rhode Island. Three states grant limited authorization (Colorado, Illinois, and Oregon), and two states prohibit filing (Georgia and Iowa), but Iowa has an exception to the prohibition. The remaining twenty-one states either are unclear or do not provide specific authorization with respect to filing as part of their state law. The District of Columbia and Puerto Rico, including municipalities in Puerto Rico, are not permitted to file Chapter 9 pursuant to the terms of the Bankruptcy Code, although a special statute known as PROMESA governs the insolvency of Puerto Rico. Pub. L. No. 114-187, 130 Stat. 549 (2016).

35. *In re City of Detroit, Mich.*, 504 B.R. 97 (Bankr. E.D. Mich. 2013); *In re City of Stockton, Cal.*, 478 B.R. 8, 23 (Bankr. E.D. Cal. 2012).

36. Alex Emslie, *Vallejo City Manager Responds to Questions about Police Shootings*, KQED News (May 20, 2014), https: 11ww2.org/news/2014/05/20/vallejo-city-manager-responds-to-questions-about-police-shootings.

37. Alison Vekshin and Martin Z. Braun, *Vallejo's Bankruptcy "Failure" Scares Cities into Cutting Costs*, Bloomberg (December 13, 2010), www.bloomberg.com/

news/articles/2010-12-14/vallejo-s-california-bankruptcy-failure-scares-cities-into
-cost-cutting. Others report a higher number, $13 million, for legal costs. *See* Hannah Dreier, *Vallejo Bankruptcy: California City Emerges from Financial Disaster*, Huffington Post (July 23, 2012), http://www.huffingtonpost.com/2012/07/23/vallejo
-bankruptcy_n_1693863.html.

38. Mike Shedlock, *Vallejo Faces 2nd Bankruptcy Because They Didn't Restructure Pensions*, Union Watch (October 2, 2013), http://unionwatch.org/vallejo-faces-2nd
-bankruptcy-because-they-didnt-restructure-pensions. Vallejo had a budget deficit for 2014 and a projected budget deficit of $9 million for 2015. Adan Shapiro, *Back to the (Bankruptcy) Drawing Board for California Towns?*, Fox Business News (February 21, 2014), www.foxbusiness.com/politics/2014/02/21/back-to-bankruptcy-drawing
-board-for-california-towns.html.

39. Melanie Hicken, *Once Bankrupt, Vallejo Still Can't Afford Its Pricey Pensions*, CNN Money (March 10, 2014). The adverse effect of unaffordable public pension costs for Vallejo has continued. The City of Vallejo saw its pension contributions zoom from 3.1 percent of operating expenses in 2003–4 to 15.2 percent in 2017–18. *Nation Report* at 58. As noted above, in note 26, to pay for that astronomical increase and other rising costs, the city had no choice but to slash its workforce from 2004 to 2014. *Id.* at 60. By 2029–30, the city will likely be spending between 23.7 percent and 27.3 percent of its total budget on pensions—an increase of 665 percent to 781 percent. *Id.* That could force the city to cut the police and fire departments by another 33 percent, or cut the budget by 12 percent across the board. *Id.* at 61. This threatens not only the health and safety of its citizens but also the long-term sustainability of government, which is the predicate for continued public employment and pension payments.

40. *In re City of Stockton, Cal.*, 478 B.R. 8, 20 (Bankr. E.D. Cal. 2012).

41. Amended Opinion Regarding Confirmation and Status of CalPERS, *In re City of Stockton, Cal.*, 526 B.R. 35 (Bankr. E.D. Cal. 2015, *aff'd* 542 B.R. 261 (9th Cir. BAP Dec. 11, 2015).

42. Mary Williams Walsh, *Judge Approves Bankruptcy Exit for Stockton, Calif.*, New York Times (October 30, 2014), https://dealbook.nytimes.com/2014/10/30/judge-approves
-bankruptcy-exit-for-stockton-calif/. In Stockton,

> The termination fee has been contentious issue for years, surfacing most notably in the Stockton bankruptcy case. The city tried to get out from underneath its $370 million unfunded liabilities by switching pension providers. In response, CalPERS produced a bill for $1.6 billion, which Judge Christopher Klein likened to at 'poison pill'.
>
> Out of the ashes of the Great Recession—after losing about $100 billion in investments—CalPERS began thinking more conservatively. In 2011, it slashed the anticipated rate of returns on investments, from 7.75 to 3.8 percent, for agencies looking to quit the system. In which case CalPERS would continue to manage the pensions of retired employees but shift the funds to a lower yield account. It wound up raising the termination fee. By a lot.

Jesse Marx, *Leaving CalPERS Could Cost Agency One-Third of Its Budget*, Desert Sun (May 17, 2016), www.desertsun.com/story/news/2016/05/12/leave-calpers-citrus

-district-nees-half-million/81666626/. Four retired city employees of the town of Loyalton, California, had their pensions sliced by CalPERS because the town defaulted on its payment to the fund. CalPERS levied a $1.66 million "termination fee" on the town of Loyalton with about 760 population and an annual budget of less than $1 million, and "hundreds of other government employees across the state may soon face a similar fate." Phil Willon, *This Tiny Sierra Valley Town Voted to Pull Out of CalPERS: Now Retirees Are Seeing Their Pensions Slashed*, Los Angeles Times (August 2017), www.latimes.com/politics/la-pol-ca-loyalton-calpers-pension-problems -20170806-htmlstory.html. *See also*, How to Leave CalPERS without Paying a Huge Fee, Calpension (August 11, 2015), https://calpension.com/2015/08/10/how-to -leave-calpers-without-paying-huge-fee/.

Riverside County Pest Control District No. 2 in September 2015 "decided to walk away from California Public Employees' Retirement System which manages the investment and retirement benefits. Although the District account was more than 140 percent funded in 2014." The district thought the termination fee would be $90,000, but by March 2016 "the fee climbed to $447,000—a third of the agency's annual budget." Marx, *Leaving CalPERS*.

43. Order Confirming Third Amended Plan for the Adjustment of Debts of the City of San Bernardino, Cal. (JULY 29, 2016), As Modified; Findings of Fact and Conclusions of Law in Respect Thereof, *In re City of San Bernardino, Cal.*, No. 6:12-28006 (Bankr. C.D. Cal. Feb. 7, 2017), ECF No. 2164.

44. *In re City of Detroit, Mich.*, 504 B.R. 97, 150 (Bankr. E.D. Mich. 2013).

45. Order Confirming Eighth Amended Plan for the Adjustment of Debts of the City of Detroit, *In re City of Detroit, Mich.*, No. 13-53846 (Bankr. E.D. Mich. Nov. 12, 2014), ECF No. 8272; *see also* Supplemental Opinion Regarding Plan Confirmation, *In re City of Detroit, Mich.*, No. 13-53846 (Bankr. E.D. Mich. Dec. 31, 2014), ECF No. 8993.

46. Marc Lifsher and Melody Petersen, *Judge Approves Stockton Bankruptcy Plan; Worker's Pensions Safe*, LA Times (October 30, 2014), www.latimes.com/business/ la-fi-stockton-pension-court-ruling-cuts-20141029-story.html.

47. *See* Amended Opinion and Order Regarding the Reasonableness of Fees Under 11 U.S.C. Sec. 943(b)(3), *In re City of Detroit, Mich.*, Case No. 13-53846 (Bankr. E.D. Mich. Feb. 12, 2015), ECF No. 9257.

48. It should be noted that since July 2013, when Detroit filed for Chapter 9, no city, county, village, or town has filed for Chapter 9 except Hillview, Kentucky, a town with a population of approximately eight thousand. Hillview dismissed the case without filing a plan of debt adjustment (having settled with a judgment creditor that was the primary cause for filing the Chapter 9). *In re City of Hillview, Ken.*, Case No. 15-32679 (Bankr. W.D. Ken. 2015).

49. As noted, the *Marin County* and *CalFire* cases, pending in the California Supreme Court, will provide the opportunity for the clarification of the California Rule to eliminate the need for a comparable new advantage for any disadvantage the pension beneficiary may suffer, thereby allowing reasonable and necessary modification of the pension benefits.

50. *See, e.g., In re Southland Corp.*, 124 B.R. 211 (Bankr. N.D. Tx. 1991).

51. 11 U.S.C. § 901.

52. *See* the *City of Detroit* and *City of Stockton* cases cited in note 35 and *In re City of San Bernardino, Cal.*, 530 B.R. 474 (Bankr. C.D. Cal. 2015).

53. Barnett Wright, *How Jefferson County's $30 Million Legal Tab for Bankruptcy May Now Seem Like a Bargain*, Real Time News from Birmingham (January 5, 2015), www .al.com/news/birmingham/index.ssf/2015/01/how_jefferson_countys_30_milli.html.

54. Vekshin and Braun, *Vallejo's Bankruptcy "Failure" Scares Cities into Cutting Costs*. Others report a higher number, $13 million, for legal costs. *See* Dreier, *Vallejo Bankruptcy*.

55. "The Congress shall have Power To . . . establish uniform Laws on the subject of Bankruptcies throughout the United States." U.S. Constit. Art. I, § 8, Cl. 4.

56. James Madison, *Federalist*, No. 42, in *The Federalist Papers*, ed. J. Miller (Mineola, NY: Dover, 2014), 208.

57. 11 U.S.C. § 903.

58. 11 U.S.C. § 1 *et seq.*

59. *Northern Pipeline Construction Co. v. Marathon Pipe Line Co.*, 458 U.S. 50 (1982).

60. The state or local government as the government employer would be consenting to the court's ruling on the proposed plan, including the sufficiency of taxes levied, the need for adjustment to pension contributions, and pension benefits as such relate to the revenues, property, and political affairs of the government. The state, in specifically authorizing the use of the Public Pension Fund Bankruptcy Court, will be waiving any sovereignty and jurisdictional issues related to the federal court ruling on such matters. This is intended to avoid Tenth Amendment issues, as was the problem facing the drafters of the municipal bankruptcy provisions to comply with the constitutional tests set forth in *Ashton v. Cameron Cnty. Water Imp. Dist. No. 1*, 298 U.S. 513 (1936), and *U.S. v. Bekins*, 304 U.S. 27 (1938).

61. For a more detailed description of GORDAC, how it would operate, and why it addresses the deficiencies in other governmental debt adjustment mechanisms, *see* Spiotto, *Municipalities in Distress*, 102–12.

62. Alicia H. Munnell and Laura Quinby, *Legal Constraints on Changes in State and Local Pensions*, 25 Center for Retirement Research at Boston College, August 2012.

63. Similarly, although the Fifth Amendment provides that "private property [shall not] be taken for public use, without just compensation," the right to compensation does not extend to the loss of property as the result of necessary exercises of the police power. A state's discretionary decision to take private land to build a road requires compensation, but taking private property in response to an emergency—even seizing or destroying property or rendering it completely valueless—does not. For example, a state's action to prevent a public nuisance is categorically never a taking requiring compensation. David A. Dana and Thomas W. Merrill, Property: Takings 111 (2002). Nor, more broadly, is a state's destruction of private property "to forestall * * * grave threats to the lives and property of others." *Lucas v. S.C. Coastal Council*, 505 U.S. 1003, 1029 n. 16 (1992). The test is whether there is an "actual necessity" for

the state to take property to forestall threats to its citizens. *Id.* Examples of public necessity include "to prevent the spreading of a fire" (*Bowditch v. City of Boston*, 101 U.S. 16, 18–19 [1880]), preventing the spread of disease (*Juragua Iron Co. v. U.S.*, 212 U.S. 297, 308–9 [1909]), or preventing property from falling into the hands of an enemy (*U.S. v. Caltex, Inc.*, 344 U.S. 149, 155–56 [1952]).

One more example. The public trust doctrine generally forbids states from alienating trust property to the prejudice of the general public. *Illinois Cent. R.R. Co.*, 146 U.S. at 453–54. Indeed, the US Supreme Court has specifically analogized the public trust to reserved sovereign police powers in holding that a state may alienate neither. See *Id.* at 453 ("The state can no more abdicate its trust over property in which the whole people are interested, like navigable waters and soils under them, so as to leave them entirely under the use and control of private parties * * * than it can abdicate its police powers in the administration of government and the preservation of the peace").

64. *See* Preamble to the US Constitution, 42 U.S.C. § 1983, Article IV, Section 4 (Guarantee Clause), of the Constitution and notes *infra*.

65. Traditionally, the spread in the municipal market between strong credits (top investment grade) and significantly weak credits (lower noninvestment grade) was 200–300 basis points. *See, e.g.,* the approximately 200 basis-point trading spread between Detroit sewer and water with and without Chapter 9 threat and the Chicago sales tax securitization, which was approximately 275 basis points lower than similar Chicago maturities. https://fixedincome.fidelity.com/ftgw/fi/FINewsArticle?id=2018 01251903SM_____BNDBYER_00000161-2a4f-dad2-a779-ff4fc963_110.1. Even if weaker creditor or past defaulters suffer only a 200 to 300 basis-point rise in annual interest expense, that is 60 percent to 90 percent more payment of principal over a thirty-year period. (Spread between AAA and BBB can vary 100 to 150 basis points. Baird Fixed Income Study, 4/7/14, p. 8.) February 28, 2018, S&P Municipal Bond Index AAA (average duration 4.9 years) to B (average duration 6.08 years) on average 230 basis-point yield difference. Bloomberg Barclay BVAL scale ten years AAA-rated bond to BBB-rated bond, a difference of 97 basis points in yield (March 21, 2018). That additional cost could have been used to reduce taxes, pay for needed infrastructure or services, or pay unfunded pension obligations. In the near term, the spread may widen, thereby increasing the cost of borrowing for weaker credits.

66. According to a study done by the National Conference of State Legislatures, all states but one (Vermont) have constitutional provisions or state statutes generally dealing with balanced-budget requirements. There are forty-four states that require the governor to submit a balanced budget, forty-one states where the legislature must pass a balanced budget, and thirty-eight states where the state cannot carry over a deficit to the next fiscal year. *See* www.ncsl.org/documents/fiscal/StateBalancedBudget Provisions2010.pdf.

67. State courts therefore "generally defer to the legislature." Buenger, *Friction by Design*, 43 U. Rich. L. Rev. 571, 603 (2009). *See* Robert F. Williams, The Law of American State Constitutions 346–347 (2009) (observing that state courts have "expressed

deference to interpretation of the state constitution by the state legislature," including "specific legislative interpretations of the state constitution"); *Nelson v. Miller*, 170 F.3d 641, 653 (6th Cir. 1999) (*"Nelson"*) (state legislatures are charged with "understand-ing" and "interpreting" state constitutions and are presumed to have "acted within the scope of their authority" in passing legislation); *Sturgeon v. County of L.A.*, 167 Cal. App. 4th 630, 644 (2008) ("We recognize we owe deference to interpretations of constitutional provisions enacted by the Legislature"); *cf. Turner Broad. Sys., Inc. v. FCC*, 520 U.S. 180, 196 (1997) (affording Congress "an additional measure of defer-ence out of respect for its authority to exercise the legislative power").

68. *See* Paul Bairoch, Cities and Economic Development (Chicago: University of Chicago Press, 1998); and Brendan O'Flaherty, City Economics (Cambridge, MA: Harvard University Press, 2005).

69. Amy B. Monahan, *Public Pension Plan Reform: The Legal Framework*, 5 Educ. Fin. & Pol'y 617 (2010) (*Monahan*).

70. *See Monahan* at pp. 3–10; Munnell and Quinby at pp. 1–3, available at http://crr.bc.edu/briefs/legal-constraints-on-changes-in-state-and-local-pensions; and *Willamette*.

71. *E.g., Chicago, R. I. & P. Ry. Co. v. Taylor*, 192 P. 349,356 (Okla. 1920) ("As neither the state nor the municipality can surrender by contract the [police] power * * *, a contract purporting to do so is void ab initio, and, being void, it is impossible to speak of laws in conflict with its terms as impairing the obligations of a contract"); *Brick Presbyterian Church v. City of N.Y.*, 5 Cow. 538, 542 (N.Y. Sup. Ct. 1826). And it has been described in leading treatises. *E.g.,* Thomas M. Cooley, A Treatise on the Constitutional Limitations which Rest upon the Legislative Power of the States of the American Union 283 (1868) (hereafter cited as "Cooley, Treatise") ("the prevail-ing opinion" is "that the State could not barter away, or in any manner abridge or weaken, any of those essential powers which are inherent in all governments" and "that any contracts to that end cannot be enforced under the provision of the na-tional Constitution now under consideration"); Christopher G. Tiedman, A Treatise on the Limitations of Police Power in the United States 580–581 (1886) (it has "been often decided, in the American courts, Federal and State, that the State cannot * * * in any way curtail its exercise of any of those powers, which are essential attributes of sovereignty, and particularly the police power").

72. A state's "police power" includes both "state power to deal with the health, safety and morals of the people" (*Dakota Cent. Tel. Co. v. S. Kakota ex rel. Payne*, 250 U.S. 163, 186 [1919]) and more broadly "the residuary sovereignty of the states." Santiago Legarre, *The Historical Background of the Police Power*, 9 U. Pa. J. Const. L. 745, 785 (2007) (quoting *The Federalist*, No. 39, at 186 [James Madison] [Terence Ball ed., 2003]). See Cooley, Treatise, at 572 ("The police power of a State, in a compre-hensive sense, embraces its system of internal regulation, by which it is sought not only to preserve the public order and to prevent offices against the State, but also to establish for the intercourse of citizen with citizen those rules of good manners and good neighborhood which are calculated to prevent a conflict of rights, and to insure

to each the uninterrupted enjoyment of his own, so far as is reasonably consistent with a like enjoyment of rights by others"); *Day-Brite Lighting Inc. v. Missouri*, 342 U.S. 421, 424 (1952) (the police power "extends * * * to all the great public needs").

73. In light of all these considerations, although the US Constitution does not say in so many words that a state may not alienate its core police powers necessary to the economic and social functioning of the state and its citizens, that is "an inference from structure and relation" in the constitutional scheme "just as sure as any constitutional inference could be." Black, Structure and Relationship, 40. See *The Federalist*, No. 45, at 313 (Jacob E. Cooke ed., 1961) ("The powers reserved to the several States * * * concern the lives, liberties, and properties of the people; and the internal order, improvement, and prosperity of the State"); *City of New Orleans v. Bd. of Comm'rs of Orleans Levee Dist.*, 640 S.2d 237, 249 (La. 1994) ("The principle of constitutional law that a state cannot surrender, abdicate, or abridge its police power has been recognized without exception by the state and federal courts. Because the police power is inherent in the sovereignty of each state, the power is not dependent for its existence or inalienability upon the written constitution or positive law"); *State ex rel. City of Minot v. Gronna*, 59 N.W.2d 514, 531 (N.D. 1953) ("The police power is an attribute of sovereignty inherent in the states of the American union, and exists without any reservation in the constitution, being founded on the duty of the state to protect its citizens and provide for the safety and good order of society") (internal quotation marks omitted).

74. Of a state's reserved powers, the police power is not unique in its inalienability. The US Supreme Court has refused to allow states to alienate other great powers as well. As early as 1848, the Court held that states could not surrender the power of eminent domain by contract. *West River Bridge Co. v. Dix*, 47 U.S. (6 How.) 507 (1848). See also *Backus v. Lebanon*, 11 N.H. 19, 24 (1840). Likewise, the Supreme Court has prevented states, under the public trust doctrine, from abridging the public's reasonable use of the waterways by granting title to submerged lands. *Illinois Cent. R.R. Co. v. Illinois*, 146 U.S. 387, 460 (1892) ("There can be no irrepealable contract in a conveyance of property by a grantor in disregard of a public trust, under which he was bound to hold and manage it"). The only core state powers that clearly are alienable are the taxation and spending powers. *U.S. Trust Co.*, 431 U.S. at 24; *New Jersey v. Wilson*, 11 U.S. (7 Cranch) 164 (1812).

75. In fact, the Court noted that state and local governments in financial distress may lack the ability to collect sufficient funds to pay certain unsecured obligations, and therefore there was no impairment or diminishment in the adjustment of those unsecured obligations to what can be paid. (See also note 63, that such reduction or modification is not a taking, since it is to protect a public necessity.)

76. *See* Jack M. Beermann, *The Public Crisis*, 70 Wash & Lee L. Rev. 3, 47–48 (2013).

Contributors

JERED B. CARR   is a professor and head of the Department of Public Administration at the University of Illinois at Chicago. Carr's teaching and research interests are in intergovernmental management, metropolitan governance, and local government administration. He teaches courses in intergovernmental management, public administration, urban policy, and local government administration. He has ongoing research programs focused on the formation and performance of urban governance networks, shared public services/joint ventures, and understanding the risk perceptions of public officials considering intergovernmental collaborations. He is co–editor in chief and managing editor of the *Urban Affairs Review*, a leading scholarly journal publishing conceptual and empirical research on issues of politics, policy, and governance in urban, regional, and metropolitan settings throughout the world. Carr is coeditor of *City-County Consolidation and Its Alternatives: Reshaping the Local Government Landscape* (2004). His research has been published in a wide range of journals in public administration and urban affairs, including the *American Review of Public Administration, Economic Development Quarterly, Journal of Urban Affairs, Local Government Studies, Political Research Quarterly, Public Administration Review, Publius, State and Local Government Review, Urban Affairs Review,* and *Urban Studies.* Carr earned his PhD in public administration from the Askew School at Florida State University.

REBECCA HENDRICK   is a professor and director of PhD Graduate Studies in the Department of Public Administration at the University of Illinois at Chicago. She also has an appointment at the Government Finance Research

Center in the College of Urban Planning and Public Affairs. Her PhD is in political science from Michigan State University, and her research focuses on state and local government financial condition and fiscal practices. She is the author of *Managing the Fiscal Metropolis: The Financial Polices, Practices and Health of Municipalities* (2012), which is based on her years of research on Chicago suburban municipalities. She has published widely in journals in public administration, political science, and public finance.

MARTIN J. LUBY   held academic positions at DePaul University, Ohio State University, and University of Illinois before joining the University of Texas faculty. He is an assistant professor in the LBJ School of Public Affairs. His teaching and research broadly focus on public finance with an emphasis in public financial management. Much of his research has focused on the municipal securities market and the use of debt finance by state and local governments. He has published on innovative government financial instruments, federal financing techniques, and regulation of the municipal securities market. He has extensive consultant and advisory experience with the federal government and many state and local governments. Recently, he served as a consultant to the Office of Inspector General for the US Department of Transportation, the Task Force on the State Budget Crisis cochaired by former Federal Reserve chairman Paul Volcker, the City of Chicago, and the Chicago Transit Authority. He is a registered municipal adviser representative with the Securities and Exchange Commission (Series 50 Qualification) and regulated by the Municipal Securities Rulemaking Board.

DAVID MERRIMAN   is a professor in the Department of Public Administration at the University of Illinois at Chicago. Merriman cofounded and directs the University of Illinois's Fiscal Futures Project, which monitors the fiscal condition of the state of Illinois. He served on the Illinois Council of Economic Advisors under both Governors Pat Quinn and Bruce Rauner. Merriman has done many studies on state and local public finance. Topics include Walmart's impact on local retail markets, tax-increment finance, business-tax incentives, Cook County assessment caps, telecommunications tax rates, and state budget policies. Merriman holds a PhD in economics from the University of Wisconsin–Madison.

MICHAEL A. PAGANO   is dean of the College of Urban Planning and Public Affairs at the University of Illinois at Chicago, director of UIC's Government Finance Research Center, professor of public administration, former coeditor of *Urban Affairs Review* (2001–14), and nonresident senior fellow of the Brookings Institution's Metropolitan Policy Program. He has published ten books, including *Metropolitan Resilience in a Time of Economic Turmoil, Terra Incognita, Cityscapes and Capital,* and *The Dynamics of Federalism,* and more than one hundred publications on urban finance, capital budgeting, federalism, infrastructure, urban development, and fiscal policy. Since 1991 he has written the annual *City Fiscal Conditions* report for the National League of Cities and recently published a Brookings report summarizing a multiyear project on fiscal policy space at www.brookings.edu/research/city-budgets-in-an-era-of-increased-uncertainty/.

DAVID SAUSTAD, currently a second-year master of public affairs student at the LBJ School of Public Affairs, holds a BA in economics and political science from Boston College. His professional experience includes internships with the City of Georgetown, Texas, Budget Office and the City of Baltimore's Bureau of the Budget and Management Research. He currently works as a teaching assistant at the LBJ School for a graduate-level public finance course. Upon graduation, he hopes to pursue a career in public finance at the state or local level.

CASEY SEBETTO is a research assistant working for the Dean's Office in the College of Urban Planning and Public Affairs at the University of Illinois at Chicago. She is currently working toward her master's of urban planning and policy and is appointed a Stukel Fellow with the Great Cities Institute. Sebetto's studies are concentrated in environmental planning and policy with a focus on water resources and sustainable development both nationally and internationally. She is looking forward to graduating in 2019 and hopefully not being unemployed.

MICHAEL D. SICILIANO is assistant professor in the Department of Public Administration at the University of Illinois at Chicago. Siciliano's research interests are interdisciplinary and center on the policy-making and administrative implications of human and interorganizational networks. His work investigates the factors influencing network formation as well as the effect of social structure on individual and collective behavior, decision making, and performance. Substantive fields of interest include education policy, disaster management, and urban governance. Michael is currently the co-PI on an NSF grant developing data management tools for mapping, querying, visualizing, and sharing underground civil infrastructure data. He is also working as the research team director for a regional benchmarking collaborative and leads local governments in the development and use of performance metrics.

JAMES E. SPIOTTO   is a managing director of Chapman Strategic Advisors LLC, the consulting subsidiary of Chapman and Cutler LLP. In this role, he is engaged in strategic and advocacy initiatives on topics of high interest to municipal market participants and the presentation of educational forums on issues impacting the financial services industry. He is also the co-owner and copublisher of MuniNetGuide.com, an online resource specializing in municipal-related research and information concerning state and local government, including public finance, infrastructure, job-market data, and economic statistics and analysis. He is a member of the Advisory Board of the Center for Municipal Finance Harris School of Public Policy, University of Chicago, and a member of the Board of Visitors for the College of Urban Planning and Policy, University of Illinois at Chicago. He received his JD from the University of Chicago Law School. Prior to joining Chapman Strategic Advisors LLC, Spiotto was a partner in the law firm of Chapman and Cutler LLP, where he represented issuers, indenture trustees, bondholders, banks, insurance companies, institutional investors, and funds in litigation, bankruptcy, or workouts of more than four hundred troubled debt financings in over thirty-five states and in foreign countries as well. Over the past thirty years, Spiotto represented clients in the resolution of troubled state and local debt financings. He has written numerous books and articles on municipal defaults and bankruptcy, including *Municipalities in Distress? How States and Investors Deal with Local Government Financial Emergencies* (2012) and *Defaulted Securities: The Guide for Trustees and Bondholders* (2018).

GARY STRONG   is the legislative director for Texas state representative Chris Turner and received a master's of public affairs from the LBJ School at the University of Texas at Austin, where he focused on public financial management and municipal securities. Gary worked in the financial services industry for ten years prior to entering public service and witnessed, firsthand, the negative impact of imprudent fiscal policy.

SHU WANG   is an assistant professor in the Department of Agricultural, Food, and Resource Economics at Michigan State University. Wang's research focuses on institutional and economic factors that affect the fiscal condition of local governments and the sustainability of service provision. Her current projects investigate state-imposed constraints on local revenue raising and state intervention when local governments are in distress. Her work has been published in *Public Budgeting and Finance,* the *American Review of Public Administration, State and Local Government Review,* and *Publius: The Journal of Federalism.* She teaches public policy courses at the undergraduate and graduate levels and also delivers educational programs to local governments in Michigan.

YONGHONG WU   is the director of the International Program and an associate professor in the Department of Public Administration at the University of Illinois at Chicago. He received his PhD in public administration from the Maxwell School of Syracuse University. His fields of specialization include state and local public finance and science and technology policy. Wu's recent research has focused on municipal government fiscal policy making, financial management issues, and government financing of research and development activities.

THE URBAN AGENDA

Metropolitan Resilience in a Time of Economic Turmoil
Edited by Michael A. Pagano

Technology and the Resilience of Metropolitan Regions
Edited by Michael A. Pagano

The Return of the Neighborhood as an Urban Strategy
Edited by Michael A. Pagano

Remaking the Urban Social Contract: Health, Energy, and the Environment
Edited by Michael A. Pagano

Jobs and the Labor Force of Tomorrow: Migration, Training, Education
Edited by Michael A. Pagano

The Public Infrastructure of Work and Play
Edited by Michael A. Pagano

The People's Money: Pensions, Debt, and Government Services
Edited by Michael A. Pagano

The University of Illinois Press
is a founding member of the
Association of American University Presses.

Composed in 10.5/13 Minion Pro
with Franklin Gothic display
by Lisa Connery
at the University of Illinois Press
Cover design by Dustin J. Hubbart
Manufactured by Sheridan Books, Inc.

University of Illinois Press
1325 South Oak Street
Champaign, IL 61820-6903
www.press.uillinois.edu